THE INNOCENCE OF
JOAN LITTLE

THE
INNOCENCE
OF
JOAN LITTLE

A SOUTHERN MYSTERY

James Reston, Jr.

Times
BOOKS

All rights reserved, including the right to reproduce this book or portions thereof in any form. For information, address: Times Books, a division of Quadrangle/The New York Times Book Company, Inc., Three Park Avenue, New York, N.Y. 10016. Manufactured in the United States of America. Published simultaneously in Canada by Fitzhenry & Whiteside, Ltd., Toronto.

Third printing, January 1978

Library of Congress Cataloging in Publication Data

Reston, James, 1941–
    The innocence of Joan Little.

    1. Little, Joan. I. Title.
KF224.L52R47   364.1′523′0924 [B]   77-79038
ISBN 0-8129-0714-0

For Henry Mayer
with love and thanks

CONTENTS

INTRODUCTION

In the preface to the first edition of his great mystery, *The Moonstone*, published in 1868, Wilkie Collins wrote that his new book reversed the technique of his previous novels. Before, he had been concerned with the influence of circumstances upon character, but with *The Moonstone*, he was preoccupied with the impact of character upon events. The characters' "course of thought and action under the circumstances which surround them," he wrote, "is shown to be sometimes right, and sometimes wrong. Right or wrong, their conduct, in either event, equally directs the course of those portions of the story in which they are concerned."

In my previous work, both my fiction and my factual writing, the emphasis has also been on the stamp of events on personality, and so this book represents a reversal for me as well. In the chronicles which comprise the chapters, I have adapted Wilkie Collins's narrative approach (with some alterations) to a real case. Each chapter concentrates on a participant in the Joan Little story at the period when the participant is most intimately involved with the events. The perception of what is happening by the participants, colored by their values, prejudices, and sentimentalities, is so different, and this very difference of perception often influences the course of events, and so proves in fact what Wilkie Collins proved in fiction.

There may never be a better set of actual circumstances to adapt the Collins approach than the Joan Little case. It was circumstantial case of murder and rape, with two distinct theories of how the crime(s) happened, each supported by considerable evidence (not all of which was presented to the jury or reported to the public in the press). As the chronicler, I have endeavored to relate both theories with equal passion. Each theory of the case was based largely on a view of the character of Miss Joan Little—heroic or villainous—and judging the defendant was largely a matter of predisposition. It was a case whose elements were novelistic, almost surpassing the novel in intrigue, for what novelist can construct a believable set of circumstances that contains so much mystery and at the same time bears so importantly on five crucial questions? In a sexual assault, does a woman (or a man) have the right to kill her (or his) attacker? Is the level of decency in North Carolina and the nation above the spectacle of human executions? What recourse does a prisoner in jail have to the brutality of jail authorities? How has the lot of the black citizen changed in the rural South? And finally, despite the flood of flowery acclaim for the South that Jimmy Carter's election has brought, how new is the New South? The interplay of these themes in the Joan Little case was fascinating.

But so too were the characters. This case was distinctly Southern. The manipulation of the national press was possible only because the national press brought to North Carolina the nostalgic, fixed view of an Old South of helpless black victims, and gross, ignorant, white law enforcement. This was the sixties revisited, and it brought out of the closet a lot of those dusty trappings. The Joan Little defense played this theme to a fare-thee-well, and it was lapped up by the press and the nation. But if the tone of Southern life has changed since the days of segregation, the people of the region retain a unique and rich turn of phrase and demeanor, and the original Southerners, the Old Southerners, have been joined by migrants, like myself, whose upbringing was in other regions, but who appreciate the beauty and the diversity and the struggle of the South. In the Joan Little extravaganza, the characters became as interesting as the legalities or the philosophical issues that the case raised. In these chronicles, the range is diverse: a sheriff and his deputy, a scientist and an undertaker, a psychic and a psychopath, the competing lawyers of vastly different outlooks, a feminist and a black activist over the hill, and Joan Little herself, whose true character, by design, remained indistinct to the end.

The result allows the reader to judge the guilt or innocence of Joan Little, in possession of far more facts than the real jury had—in a sense, to act as a superjuror. But the issue, of course, is far broader than the legal question of guilt or innocence. One hardly knows what that means in this case. The show prodded and pushed the legal system out of recognition. As a nationally followed case, it became a stage where only lawyer-publicists belong. As a psychodrama of desire and hate, the jurors expected the lawyers and the witnesses to act like the characters from their favorite television series. When they did not, they were less believable. If the behavior of the defense lawyer, Jerry Paul, was extreme and outrageous, he was reacting to the extremity and outrageousness of the charge and the punishment. It was the excess of it all—on all sides, including the press and the jury—that stands out.

These are the facts. In the early morning hours of August 27, 1974, a policeman bringing a drunken prisoner to the Beaufort County Jail in Washington, North Carolina, discovered the dead body of the white jailer, Clarence Alligood, lying on the bunk bed of the sole female prisoner in the jail, Miss Joan Little, twenty-one years old and black. Alligood's body was naked from the waist down. Sperm was present on his leg, and an icepick lay loosely cupped in his hand. He had icepick wounds around his temple and his heart. Joan Little was gone.

Over a week later, she turned herself in to the North Carolina authorities, saying that she had acted in self-defense against a sexual assault, and she was immediately charged with first-degree murder. If she were convicted on that charge under existing North Carolina law, she would automatically be executed in the gas chamber. In the months that followed, she became a symbol of women's groups, civil-rights groups, prisoners'-rights groups, and the opponents of capital punishment. At the time of the crime and the trial, North Carolina had over a third of the nation's entire death-row population. In the course of the Joan Little case, through the use of highly sophisticated money-raising techniques, over $350,000 was raised nationally and worldwide for her defense.

On August 14, 1975, she was acquitted.

James Reston, Jr.
Hillsborough, N. C.
February 1977

PART 1

In some of my former novels, the object pro-
posed has been to trace the influence of cir-
cumstances upon character. In the present
story I have reversed the process. The at-
tempt made, here, is to trace the influence of
character on circumstances. The conduct
pursued, under sudden emergency, by a
young girl, supplies the foundation on which
I have built this book.

The same object has been kept in view, in
the handling of the other characters which
appear in these pages. Their course of
thought and action under the circumstances
which surround them, is shown to be some-
times right, and sometimes wrong. Right or
wrong, their conduct, in either event, equally
directs the course of those portions of the
story in which they are concerned. . . .

Wilkie Collins, Preface to the
first edition of *The Moonstone*,
1868

CHAPTER 1

SHERIFF OTTIS (RED) DAVIS

. . . The encounter did not leave behind with Chief Inspector Heat that satisfactory sense of superiority that members of the police force get from the unofficial but intimate side of their intercourse with the criminal classes, by which the vanity of power is soothed, and the vulgar love of domination over our fellow creatures is flattered as worthily as it deserves.

Joseph Conrad, *The Secret Agent*

EAST from the Piedmont, speckled with crossroads called Pinetops, Crisp, and Penny Hill, the flat, sandy tobacco country stretches away from the highway in vast gray fields with shacks off in the distance, marooned amid orderly furrows, past Conetoe and Bethel —"first at Bethel, fartherest at Gettysburg and Chickamauga, last at Appomattox" the excuse ran— through the swamps and endless corridors of high-standing pine to the bridge across the Pamlico, where it and the Tar River converge into a wide, baylike, brackish expanse. "Original Washington," 1776–1976, the first town in the United States named after George Washington, but the claim was disputed by Washington, New Hampshire. At Main Street, the black raised letters against the steely background impart the news that this was the town where Cecil B.

De Mille grew up—a fact that had always seemed appropriate, for the whole affair had been a kind of Cecil B. De Mille extravaganza.

Past the old railroad station, now a community art gallery in celebration of the Bicentennial, along the new waterfront plaza that the town had made in the sixties where dilapidated wharf warehouses once sagged toward the brackish water, along the clean main street, newly landscaped with garden plots, to the old hotel that now housed the aged: clean, well-kept . . . and integrated. The mayor had been proud of that.

"They take their cane poles down to the river and fish together," he had said, two doors down at Harris Hardware, his Windsor knot loosened around his brief neck, his stocky legs raised from the wooden floor as he leaned back in his chair. He had been surprisingly calm about Washington's ordeal; few others in the town were calm about it.

When the marchers had come a week after the incident, Max the mayor, Max Roebuck, stood across the street, watched them "raise a little hell," but heard nothing "out of the way," nothing he could take offense to, and he did not blame the "self-interest groups" for taking advantage of the case, thought they'd be foolish not to, but it was being done at the expense of his community's reputation. Still he had jumped six inches when a motorcycle backfired, as Golden Frinks, the civil-rights man, exhorted his small group of followers. The mayor had a fondness for the phrase "dad-burn." He knew who the town "ruffians" were, but they'd be dad-burn brave to try something. "We white people" didn't like it when integration was forced on us in 1965; it made him madder 'n hell, and he wouldn't have cried if the judge who ordered it, Judge John D. Larkins (Federal District Judge), had gotten in an accident—though he wished him no harm—but now,

"We've done more around here in the last ten years than we did in the forty before that, and I have to admit that integration is one of the finest things that ever happened to this town. We've had less trouble now than when we were totally segregated, and it's because we've got dad-burn good young people."

Max had said that—in March 1975—when the uncertainty was the greatest, before the trial had been moved to Raleigh, when people lamely joked that their biggest problem would be where to put all the people when they descended upon the town. In July, the week before the trial began, a television crew had flown in from Washington, Big Washington, and seemed quizzical, though hardly amused, about having to spend all this effort and expense to fly all the way into this backward Eastern North Carolina town —they referred to it as Noplace, North Carolina—to interview this stubby, pleasant man, but it was getting to be the dog days on Capitol Hill, and there was little news there. Max had been wired for his interview up behind the nail counter, with the shovels to the left by the mule collars ("We don't sell many of 'em," he said), and the wooden drawers for plumbing fixtures behind; and overhead, the old pulley system, devised around the turn of the century, would shuttle the cash sales to the cashier upstairs on the second level, and with this quaint background for the amusement of millions, Max had said calmly, sweating a little under the lights, that, yes, it was valid for some people to conclude that the transfer of the trial from Beaufort County to Raleigh *did* imply more prejudice here, but there was no meanness in what he said, no sharpness, just resignation, a touch of sadness, a desire to do better in the coming years.

Afterwards, outside the mayor's office, Bee Morton, a pert, scrubbed, attractive spinster stood in front of the stand-up safe, circa 1890, and buzzed to the visitors for twenty minutes about how the news media were playing up one side of the issue, how they ought to investigate the background of Joan Little some more, how Jerry Paul, her lawyer, had made a lot of money defending colored people, but that he was a nice boy growing up there, when he played football and all that. She'd told Max the day before that she hoped the outsiders would come by and talk to her—news travels fast in Washington—and she'd give them an earful, and she had, ending with the plea only to be fair to her little town.

Other ladies would talk about nothing else, at the high school football game or over weak coffee at Adams Soda Shop next to the movie house. The talk was usually guarded with strangers, although a Coca-Cola plant manager, doing most of the talking with his wife beside him, allowed as to how impressed he was that Clarence Alligood had held the jailer's job as long as he had, given his intelligence—that he should know because he often drank coffee with Alligood in the mornings, and

"I thought he was so racially biased that he wouldn't want a colored woman."

But if he did, it didn't seem to matter to some, for any notion of morality or "honor" to black women was a source of amusement.

"Hell, to them," said a car dealer, "fucking is like saying good morning or having a Pepsi-Cola," and a textile executive confided, "I'll tell you one thing, she didn't lose her honor in that cell, she'd lost that years ago at Camp Lejeune," lending his belief to the rumor that Joan Little had ferried her girl friends to the Marine Base for prostitution.

Several doors up, at the Cinderella Beauty Salon, Maggie Buck, the wonderful Maggie Buck, was curling and prodding and teasing her customer's hair into a fashion of the early 1960s, but she was also holding forth on a woman's right to defend herself, among

other issues, like the jewelry-store robbery where the
thieves had cut through two firewalls to get to the stuff
in the safe. She shook her head,
"We've been having a lot of things going on recently that we never had before."
Maggie had taken karate once, because she was
often the last person to walk down deserted Main
Street at night after closing, sometimes as late as nine
o'clock, and thought every woman should know how
to protect herself, but there were limits. Once a man
had come to the salon to demonstrate a tear-gas pencil
to go in women's purses, when she had a new customer
in the chair, and it had gone off when he dropped it
by accident—gassed her, gassed the new customer,
gassed him—and it took three days to get that smell
out. After crying for a week, she had decided against
having one of *them* around.

The days of Uncle Tom were over, Maggie was sure.
"They say we have slaves in Washington, but that's
not true. I just hired a colored woman to do the cleaning up around here. She's not treated like a slave. I
pick her up. I take her to the grocery, to the fish
market, and I take her home . . . and I pay her well."
And finally, getting to the issue, Maggie had her
maid's story too. Her maid had told her that Joan
Little was so mean, she stole her own aunt's color TV.
But still she was plenty interested in the case; she'd
love to be a "fly on the wall" for the trial, and she
remembered Jerry Paul from childhood. "He was a
cute little boy then, but I don't know that I can say
that about him now." And then the statement that
seemed to sum up the whole affair.
"Even if a girl has loose morals, she should be able
to pick the man she wants to be raped by."
In the Cinderella Beauty Salon, the significance of
the case began to emerge. It involved so many issues in
a unique package: civil rights; prison rights; women's

rights; capital punishment, for the girl faced death in
the gas chamber; and the character of the New South,
or Old South, or just the South, whatever it was.
(There is even a promotional magazine now for Eastern North Carolina called *New East*.) And the issues
worked at cross-purposes; they confused the old Southern categories. Sympathy for her as a woman diluted
prejudice against her as a black. The gas chamber
scared people in their surety about getting tough with
criminals.

Maggie had said, "*We* should be protected when
we're in prison," and she didn't care if a person was
"black, white, or indigo pink," there should have been
a matron on duty in that jail that night. And the
yearning to be modern could be stronger than the
yearning for justice. Max had said that the local
people leaned toward a verdict of acquittal.

"They're leaning in her direction, rather than the
truth. They're biased in her favor, if only to prove
that we're not like they're saying we are."

At the corner of Main and Market streets, away
from the Chamber of Commerce, whose pamphlet de-
scribes the county as "historic but hyperactive," past
John Wilkinson's modest law office, past the police
station, the spanking new courthouse comes into view.
The building is egregious, set apart by its height and
size, its manicured patch of grass, and moat of parking
spaces from the two-story, turn-of-the-century struc-
tures that form the rest of the downtown. It has the
feel of newness and aspires to importance with its
brick veneer and mixtures of cultures. The portico,
above the steps, combines Williamsburg colonial with
a Romanesque arch and Corinthian columns. Corinthian columns for new courthouses were certainly out
in the Piedmont; that is a difference.

The double doors open to the carpeted stairs leading to the basement. Impeccably clean throughout,

the linoleum basement floor is waxed and buffed, the yellow cinder-block walls washed and immaculate. The basement is given over to police functions, nearly all of which, except for the civil-defense office, became involved in the events of August 26–27, 1974: the magistrate's office where the jailer, Clarence T. Alligood, guided a woman at about 10:30 P.M. so that she could swear out a warrant; the dispatch room, with its maps of Beaufort County and of the town of Washington beside it, boldly lit, where the round-faced, pleasant coffee-colored lady, Beverly King, was working when the jailer came back to ask her at 2:55 A.M. if all the deputies had gone in for the night; the sheriff's office, with its glass partition, behind which the daytime matron, Mrs. Louise Stokes, a large leathery woman, shares the hostility to outsiders. Occasionally she would contribute an unfriendly remark to a conversation,

"If you look at the jailers we usually have around here, they're not exactly lady-killers."

It was not easy to get Sheriff Red Davis to talk openly about the case. He had been stung early by his openness, when, several months after the event, he spent an hour and a half with a reporter relating everything he knew about the case, and then the writer went home and "ran me down like a dog." Only reluctantly, in March 1975, had he consented to a tour of his jail, across the hall from his office, but he should have done so more often, for it was no miniature version of Old Bailey, no tiny convict hulk, as most visitors were primed to expect. The basement jail was new and clean, the work of a Texas company that specializes in jails nationwide. Alligood had taken on immense, grotesque proportions, but the harmless-looking, slight, almost wizened daytime jailer who stood before the bank of video screens seemingly unnoticing, as the sheriff gave his tour, was hardly that. And the woman's section of the small facility, set off from the rest down a short corridor, a turn to the left through a barred door . . .

"Did you announce yourself?" Jerry Paul blasted at Detective Jerry Helms at her trial, as the officer explained his entrance into that short corridor on the night of the killing.

"No."

"You did not!"

"No."

. . . a turn to the left, through a barred door, Helms caught sight of the jailer's feet, with his brown socks still on, his shoes in the corridor, a bra and negligée tied to the bars on one side of the cell, a blanket tied to a bar on the other . . .

"When you peeped around the corner . . ." Paul persisted in his cross-examination, relentlessly painting the whole crew as peeping Toms, oafs, voyeurs; it had been overkill, but the lawyer is not a subtle man. Helms had ventured no farther; he went to the dispatcher's office to get Beverly King and another officer. But the sheriff, in March, was proud of the cell. It was tiny—no more than seven feet long and five feet wide, the bunk on the left, where the jailer's body was found at 4:00 A.M., slumped, lying on its left side, two streams of blood flowing from the right temple across the cheek; the outer, short-sleeved shirt unbuttoned, revealing the T-shirt beneath, discolored, but not soaked in blood—"a thick, dark, red substance" it was always called at the trial—arms extending diagonally to the floor, where a pair of underpants lay on top of a negligée; in one hand, a pair of pants, in the other hand, the left, loosely held—"cupped, but not gripped tightly," one witness testified—an icepick. Below the shirt line, his fleshy thighs were exposed. Two puncture wounds in the outer left thigh were not bleeding —later it was explained why puncture wounds do not bleed profusely—and on the inner thigh, spermatoza.

For once, the language of the autopsy report seemed to accentuate the significance:

"Smears were made from fluid in the anterior urethra. The smears were teeming with spermatoza."

To the right of the bunk stood a combination commode and sink, made of stainless steel and reminiscent of a sink in a railroad car. In March, it was spotless, but on the morning of August 27 it was found with a pack of Salem cigarettes on it, a jar of Vaseline, and in the bowl, clumps of wadded, bloodstained toilet paper, conjuring up the image of a dying man, thrashing about in a locked cell, frantically dabbing toilet tissue on a puncture to his heart where the bleeding was internal rather than external, where the wall around the heart would fill in five minutes and collapse the heart.

In September, the sheriff was anxious to show off the new system that he himself had devised for the protection of female inmates. The county had not allotted any new money for a full-time matron, nor did such money seem justifiable, since women were incarcerated in the Beaufort County jail on a sporadic basis. Sheriff Davis had devised a new video system whereby television screens covering the women's cells and the corridor to it were placed in the dispatcher's office, and when a woman was locked up, no males were allowed in the dispatcher's room. The authority for this innovation rested solely with the sheriff. The head of the whole jail system in North Carolina could only offer advice. He felt that the real answer to women's privacy in jails had been provided by the Asheville jail, where the sheriff had put up a sign by the monitor covering the women's section:

Any person caught watching this monitor will be discharged immediately.

Once the case was over, the sheriff felt his obligation had ended.

"People around here tell me the case is over, the court has ruled, and you don't have to say nothin'; I get more criticism for talking to any outsider now than I do for anything I did in the entire year of the Joan Little case."

And he didn't like writers trying to soften him up by fancy introductions either. That was a "big mistake" with Red Davis. It reminded him of the time he'd stopped a man in a truck loaded with watermelons, driving a little too fast, and decided to give the driver a break, until he offered a watermelon in thanks. "Next thing he'd be comin' around here wanting a favor, saying 'Remember that watermelon I gave you.' "

When the piqued, thin-skinned, publicity-weary man finally submitted to a few questions, he wanted the author's scribbled notes afterward to Xerox, a gesture with the smell of lawsuit, intended to compel the accuracy of the chronicle. But suddenly he would soften,

"Let's talk a little bullshit," he said benignly. "You pay me a hundred thousand dollars, and I'll quit this job tomorrow, and we'll write a hell of a book together."

First the local press, then the national press, then the authors—they had worked their way through three-fourths of the process. Yet to come were the moviemakers, complete with Robert Redford, who would need some pudges in his cheeks to play Jerry Paul (though Paul later would promote Gene Hackman, who would be better at playing his rough side, and later still he switched his allegiance to Marlon Brando), Cicely Tyson as the heroine, and Rod Steiger as the villain. It was all a bad joke on a town, they insisted, which had never had racial troubles before, when towns all around them were having problems in the sixties. The dimensions of the joke were outlined by David Milligan, the editor of the *Beaufort-Hyde News*:

"This is the South. Here's a rinky-dink town with its shacks and shanties. You got this old redneck sheriff and this old redneck jailer and this pore little ol' colored gal. She's there in jail, so defenseless, so innocent, and she gets raped and ravaged by this gross jailer, and all of a sudden, out of nowhere, she struck out, trying to defend herself. She had to kill the jailer, and now those ignorant old rednecks are gonna get their revenge on her. They're gonna make her pay for it with her life."

Milligan and Davis are close, and indeed, the editor had acted as the public-relations man for the sheriff once in the winter of 1975, and with the image of the Southern sheriff as Joe Higgins, the Dodge safety sheriff, and his deputy, lamentably called "Buford," and the movies like *Cool Hand Luke* and *Easy Rider* so firmly planted in the American mind, more rural Southern sheriffs could use public-relations men. Milligan wrote the statement for Davis after a talk and then printed it in his paper on February 20, 1975:

"Hardly a day goes by that I am not contacted by the big newspapers, the wire services, television or radio, and while I certainly do not intend to discuss the details of the case, those matters will come out during the trial, I have tried to cooperate with these people as much as possible.

"So naturally I'm offended when I read a story that pictures us as ignorant rednecks living on Tobacco Road. In each case when the question of race came up I made a very special point of emphasizing that after twenty-nine years of working with both black and white in the county I was supported in my election by ninety percent of the black voters of the county. As far as I can tell every newsman I talked to completely brushed that aside, insisted on making this a case of racial discrimination, and in some cases there were strong insinuations that I myself am a racist.

"I don't really care how much they write about the story, but I am distressed when a writer comes to town with his story all written, and all he wants from us is a dateline, a few names to tag to his bad grammar quotes, and a picture or two of our slums. . . .

"The final irony is that while much of the country is led to wonder whether we're intelligent or decent enough to conduct a fair trial, one of the most consistent complaints . . . is not our so-called meanness, or bigotry or lack of compassion, but is the laxity of our jurors and the leniency of our courts."

Odd language for Red, but the sentiments were all his.

Inside the glass partition of the sheriff's office, there is customarily a set cast of characters, deputies and assorted friends of the law, like former sheriff Jack D. Harris, Davis's predecessor, who snarled in March, "Why would Alligood want such as that anyway, all eat up with syphilis like she was?" and Deputy Willis Peachey, the investigative officer on the case, who told a member of the defense team that he was tired of people in Washington making fun of him—"Goin' down to the jail and fuck some?" they asked—and Jennings Bryant Freeman, the thin, sallow bondsman, who seldom talked but watched attentively whenever the author came, as if he wondered whether his little secret would be discovered.

The sheriff's mind was not on the Joan Little affair when he finally closed the door. He was aggravated that day by something else for a change, his red hair above his freckled face mussed, his glasses sliding down his nose some. "Take this case," he began, putting the stub of his cigar down in a cluttered ashtray. "A farmer out here in the county has a little safe, and he's got fifteen hundred dollars in it. It's his life savings, earned with his own sweat over the years. Now you and I would say he's a damn fool for keeping it out there on his farm, and he *is* a damn fool. Someone goes out there and takes that safe, and several weeks ago I get some pretty good information who it is. It's two people in fact, and I go to 'em and they deny it, and I say, 'All right, if you didn't do it, you won't mind taking this lie-detector test I've got for you,' and they say OK. So I make all the arrangements, get it all set up, and I call 'em up—to tell them to come down here at ten o'clock this morning. Meanwhile, they go out and get 'em a lawyer, and the lawyer says, 'Don't say nothin'.'

"So I'm grounded. I'm not going to get too excited about it. I'm going to the high-school football game tonight and have just as good a time as I would have if this hadn't happened. But I can't interrogate 'em, because that would be violating the law. So I'm asking you: what's the answer? Should lawyers have that much power? How am I going to protect that man out there in the county?"

His speech has the sound of the sea in it, influenced by the Devonshire English that remains purest on Ocracoke in the Outer Banks. "High tide" was *"hoi toid,"* as John Fry in *Lorna Doone* might say, pronounced deep in the throat, and the county adjoining Beaufort, Hyde, was "Hoid" county. But Devonshire was not the only influence on the sheriff's speech. There was also a touch of "Bunyanese," named after the crossroads in the northeastern part of the county, and it is distinctive for its cockney *ow* in "flounder" and "sound." The third accent of Beaufort County, "plantation Southern," seemed to have had no influence on Red Davis. So between Devonshire and Bunyon, combined with rural Southernisms, Red Davis was an easy mark. His reputation as an investigator is good, but the feeling among the prosecutors was, "Let Red do the investigating, and someone else do the testifying." On the stand, his delivery, flat and often imprecise, did not carry the outrage against the evils of crime that prosecutors like in their witnesses.

The sheriff continued: "I'm what you call an old-timer, believe in good, clean law enforcement, believe in making it safe for your mother to walk down the street, believe that if you do something you should pay for it. I've always believed that, since 1946 when I joined the police department in the little town of Belhaven, east of here, at the age of twenty-two, since 1950 when I moved to the Washington police, and 1956 when I became a deputy sheriff in Beaufort County. In the old days, there were only a few positions, and if a man showed up well, then he'd become a sheriff's deputy. Things have changed now, and the standards are going down all the time, and that's because of the pressure to have more colored on the force. I'm speaking generally. Since I became sheriff in December 1974, I've hired three new people and two have been black. One of the two already improved his situation by getting hired by the State Bureau of Investigation.

"Of course, there's always a number of folks who want to become sheriff. I ran for the job for the first time in 1962 against Sheriff Harris, ran against him and four others. All the deputies supported Harris, and they even had a man run in that election from a little community of five hundred people out in the county where I was solid as a dollar—just to cut votes away from me. Still I got to the second primary with Harris. Before the vote I went to him, said,

" 'If you'll give me a little security, if you'll look out for me after the election, then it's over.' And we got in a car together and went out in the county to see a big politician, and made an agreement: that as long as Harris wanted to be sheriff, I wouldn't interfere.

"Nineteen seventy-one was when I began to get a little recognition. They had a strike out at Hamilton Beach and Scovil Company—they manufacture electrical appliances—and I had the authority to keep a driveway open, for the employees and the strikers, and I was making some right sharp arrests out there, even arrested a twenty-thousand-dollar man, an official for the union. After it was finished, some people thought I showed up well, and the National Spinning Company offered me a job as their security man, offered a salary that was *within* five hundred dollars of what the sheriff of Beaufort County made. I thought that was a little ridiculous, even though, with five children, I could use the money—and I told them that within a thousand dollars of the sheriff's salary would be OK. But Sheriff Harris went out there and asked them please, not to consider me for the job, because he didn't want to lose me. He began to recognize me a little more after that; actually I got a raise out of it, and in the press when I'd be the arresting officer on a case, I'd be called the chief deputy, though Harris never officially designated me as such.

"In 1974, Sheriff Harris got very sick and decided not to run, so in May I ran for his job. In fact, he went into surgery on the very morning that Alligood was killed. Since his term did not officially expire until December, I had to please him and the public too in the way I handled the case. Now when I'm politicking, I don't stoop to the scrapings, black or white. I talk to the leaders and to the average class of folks. I know if I'm caught talking to, say, a white bootlegger, people will say I'm obligated to him, and I don't want to be obligated to nobody. So I don't get seen with folks like that. You don't catch me politicking in these honky-tonk places, talking with scum. I try to keep my standards up.

"So I ran on my record in 1974 and won. Got ninety

percent of the black vote, so apparently I wasn't disliked. I get along with the black, and that's why it hurt me when Joan Little's lawyers said she'd be taken advantage of in Beaufort County. I knew I couldn't afford to take advantage of her, not with the support of the black votes like I've got. Besides that, I'm a family man. I've got five kids who are proud of me. I can't be out there pushing people around. She'd have been a damn sight safer in my hands than running around the county at the mercy of the world. Out there, anybody can take a whack at her. Hell, after she was in custody, her lawyers argued [September 18, 1974] that her case should be moved because the acting sheriff of Beaufort County had 'undue influence with the public' and I took that as one of the best damn compliments I'd ever had.

"They called us excitable, but I only really get excited when people aggravate me. If someone dropped dead of a heart attack in the next office I'd walk over there in a normal pace. In a high-speed chase, I don't get excited, no matter how fast I'm going. If I think I'm losing control of myself, I just stop. There were things in that year that aggravated me, but they weren't in those first few days when we were looking for Joan Little in Beaufort County. After all, it was just a jailer who had been killed by an inmate. To this day I can't understand what all the fuss was about. If it had been the president or a high official that had been killed, I could understand, but it was just a jailer. If a black man came in here and killed me dead, do you think there'd be much interest? Oh, there'd be a box in the paper: SHERIFF OF BEAUFORT COUNTY KILLED BY A BLACK. But if I went out and killed a black man, it would be all over the papers. They'd be all over me, probably burn down this town. In September '75, a black killed a highway patrolman in cold blood. He had had twenty-eight years of experience, one less than me, and you could not find a finer man around here. He even had a ballpark named after him, and I understand he was praying in his church on the day he was killed. Nobody got excited about that.

"So you see, I could not afford to have Joan Little killed in Beaufort County. I had too much to lose. People here are not going to elect a sheriff who lets that happen, and I've got a seventeen-year-old daughter who's watching everything I do.

"The call came to my house at about four A.M., August 27, from Detective Jerry Helms of the Washington Police Department. Helms had discovered Alligood's body in Joan Little's cell, and in the call to me he said he did not know if the jailer was still alive or not. He had called the rescue squad. I was at the jail ten minutes later. I was flat movin' on the way in there. I took a look at the body, but I did not study the evidence. Deputy Willis Peachey came in a few minutes later, and I told him to guard the body. Several hours later, sometime between seven and eight A.M., I made him the chief investigative officer on the case, and he remained so through her trial nearly a year later. At that time, of the men available, he was my most experienced deputy, with four years of experience.

"My first concern, meanwhile, was about the other prisoners, and then about the whereabouts of Joan Little. I asked for the key of rings to the cells and found that they had been carried off. That meant that while we could get into the woman's cell by an automatic release outside the cell block, we could not get to the male prisoners because a key was required to open a safety door to the men's section. So while Peachey was in charge of the crime scene, I went off to call the Texas company that had constructed the

Beaufort County Jail—to have them send us an extra set of keys—and then I called a local torch man to come and cut through the safety door to the men's lockup.

"They painted a picture later at the trial of chaos in the jail in those first few hours, of how the investigation was 'blown' or 'sloppy,' but I don't think the public really bought it. There was some excitement, sure, just the same as there is in most killings, but I would not call it chaos. Oh, there's always improvements that can be made. If I had been in charge of the crime scene instead of Peachey, for example, I might not have let Gordon Edwards, the cameraman from Channel Seven in Greenville, inside the jail that morning to do his filming. But later, I thought the filming had been to my good, when they started saying we were hiding the evidence. With the experience of this case behind me now, I might have called in the State Bureau of Investigation the minute I learned of the killing, instead of five hours later. We might have gone over a few things a little more just to satisfy people. But there's always improvements that can be made.

"They made a lot later about the jailer's pants, and accused us of stealing 'em. The truth is that the pants were put on top of the body as it was wheeled out on a stretcher by the rescue squad, and later Peachey brought them back and locked them in his locker. So we had the pants all the time.

"In that first hour I contacted Mrs. Louise Stokes, the matron for the jail, and had her go to the Alligood house to convey the news. Within three hours of the stabbing, the family was in the sheriff's office, and I told them dead straight all the facts about how Clarence Alligood was found, and said,

" 'I don't want you to hear the details on the street

and come back here asking me why I did not tell you, why you did not hear it from me.'

"By eight A.M. the reporters were all over me, and I did not reveal to them the fact that Alligood was found with his pants off. They would be asking questions about whether Alligood was screwing Little or if Alligood screwed prisoners regularly, and I didn't know the answers to those questions. Now Alligood wasn't all lily-white. If I had known he was a ladies' man, he wouldn't have stayed around here ten minutes. But as far as I knew then, he was the most security-minded man we ever had back there. Likewise, people came around talking about *her* reputation, about how she was a prostitute and had the clap, but I never said a thing about that either, but I didn't know anything about her reputation.

"By nine-thirty or ten o'clock I realized that this was going to be a big case. There was a chance that she would go abroad—to New York or Philadelphia—and I called in the SBI. Ten-fifteen A.M. is the official time when the SBI was directed to help the Beaufort County Sheriff's department. Meanwhile, we already were getting information from people who had seen her that morning—on a street corner or wherever. I expected that we would make a pickup shortly, and I told the deputies to check out the leads as they came in. Unfortunately, you cannot pick and choose which leads to check out. You've got to check them all out.

"After the SBI came on the case that morning, I began cruising Back of Town, colored town. Now I've got certain people in Back of Town I can drop the word to, people who can be helpful. I assured them and others as I cruised around that the case would be handled in a safe way, that Joan Little would not be treated badly, regardless of what she had done. But people were already playing this case up, and my policy is always to play cases down. So I let it pass when the *Washington Daily News* printed its editorial the following afternoon, August 28, 1975:

Brutal Murder

The murder of Clarence G. Alligood, age 62, Beaufort County night jailer, is one of the most brutal ever to happen in this county.

At this very moment we look at what has happened, we look at his family and loved ones, and what is there to say? Here is a man who gave his life in the line of duty. Here is a good man who never made the headlines in life, but in death there must be an appreciation for him and what he did that he never lived to realize.

We look so often at the death of a law enforcement officer, and within a day the story belongs to history. We express great sympathy at the time, but all too soon the story fades away.

Clarence Alligood gave his best to his job. He gave his life in the performance of his duties. What more can any man give?

It is with deeper sympathy than words can express that we feel a part of this story. There will be other Clarence Alligoods who give their lives, and there will be other stories of a similar nature. But this one is here at home, and it represents a brutal chapter of a continuing story.

He was a good man.

"I didn't feel too bad about that. Ashley Futrell, the editor, is a friend of mine, and I told him three or four days later how the body was found. But if a man wants to stick his neck out without knowing all the facts, it's his own damn problem. For the rest of the week we continued on routine patrol, following leads, interviewing local people. Sheriff Harris came back from the hospital later that week, and I told him that a lot of rumors were going around about what was going on in the jail. They involved not only Alligood, but deputies and bondsmen. Later, a local civil-rights man, James Barrow, went to Ashley Futrell and demanded he print a story that one of my deputies had held the icepick on Joan Little while the jailer screwed her, and then they had reversed roles. I told Harris, 'I'm not the boss, but if I were you, I would ask for a complete investigation of the jail.' This was done, and the SBI interviewed ninety-one female inmates who had served time in the Beaufort County jail, and all of them said they'd been treated nice."

The sheriff did not mention that two black inmates, Rosa Roberson and Annie Marie Gardner, had complained about sexual advances by Clarence Alligood. With Roberson, Alligood wondered if she hadn't been in jail so long that she was ready for sex with him. Roberson told him to go away, said if he tried something like that, "she'd kill him," and that was the end of it. Annie Marie Gardner was somewhat more timid, and Alligood got as far as fondling her breasts when she was down on her knees scrubbing the floor. But she slapped his hands, told him she didn't "play that mess," and the jailer went away.

"When we did not succeed in picking her up immediately, the talk began about declaring her an outlaw. People in the general public, just John Does, started coming to me, maybe twelve or fifteen of them, urging me on the outlaw statute. They'd say, 'Let's get her, get her any way we can.'

"This pressure increased towards the weekend, and on Sunday, William Griffin, the district attorney, who got back from vacation, came to Washington, and we discussed it. Now I've got a few lawyers who advise me, not for a fee, who're just there to steer me right. And I asked them, " 'Wouldn't I be pressing the issue if I supported the outlaw statute in this case?' and they agreed with me. So when Griffin came I took the position that there was no need of it, that it was too much trouble, and he agreed. You see, if I had let Little be declared an outlaw, and someone had killed her, I would have been cutting her down like a weed. It would have trimmed the feet right out from under us. Someone might have killed her and then said, 'Aw, she was giving me a little trouble.' "

The sheriff paused in his narrative, taking a call— routine business about the arrangements for a "client" who wanted to commit himself to a state mental institution.

Sam Grimes, the assistant district attorney and Joan Little's prosecutor in the breaking-and-entering case, told a slightly different version of the outlaw-statute negotiations in the week Joan Little was at large. Grimes descends from an old, fine family in Beaufort County. His great-great-grandfather, Bryan Grimes, was the highest-ranking North Carolinian in the Confederate Army, and "first at Bethel." In 1880, Major General Grimes was found dead, shot in the back, and a year later, down on Water Street in Washington, where the waterfront dives teemed with sailors, ruffians, and ne'er-do-wells, a stranger got drunk and bragged about being the man who shot General Grimes. The next day the stranger was found hanging from the bridge across the Pamlico, the bridge that Grimes had built for the town after the war.

Sam Grimes had found Sheriff Davis not entirely uninterested in the outlaw statute on the day Alligood's body was discovered. There was a good deal of "hot talk" around the sheriff's office about getting Joan Little. Indeed, the sheriff had talked with William Griffin, the chief prosecutor, who was out of town, and Griffin, while not saying to "do it," had not discouraged it either. With this ambivalent instruc-

tion from Griffin, Sam Grimes drafted an outlaw
proclamation against Joan Little. As his guide, the
assistant prosecutor used the language of the last outlaw statute declared in Beaufort County. It had been
requested by William Griffin in June 1973, when one
Samuel Nick Moore, a convicted murderer, escaped
from Central Prison in Raleigh and threatened the
lives of several local citizens, including the officers of
the court who had convicted him. The application for
the outlawry proclamation called Moore "a violent
and dangerous man," and the proclamation itself
read:

> If the said fugitive, Samuel Nick Moore, contin-
> ues to conceal himself and does not immediately
> surrender himself as herein directed, any citizen
> of this State may capture, arrest and bring the
> said fugitive to justice; and in case the said fugi-
> tive attempts to flee or to resist capture when
> called on to surrender, any citizen may slay him,
> the said Samuel Nick Moore, without accusation
> or impeachment for any crime.

But as Grimes substituted Joan Little's name for
Samuel Nick Moore's, the language of the proclamation bothered him. After lunch, Grimes discussed it
with Judge Hallett Ward, a district-court judge in
Washington whose signature on the proclamation
could have set it into effect. Grimes and Ward came to
the conclusion that Joan Little did not have the background that made her dangerous to society when she
was at large, and the sheriff was told that the statute
would not be used.

"Anyway," the sheriff resumed, "on Labor Day an
SBI man contacted me, said it was his understanding
that she was going to surrender in Raleigh the next

day. He did not say, 'Quit looking for her.' That would have been spitting in my face. I had the warrant for her arrest, and so we continued our routine patrolling. The next day I carried the warrant to Raleigh to the SBI headquarters. I was in the building when she entered, but not in Charles Dunn's [Director of the North Carolina State Bureau of Investigation] office. They asked me to wait a few rooms away at first, while they had a quick conversation with her and her attorney before I saw her. I don't know if she was asked whether she wanted me present in the formal arrest or not, but soon after, I was called into Dunn's office, and an SBI agent read her rights to her. I was representing the forty thousand people of Beaufort County at that meeting, and I felt I should have been in Dunn's office when she first came in the building."

CHAPTER 2

ERNEST (PAPS) BARNES AND MARGIE WRIGHT

BACK of Town. It begins a block behind the court house, the classic scene across tracks that actually exist, of shacks and dusty streets, block after block, alive with activity, dead with decay. Fourth Street is the town's 125th Street, but the difference is that it is close, very close by, so there is no hiding it. As there is no hiding it, there must be stock explanations.

Manhattan Transfer, or the honesty of the South: "In New York it seethes, here it's out in the open . . . If you want to see hypocrisy, look at them, or go to the Midwest. Now, that's where the real hypocrisy is." So said Jim Crooks, the Unemployment Insurance man in town, pointing to the lines of applicants at his counter, complaining about how many of New York's welfare clients have come down here, or perhaps "come back" would be the more precise description. Sixty percent black applicants now, when there is only thirty percent black in the Beaufort County population, worse since the recession, bad in all seasons, where the permanent jobs are limited to the mills like National Spinning Company's, or the phosphate plant out in the county, and the seasonal work is the rule: for the men in the winter, logging for Weyerhaeuser, and in the summer, tobacco; for the women, "our oyster shuckers and crab pickers,"

Crooks called them, who like the early work, starting
at five or six in the morning, so they can get back to
all those children by noon.

Silence Is Golden, but not Golden Frinks:

All around Washington, through the sixties, other
towns had racial troubles, but not Washington:
Ayden, twenty-five miles to the west, months of tur-
moil in 1971 followed the killing of a black laborer by
a white policeman and the sentencing of a seventeen-
year-old, Donald Smith, to forty years for bombing a
rest room in the Ayden High School, in which no one
was hurt; Williamston, twenty miles north, massive
organizing by Golden Frinks in 1962 around a dispute
over garbage collection in the black community and
the killing of a black farm hand by his white boss, the
Klan contributing the biggest cross ever burnt (ninety-
two feet); Swanquarter, seventy-five miles east, black
children missed an entire year of school as the closing
of two black schools was protested, and Golden Frinks
turned hundreds of chickens loose in the streets and
834 people were arrested; Windsor, thirty-four miles
north, Klan burnings responded to the protest over
the execution of a black for the attempted rape of a
white woman in 1964; Plymouth and Creswell, thirty-
two miles northeast, Golden Frinks called it the "Second Battle of Plymouth" after the first battle in Massachusetts (wasn't Plymouth a symbol of amity),
when five hundred Klansmen descended on the area
in 1965 and shootouts resulted, as Frinks and Floyd
McKissick, now the developer of Soul City, North
Carolina, supporter of Richard Nixon, leading black
Republican in the state, led a protest over jobs.

But Little Washington never had anything of the
kind. "This is not Meridian, Mississippi," said editor
Dave Milligan. "We've never killed a civil rights
worker here . . . But it's not New York either." Manhattan Transfer within Golden Silence.

But it is true enough that the town wanted to maintain its record of peace. When Golden Frinks announced his march for September 8, 1974, the day before Joan Little was indicted for first-degree murder, a group from Wilmington, North Carolina, called the Rights of White People announced that they were coming to Washington to aid the police force in doing its duty. The Washington Chief of Police, Philip Paul, phoned the group, assured it he needed no help, and added that if its goons came to Washington stirring up trouble, he would do his job. The Rights of White People never showed up, and its leader, Leroy Gibson, is now in prison for a bombing conviction.

THINK POSITIVE, or take a picture of our projects too:

It was a fair point. For the town had demolished four hundred substandard houses, had constructed an equal number of new units, and had repaired five hundred more since 1962—but then, the 1960 census had declared forty-six percent of the entire housing in Washington substandard. Still, its Redevelopment Commission had received an award from HUD for superior achievement in urban renewal, but that was before the malaise of the 1970s, and the Commission director, William I. Cochran, complained that they would have built even more units "if Nixon hadn't frozen the funds."

"The Administration," Cochran wrote the author, "has effectively done away with urban renewal. . . . It was calculated and contrived. The poor and underprivileged have few lobbyists to protect their interests."

At the pretrial hearing in April 1975, the cadre of sociologists, psychologists, and statisticians that the defense had gathered was delighted with the classic case of "dissonance" that the town of Washington exhibited. The theory of dissonance in psychology applies to a situation where there is suddenly a dilemma to which there is no solution, and a person is forced to make a decision. When there is uncertainty about facts, with no solution that reason can determine, dissonance is aroused, and the person leaps. Once he has leapt to an opinion, that opinion is held with ferocity; its veracity is unshakable; its rightness, obvious. For the whites of Washington, the choice was either to latch on to the "evilness" of Joan Little as a person or to acknowledge that they had a "whoremaster" as a jailer, that the system led to abuses, that Back of Town was a disgrace. It was not impossible to find someone in Washington who would manfully take on the guilt. Editor David Milligan, for example, contradicted an earlier Manhattan Transfer. "We've got no responsibility for Boston or Harlem. We've got to see to it that things are right in our own town. The point is that Joan Little is here."

But his was not a commonly held pose. Dissonance had set in with a vengeance, and in a town that was "delightful," as Milligan called it, which had a good deal of respect for itself, the whites leapt to the conclusion that was the least painful: Joan Little was evil, and she lured Alligood, no pillar of strength, into that cell. Or, stated more generally, as did William Roberson, three times Beaufort County's representative to the State legislature and the owner of the local television station, "Whatever happened in that cell happened between two sorry individuals, and it has nothing whatever to do with the other thirty-six thousand citizens of Beaufort County."

Along Fourth Street, where there is always a recession, the legitimate money is in the mortuary business, as it has always been Back of Town in all Southern villages. For death there is no medicine, and the Whitfields and the Randolphs are waiting. The Whitfield Funeral Home is at the corner of Gladden Street, where Joan Little and her boy friend had their club, a place where you could bring a bottle and it would be tagged with your name, put away while you shot pool, or had a bit to eat. Golden Frinks referred to it as a "candy store, like they have in New York," and John Wilkinson, later her prosecutor, called it, "for lack of a better word," a bistro.

The Randolph Funeral Home is down the street, presided over by Louis Randolph, often put forward as the evidence of black leadership in Washington, the man who polled more votes than any other candidate for city council, in two straight elections, but who, all agree, will never be mayor regardless. He could deliver the black vote almost in a bloc, and had been put on the Board of Governor's at the University of North Carolina. In his twenty years in business, Randolph had buried only one white person, a woman of German extraction, who in her will had designated him as her undertaker.

"She knew who I was," Randolph would say with a smile. It is a smile that might have crossed the face of a merchant in the Casbah, a knowing smile, that comes from years of watching the two cultures of a small town operate, learning to live with it and sway with it, and, eventually, to change it ever so slowly. He is always well dressed, for "you got to look good for the public." He wears a Masonic ring on one hand and a four-carat diamond ring on the other. The jeweler uptown had called him one day, saying he had a diamond ring that was "just you."

"You know," he confided, "black people have thrown away their money for so long on things that have no value. I think it's important to know what's valuable in this world." Later he had been hurt by the author's mention of the ring in a magazine article about the Little case, for such materialism tarnished his image for some of his constituency.

Randolph can talk of "negotiation and compromise" and can prove it by talking in one breath about his contributions early to the Joan Little Defense Fund (Golden Frinks was later investigated for supposedly "embezzling" a Randolph check to the Fund, but the prosecutor, Griffin, could find no basis for prosecution), and in the next about what a superb lawyer John Wilkinson, her prosecutor, is—so much better than Jerry Paul.

"There was a time when blacks could only work in the sawmills, on the farm, or in the kitchen," he says. "But the area has industrialized; over fifty percent of the workers in the industries in Beaufort County are black now, some in supervisory capacities, and we've got tellers in all the banks. We've got black policemen, and black firemen. I'm personally responsible for getting the first two black firemen hired (out of nineteen) and I'm looking for two more."

So Randolph sees his duty as watching that people are treated right, people generally, not necessarily just his own, and that things move smoothly in town. But despite that cagey smile, Randolph still could be touched, even angered, when the younger people called him an Uncle Tom, because he refers often to his problem on the city council with people from the "old school of thought." Still,

"We've got to live here together. There's all this talk about going to heaven. What's the use in that if we can't get along here?"

But the legitimate money in the small rural towns of eastern North Carolina is scarce Back of Town. How then does the illegitimate money come? Golden Frinks knew one way.

"If you're very poor, which we are, prostitution starts at a very early age. Sex is very common around the house. You've got the little thin walls. The children get up in the attic and watch the parents or the uncle or whoever. The girls start to budding out, and their breath gets short. They go into the city on a Saturday, and see all the pretty things in the window. Soon enough, someone talks to them about how, in Chicago or New York, the fast girls work. Their minds get captivated, and they turn around and become more free. They try it first with the young boys: 'I will . . . if you give me a quarter, a dollar, thirty-five cents,' and it seems to be a profitable proposition. From that, they dress in such a way; they switch their buttocks around in a different way.

"The morality decays within their conscious mind. They wind up with a tendency to sell themselves, and the money goes from a dollar thirty-five to as high as twenty dollars. From the age of sixteen to twenty, the money may be seven to twenty dollars, or if they can catch the right drunk at the right time, they might pilfer him off by rolling him, making an amount over their cost. And especially if a white man comes into the black community, takes on a good drunk, they'll wolfpack him. So a prostitute can make a pretty good living, and satisfy her man both monetarily and sexually.

"Of course, often they go along and catch their disease. News gets around that this product is a bad product, and they lose out. The community labels them, keeps their sons away from them, says, 'She's not good enough for the dogs,' and puts them in the category of a Jezebel."

Before she went to jail, Joan Little was living in a shack on dusty Pierce Street, half a block from Fourth, when she was not living with her boy friend, or when the Pierce Street house was not occupied by her brother, Jerome, and his thirteen-year-old girl friend.

When she broke out on the night of August 27, 1974, she headed in that direction. She had the heavy ring of jail keys with her, and at her trial the prosecution made fun of that.

"She ran down the street jangling the keys. Jingle, jingle, jingle, sleigh bells in the night. Phooey. Believe that?" Prosecutor Wilkinson blustered at the jury.

She threw the keys away, down by the railroad tracks, and later a youth cutting some grass found them underneath a holly tree. She saw lights and ducked behind a laundry. When the car passed, she raced on, barefoot, along the dirt streets Back of Town to her cousins' house, Annie and Raymond Cobb, and tapped on the window of their dark house on Seventh Street. Raymond Cobb let her in, and, breathless, she told them she thought she'd killed a man.

"Who?"

"The jailer."

The jailer had made her take her clothes off, tried to make her have sex with him, and when he started to take his clothes off, she had stabbed him. That was what the Cobbs told an SBI agent and Deputy Willis Peachey later that day, in the afternoon, when they came looking for Joan Little, but Deputy Peachey had heard something more specific. Joan Little told Annie Cobb (as Peachey heard it) that when Alligood started to take off his clothes, Joan Little *ran and got the icepick,* and when Alligood came at her, she stabbed him with it.

Raymond Cobb was scared. He told his young cousin she could not stay there, that he did not want any trouble with the police. But he made a gesture nonetheless. He let her call her mother, and then took her around back, to another house, where another man, Steve, lived. Raymond Cobb asked Steve if he would take Joan out into the country, but as they talked a police car came down Seventh Street and

Joan Little bolted . . . farther west down Seventh, along the row of tiny, squalid cinderblock houses, perhaps fifteen by thirty feet, easily the slummiest housing in Washington, if not the Southeast, if not the world—the row that the Redevelopment Director had said he would love to have destroyed and replaced, but the funds had run out.

Sitting outside one such house, in the middle of the block, was an old man, Ernest (Paps) Barnes. In fact, he is not that old, fifty-two, but he looks like a septuagenarian. He is a big man, about Alligood's dimensions, perhaps two hundred pounds, with a roundish moon-face and a deep, husky voice, and eyes that size a man up, with great caution, before he speaks. A sweat-stained rain hat was pulled over his head, and he let the author into his block house only after earnest protestations that his visitor had not come to lock the old man up. Paps motioned for him to have a seat on the wreck of a couch, springs broken, with a filthy pinkish terry cloth thrown over it. The living room had once upon a time been painted green, but the paint was cracked and peeling now. A small space heater against the far wall, a snowy television projecting *Sanford and Son,* a table in the center with linoleum tacked to it—Paps is a poker player—these were the accommodations. A yellowish towel hung across the entrance to the steps leading to the loft, a passageway to the kitchen, and the small room—the important room—where a box spring on the floor supports a lumpy feather mattress.

Paps allowed how he was a "hardworkin' son of a bitch," came up the hard way, and rode that damn tractor for a real-estate man in Washington for twenty years. After that he worked the power saw for Weyerhauser for ten years, and in the summer, chopped tobacco.

But now, "the doctor's got me on 'no work.' Ain't

supposed to do nothin'. High blood and kidneys. Doctor says,

" 'Sit down and be clean.'

"And so I do, and I do my drinkin' and get drunk quick now. That morning early, I was drinkin', sittin' out on my front porch, drinkin', and that was when she came by. She didn't say at first she was in trouble, said she just wanted to stay with me a while, and I said,

" 'Sure, honey, you can stay here. You could be my daughter. You could be my granddaughter. Yeah, I'll look after you.'

"But when the police came a little later—about seven or eight o'clock—and they had rifles out, rifles on their shoulders, and they got all around the house, and Joan ran for the back door, and I snatched her back, told her to go in the back bedroom and crawl under that old feather mattress . . . I knew she was in trouble then. They were gonna shoot her, first sight. They were gonna kill her. That's the truth. Go ahead, write that down.

"So they beat on the door and I opened it.

" 'We're lookin' for Joan Little,' this tall one says, tall one with slicked-back hair, and I said,

" 'You got a search warrant?' but the way they was actin', it got my temper to rise up, said, 'Can't search this house 'less you got a search warrant,' but I knew it wont no use, said,

" 'Hell, don't make no difference anyway. C'mon in and search. Don't make no difference.'

"They came in, and this short one, he slapped my pants pocket where I had my pistol, my twenty-two-caliber pistol.

" 'What's this?' and he took it away and later, someone from down there at the sheriff's office called me up.

" 'Barnes?' he said.

" 'Yassah.'

" 'C'mon downtown and get your gun. He had no business going in your house and takin' your gun.'

"Anyway, this tall one, he was the one making me mad, said,

" 'You better tell me where she's at, or I'm gonna knock the shit out of you.' I should have hit the son of a bitch right there. How I despise 'em!

"Well, up in the loft, there were two, they were up there, bald neked, fuckin', and I said to the police,

" 'Go on up there, see if that girl up there's the one you're lookin' for. Go on up there, see if that's this Little you're after.'

"They went up, come back down, looking a little silly.

" 'Is that her? Is that Little?' I asked 'em, and they said,

" 'Naw.'

"Those two up there in the loft—that's what saved Joan and me too! Go on, put that down. And this other one, he pulls out five hundred dollars, had it right there in his hand, said,

" 'Barnes, I'll give you this five hundred dollars if you tell me where she is.'

" 'I don't need no money,' I told him. 'Don't know where she is. Go ahead and lock me up,' and they went away. In those six days she stayed with me, they came back four times and each time she hid under that feather mattress, and one of 'em even sat on that bed one time when she was under it. They never found her, with their dogs and flashlights and rifles. They never found her. Haw. Haw. Haw.

"In the time she was with me, she had the fear. She said he got naked with her in that cell, tried to make her suck him, and she killed him with an icepick. He tried to make her suck his dick. You know that ain't right. It was his fault. That won't right, what he tried

to make her do. Write that down. That won't right.
"And then Marjorie Wright came and got her
about two A.M. one night, put a wig on her, and she
walked out with my old army shirt. I've never seen her
since."

Margie Wright is tough. She has seen a lot in thirty-
one years, and will not stand for much foolishness,
certainly not from no white boy like the author,
whom she referred to as a "news media." She has done
what she's had to do to make a living in Washington,
supporting herself, her daughter, her mother (Mrs.
Jessie Wrighton—pronounced Right On), and assorted others, presently by driving a community cab.
She expects to be paid when she renders a service, and
before the trial the defense considered using her to
ferry a shy, reluctant witness, Annie Gardner, to the
trial. Annie Gardner would tell the court later that
when she was in jail, Alligood would bring sandwiches to her and would often try to feel her breasts,
but when she told him she didn't play that mess and
slapped his hands away, he would stop. Morris Dees
warned Jerry Paul that they had a problem in getting
Annie Gardner to court and suggested Margie Wright
perform the chore—"if we can afford her."

Of the seamy side of social control in Beaufort
County, Margie Wright was well acquainted, and
through her, once again, the name of the sallow
bondsman, J. B. Freeman, cropped up. The State
Bureau of Investigation had been interested in Freeman shortly after Alligood's death, because the stories
began to come in that he dispensed bonds for sexual
favors. Margie Wright had a story about Freeman that
went back in time:

"About eight or nine years ago, a friend, Ruby Dud-
ley, was charged, and Freeman was her bondsman.
Since she had to have employment while on bond, he

hired her to work at his drive-in. She told me he was
attempting to have sexual relations with her and asked
me to help her avoid this by speaking to him. When I
approached him about this, he attempted the same
thing with me by stating, in substance, that I could
have anything if I had sexual relations with him."

After the Alligood death, the SBI conducted a series
of interviews with former female inmates in the Beaufort County Jail, and one of them, Sandra Davenport,
who was in the jail with Joan Little for a time, said
that J. B. Freeman came back to her cell each morning for a week and "offered to have sex." "He'd say
wasn't I getting restless for a man. He told me he was
available, but I joked it off." But then Davenport told
the SBI that Joan Little never wore clothes from the
waist up and would undress in front of anyone who
came in. She told a story of Little's prosecutor in her
breaking-and-entering case, Sam Grimes, coming for a
visit to the jail, when Joan Little was naked. At the
corridor to the women's section, Grimes at least did
announce himself,

"Are you dressed?" he called out.

"Come on in," Joan Little replied, and she put a
blanket across her lap. Grimes entered, and prosecutor
and defendant talked for a long while, with defendant
naked from the waist up, as Davenport tells it.
(Grimes denies it.) When he had gone, Little turned
to Davenport.

"If the crazy fool wants to stand and look, let him
get his eyes full."

So the defense had a quandary about calling Sandra
Davenport to the stand later. Morris Dees, the defense
investigator, wrote in a memo to chief defense lawyer
Jerry Paul,

"We face a real problem in getting her to court, if
we decide that her testimony about Freeman will
overcome what she will say about Joan Little being

naked. I'd bring the naked incident out in direct to show how court officials invade inmates' privacy. I doubt if Grimes would say he stood and talked for a long time." In the end they decided that the naked-ness incident was too damaging, and they never called Sandra Davenport to the trial.

All this maneuvering around the bondsmen went to the fact that the defense also considered J. B. Freeman a dangerous witness. He had told Morris Dees that he would "rip her up" on the stand, and he had a story of Joan Little propositioning him. In a statement to the defense, he wrote,

"I bonded out Joan Little when she was arrested for breaking and entering in Beaufort County. She failed to appear in court and her bond was called. Sheriff Davis and I went to Chapel Hill to find Joan. We tracked her around Chapel Hill. We were unable to find her but left word for her to return to Washington. When I returned home, Joan called my house. She said,

" 'Mr. Freeman, are you looking for me?'

"I told her to come back to Washington the next day. . . . The next day she returned and I turned her into the jail. She sent for me and said that she had a friend (a man) in Greenville who would put up the money for another bond. She asked me to take her to Greenville so she could see this man and get the money. I bonded her out of jail and drove her to Greenville in my car. She went to the place where the man lived but was unable to locate him. She asked me to take her to another friend's house. I did, but they would not let her have any money. We, me and Joan, then headed towards Washington in my car. On the return trip, she said,

" 'Mr. Freeman, if I have sex with you, will you let me stay out of jail until the first of the month?'

"I asked her why until the first of the month. She

replied that she would take some girls down to Jacksonville [the site of Camp Lejeune] and make some money, about a thousand dollars, because the Marines get paid on the first. I refused to remain on her bond and took her back to jail. This is the only time Joan Little ever offered sex to me or ever spoke to me about sex."

But it may not have been the only time J. B. Freeman considered sex with Joan Little. For the "man" in the statement was Bennie Roundtree, a café owner in Greenville, and Roundtree had a story about going with Joan Little to Freeman's house on another of Joan Little's difficulties, a time in 1974 when she was charged for having a concealed shotgun under the seat of a car she was driving in Jacksonville. Joan wanted Bennie to put up $150 on a bond in that case, so she could get back a ring worth $5 and a color TV set she had given Freeman for a bond, and they went to Freeman's house. Freeman invited them inside, and then took Roundtree aside and offered him a drink. Freeman asked Roundtree, according to the latter, if maybe Joan Little would swap him some sex for the bond and that Freeman did not want any money from Bennie. Bennie replied that he did not know what she would do, and offered the money instead. Freeman refused, saying, "Wait until you check out whether she will give me some sex." Bennie never talked with Freeman again, and Joan Little settled her Jacksonville case.

So the defense and the prosecution were ready with their competing stories about the sallow Mr. Freeman at the trial, but when he took the stand and started his story about the proposition, with the jury out, the whole matter was declared irrelevant, and that was the end of it. Had Freeman's testimony not been cut short, he doubtless would also have described his amazement at watching Clarence Alligood, along with another man, lift a three-hundred-pound hog into a pickup truck two weeks before he was killed. That the sixty-two-year-old jailer was that strong before his death would have given credence to the prosecutions's contention that the jailer needed no icepick to force this "slip of a girl" to do his bidding, and had she threatened him, he could have snapped her "like a twig" with his brute strength.

So Margie Wright was important to the defense as one of several counters to J. B. Freeman, should he take the stand. Her mother, Jessie Mae Wrighton, was potentially important as well, for she had a story which bore on Alligood's proclivities. Once when she went to visit her son in jail, Alligood showed her a bottle of whiskey and said, "Let's have a party."

He asked her to go to bed with him. She refused both whiskey and bed, and did not report the incident to anyone, except her daughter. However, Morris Dees, the defense investigator, did not find her an attractive witness, but thought she "might be sobered up for the trial." Dees argued in a memo,

"If we offered it [Mrs. Wrighton's testimony] and the State did not object, the State might then contend *they* could offer unrelated sexual acts of Joan Little in rebuttal, because we opened the door by showing sexual acts or practices of Alligood unrelated to female inmates. I'd argue if we used Ms. Wrighton that this involved his conduct at the jail with inmates and their families."

Jessie Mae Wrighton never took the stand, but she did make the news once and even got her picture in a Raleigh paper. During Joan Little's pretrial hearing in April 1975, when the trial was moved to Raleigh, Wrighton swore out a warrant against Golden Frinks, claiming that he had threatened her four times, when she did not show up at his tent city in Washington, which he was calling Resurrection City III. Frinks needed all the bodies he could get for his crusade, because his Resurrection City III had only twelve tents.

But Margie Wright's most important role would be in Joan Little's escape from Beaufort County. "I did not pay much attention to the Alligood talk when it first happened," Margie Wright said. "I was the assistant supervisor at the Seacrest Marine Company, making three dollars an hour, and I just didn't have the time, but when things started to get so heavy and so serious—I was scared to death that the law-enforcement officers in Beaufort County would find her and kill her—I said,

" 'Heck, she's a woman just like I am. Why don't I get out there and look out for her?' And before it was over I was fired from Seacrest. I didn't care. I was tired of working there anyway. Oh, they tried to give me the job back when I beefed about it—but for reduced pay, offered two dollars an hour instead of three, and I wasn't gonna lift no two-hundred-fifty-pound and hundred-twenty-five-pound boats for that, so I told 'em to keep it.

"I had known Joan since she was a tiny tot, and I started askin' around, and someone told me where they *thought* she was. So I *thought* she was with Paps, but I won't for sure. I went from door to door, knocking and asking along Seventh Street. I didn't know Paps that well, but I'd seen him around several times, and when I went to his house, I said,

" 'Paps, do you know me?'

" 'Yeah, Margie, I know you.'

" 'I'm lookin' for Joan. I'm trying to save her life.'

" 'C'mon back in the kitchen,' he said, 'and get yourself a glass of water,' and when I got back to the kitchen, she was the first thing that met me at the door. She grabbed me and hugged me, broke down crying. Her face was all swollen from crying, and her eyes were so swollen, they looked like they would pop out.

" 'Margie,' she said, 'I wanted to come to where you were staying, but I was scared to death to run that far.' You see, I was staying another five blocks out of town near the shopping center.

"I had to hold her up as she sobbed, and then I laid her down on the bed.

" 'Cool it, mama,' I told her, trying to calm her, because she was so hysterical that she couldn't talk plain. 'You don't have to discuss anything with anybody.'

" 'Margie,' she said, 'I don't want to go back to jail.'

" 'Don't worry about it, sugar.'

"I told her that I would be back, and I did go back every day for the next three days she was there, before I drove her out of there in a green Plymouth from New York. Nobody could get next to her but me, and I only talked with Jerry Paul, Golden Frinks, and James Barrow, who is dead now, but I was the only one who knew where she was. In those visits, she told me that she got tired of Alligood making her suck him, and she also said that in one of those searches in Paps's place, a policeman had shined a flashlight right in her face. She was trembling and carrying on, but she said,

" 'I did not kill Alligood,' and I still don't think she broke out by herself. She had help, because I've seen that key ring, and how else, except with help, could she know the precise key to use on that chain of keys to get out of the jail?

"But Paps, Lord, you ain't never seen a calmer person in your life than him, never. When I found her first, I wanted to take her away, but he said,

" 'No, wait till you've found a safe place to take her.'

"He's an old, lonely man, living by himself, mostly disabled from some disease. He don't even have the right facilities. Don't even have a decent bathroom, and his kitchen is overflowing with everything. You know how poor people are, especially if they're black. He told me,

" 'I ain't got nothin' to lose but my life. If I have to lose my life for that young girl, let it go. Because I got children out there. She might be my grandchild, and you never know what's going to happen to them.'

"About one A.M. on the night of September first, I was out at the American Legion Post No. 263. What was I doin'? I was partyin', drinkin' liquor, what in the hell's the matter with you? Some friends came and picked me up, told me they needed me at the motel. At the motel they told me to go get her in a green Plymouth with New York tags—it was a car that they would not be watching. When I got in front of Paps's house and got out of the car, here comes a police car down Seventh Street with its lights out, and I stooped down behind an old evergreen bush, and that bush saved me. After he went past, I went in and got her. She was wearing blue jeans that were big enough for me, and an old shirt that was big enough for four people. I had this short-cut wig on, and I put it on her, snatched a paper bag that she was holding away from her, and hustled her out to the car, carried her to Mr. Ed's out on the highway where Jerry Paul was waiting, and he took her off in the night.

"Several days later, after she was gone and already in Women's Prison, I went back to Paps, and he was crying:

" 'Please tell Joan to come around and see me one more time,' he said.

" 'Paps, I think you deserve that,' I told him."

CHAPTER 3

GOLDEN FRINKS

"In the last fourteen years there hasn't been a day when I haven't done something for civil rights. Ever since that day in 1962 when Dr. King came to me and said, 'Golden, can I trust you?' I've been working full time, and I've done some pretty good movements. In Eastern North Carolina: Williamston in '62, the Second Battle of Plymouth in '65, Swanquarter in '69 to '72. I've pulled more time than any other active civil-rights leader in the movement. I've had some laws changed as a result of my impatience with the system, and God knows, I've paid: 197 arrests, 71 terms in jail, been apprehended more than 295 times. I was also with Dr. King in the St. Augustine, Florida, movement in '65, and the project director in Montgomery during the Selma-to-Montgomery march. Six good years with Dr. King, and he would catch me if I got discouraged. Once I was ranting about something or other, and he turned to me, said, 'Golden, you're bitter.' His thing was Glory, Hallelujah, and that was why the Goverment could never discredit him.

"So I've done a lot of marching, and I always wear these boots. 'These boots are made for marching': I said that first in the open-housing struggle in Louisville in '65. 'Open Housing, Open Hell, or these boots will walk all over you.' That was the slogan. And I started wearing these jump suits during the Poor People's campaign in 1968. I went to this department store in Washington, D.C., and they said they had run out of the old coveralls, so the man suggested the jump suit. During the Resurrection City I, Chief Jerry Wilson in D.C. said, 'Why, Golden, you're the cleanest one of them all. You can march here any time.' Those jump suits got so popular once down here that a company in a little town down the line started to market 'Golden jump suits.' "

Golden was saying all this, walking to his motel room in Washington. The room was on the ground floor. Frinks never took a room on a balcony if he could help it. It was one of his superstitions. Dr. King had been shot on a motel balcony. He is not commanding in appearance, his thick black glasses often sliding down his nose and sometimes askew. At fifty-five, he is spreading out within his loose-fitting jump suits. His speech sometimes requires an effort at translation, and seldom did the reporters who covered him think the effort worthwhile. For Frinks was another character in the piece that was easy to make fun of. One magazine article during the year of Joan Little had referred to him as "a crack-brained civil-rights activist," and many had gleefully latched onto the label.

"My activities as an organizer were good," he began, "but the credit was always sopped up by someone else; someone else always got the credit. The reason was that I did not come into civil rights by the respectable route, through the ministry. I'm a photographer and journalist by trade, but I ran a nightclub in Edenton, North Carolina, in the late fifties and early sixties, and when I started to get active in civil rights they took my beer license away. There was a navy base in Edenton in those days, and they claimed that I was running in girls from New York and Philadelphia for fornication purposes on paydays at the base. The news media developed a reputation on me, and that reputation was worse than my character. Rather than rise above the average civil-rights leader for my work, I lagged behind—in reputation, not in work, for I have been consistent in my fight against evil. I didn't look for fanfare. If the publicity came, fine. Why, I used to call up UPI and say, I just did this and I just did that. Print it if you want to. I guess my greatest downfall was that I was my own publicity agent.

"When I took the Joan Little case, I understood from my own life certain aspects of her situation. The way the case developed, however, was a little different from what we as black people would like to have had. You see, in the South we've been subjected to injustices to a degree that is astronomical. For a person to understand that, he would have to walk in our shoes. It's very difficult for other than a black to recognize this, unless he is really true blue all the way through. Jerry Paul thought he was true blue, but then he jumped the fence. He wasn't paying attention to the surroundings. He lost sight of the moral issue of the treatment of black women in the South.

"Now when I agreed to develop a movement around Joan Little, it was the first time I could remember when a civil-rights organization went out on a case, where murder was the spark . . . other than when a murder occurred during the act of civil disobedience. It was a brand-new area of civil rights, if there was any civil rights in the beginning, because when I went to investigate it, I had no idea there was any civil rights about it.

"On the evening of August 27, 1974, I was incarcerated in the Maury State Prison on a six-month sentence for blocking traffic on the streets of Edenton, North Carolina, protesting the firing of a black band director at the local high school, when a special newscast came on the TV, saying that a black woman had escaped from the Beaufort County jail, and the jailer was found dead in the cell block. The newscast was immediately followed by a telephone call, asking for the use of the prison tracking dogs, to be taken to an area of adjoining Pitt County, where a car had been seen with a woman answering to the description of Miss Little. At the time I was talking to the Eastern Area correctional director. My visit ended, and I was taken back in and locked up for the night. Once back in the cell block, several inmates surrounded me and began asking questions about whether SCLC would enter the case. At that time I only offered some information about SCLC's program of nonviolence, said I did not see that murder and jailbreak had anything to do with basic civil liberties.

"What I did not expect to see on the TV, however, was police officers peering into an abandoned car with high-powered rifles. At that moment I knew something was amiss. I asked the inmates,

" 'Do you think she killed the jailer in a cold-blooded plan to escape?'

"They answered they thought there was a little more to the story than a black woman breaking out of jail, and a wide-ranging discussion of what might have happened ensued. The inmates felt that Miss Little was in great danger of her life. Some were aggravated to a great degree to see black officers searching for Miss Little with high-powered rifles at the ready.

"For the next few days the whole cell block continued to discuss the jailbreak, and on August 30 a report reached the prison that Miss Little had been found. This report was ungrounded, but later, a better-grounded and happier report came: Jerry Paul, SCLC's attorney, had gone before the Appeals Court and a bond had been set for my release. It was near ten P.M. that night when Jerry finally came for me.

We drove over to Greenville for a steak at R. B. Junior's Bar and Grill, and after that we went on to Edenton for the night. We did not discuss the Little case, because, I suppose, we were caught up in my own pending legal matters.

"On Saturday, August 31, I got a call from the late Mr. James Barrow, the SCLC's area field coordinator in Washington, North Carolina, asking if I would come over to Washington and look into the facts of the girl breaking jail. He said he had been able to compile a few things that I could look over. You see, that's always the first step in building a movement: it's the old tactics of the sixties. First you get whatever information you can, then you go out and survey the community to see if you can build support.

"After talking with Mr. Barrow for over an hour, the phone rang again, and it was Miss Margie Wright. She was very excited, and said,

" 'You've got to come and help us.'

"I asked her what was the matter.

" 'The cops are about to catch Joan, and if they do they'll kill her.'

"She thought that if I could come, I could be of some help. I told her that I'd be over within the day, and also related that Jerry was right there in Edenton.

" 'Perhaps you can get him to come over to Washington on his way back to Durham,' I said, trying to soothe her, and I gave her his number.

"Shortly thereafter Jerry called and asked if I was going to Washington. I said I was, and for him to come over from his motel, that it was time for breakfast. When he got there, we talked over Miss Little's case, and what if anything we could do. At that point Miss Wright called again. I told her to get ahold of Mrs. Williams, Joan's mother, and she said Mrs. Williams was right there. I said, fine, I will see you after lunch.

"Jerry and I then drove to Washington by different routes, with plans to meet at the Quality Motel in Washington after I had seen Mr. Barrow. When I arrived at Mr. Barrow's house, he was taking a lady to the supermarket, and we agreed to meet later in my motel room.

"At about one-thirty that afternoon, Mr. Barrow came to my motel room, and shortly afterwards Jerry arrived. Barrow called Miss Wright and she came out with another daughter, her mother, Ms. Jessie Wrighton, two other young ladies, and Mrs. Jessie Williams, Joan's mother. We asked Mrs. Williams to tell us all she knew about her daughter Joan, and all about her daughter's legal troubles. She began, but she was overcome with grief, and she started to cry. It was a concerned little cry that would have sold anybody. She put on the little cry, impressed me as naïve-sounding, but later I found out she wasn't so naïve at all. She lives in a nice house, nicer than mine, and she knows a lot. I asked if she knew where her daughter was. She did not. I spoke of the cost involved in finding her daughter and then defending her. I was stone broke, I told her, but said I would do all I could to help her.

" 'Do you want SCLC's lawyer, Jerry Paul, to represent her?' I asked.

"She said yes.

" 'Well, go ahead, Jessie Ruth, ask him,' Miss Wright said to Joan's mother.

"She turned to Jerry. 'Will you help my daughter?' she asked.

" 'I will. I'll do all I can,' Jerry replied.

"Now the problem was how to find Joan Little. I asked Miss Wright if she would go out in the community and sell some books to raise money for telephoning. I always have books from SCLC conventions if I need to raise money on the spot. They are handed out at our conventions, so that the field secretaries can sell them in black communities on their way home for gas money . . . you know, living off the land like General Sherman in the Civil War. Margie organized a team of young people to do the selling, and in about an hour they returned with sixty dollars.

"Even though we were close on Joan Little's trail, I had no success finding her, and so our little group decided to send out a call for Miss Little to surrender herself. But who should she surrender herself to? Certainly not the police, for we felt she was surely in terror for her life—and with good reason. The group agreed that she should surrender herself to me . . . or to SCLC Attorney Paul, and that we would provide her with safety. So I drafted a news release and Mr. Barrow placed the call to UPI. It was getting towards six-fifteen, and Mr. Paul said he would be off to Durham. He left with the understanding that I would build a movement around Joan Little's case, and that SCLC would not meddle in any way with the legal aspects of the case.

"You ask if it is not dangerous to decide to build a movement around a woman whom I did not know. But the movement was not built around Joan Little as such at this time. It was built around saving her from getting shot on sight, so that the facts could be brought out, so that the truth could be known. Neither I nor Jerry ever did talk to Joan, until I got her to surrender. But I knew more about Joan Little in an hour after Jerry had departed than I needed to know—by conjecture, you know, conjecture as a black person and from what I could glean from the community. What the police knew about her did not help, because they themselves were withholding information. The secrecy surrounding Joan, however, was a great deterrent to building a movement in those first days.

"You see, she was in a community that had rejected

her. Because of little accidents in her life, because of
her past life which the local people did not exactly
feel was up to the general moral standard of the community, they had ostracized her. She had led what I
would call a 'fast life,' and she had fallen into the
obedience of friends that did not care for what Joan
was trying to seek herself. They used her, exploited
her because of her age, seventeen or eighteen, and that
was where her troubles began. Her contacts were leading her in a direction that her mother and others in
the community did not appreciate, running that little
ole café and poolroom down there on Fourth Street—
in New York, they would call it a candy store. She had
fallen into bad repute, getting the reputation of a
'wayward girl,' but so far as I could tell in making my
investigation, she never did solicit. Joan herself is not
basically bad. It was her associates and the system that
were bad.

"Washington, North Carolina, is a backward, un-
developed little place, almost, how do you say, on the
border of heathenism. It has always been a compla-
cent and pathetic place, even in Eastern North Carolina terms. There's always been a stagnation of black
leadership there, and when there is no black leadership, there's always more hustlers and hoodlums. Why,
I went in there at the end of 1961 with the NAACP
under the commands of Floyd B. McKissick. I lent my
corps of youths to organize there, and we made Washington the first city in Eastern North Carolina where
they would let a black work in the five-and-dime store
downtown. Do you know, we couldn't get a single
black in Washington to let their children work in that
downtown store?

"So I stayed up night and day trying to decide if
this case was worth it, with the community rejecting
her automatically. But when her mother said she did
not think Joan had killed Mr. Alligood, *there* was
something that we could go to work with; we could

focus on the treatment of black women in the state, the abuses in the jails, especially of a woman who had overstayed her time in jail, for her case was on appeal, and we could work on saving her from being killed. There was something that we could sell to the community . . . and the nation.

"I determined that I would write a little pamphlet that would introduce the case to the minds of the people. I took the tack that 'God had chosen this girl with all her little happenings to be the savior of black women who are incarcerated.' I described her as a meek little girl who had been swept up in this cause. I wrote,

" 'Joan had one goal in mind: she wanted to be intelligent and she endeavored to this end; falling short, she became trapped in the cage of the deprived black community. Listening to the fast beat of pop records, and the desire for fancy clothes, brought her into contact with others who did not share with her the goals she had set—and she moved to the obedience of her new-found friends. The strongest evidence yet to support the Free Joan Little Committee's faith in their efforts in her behalf is that she attended church very often and was involved in the Tenants' Rights Movement.'

"I continued that the authorities were not taking into account the individual's right to be 'secure in security,' and wrote,

" 'The question is, Why did Mr. Alligood go to Joan's cell at such an hour (three-twenty-eight) in the morning? Why did he take the icepick? Is the sheriff's department holding back information? Did not Mr. Alligood commit a capital crime?* Could sex and

---

* In 1974, under first-degree rape in North Carolina Law, a defendant could get death under two circumstances: (a) if the defendant was over sixteen and the victim under twelve,

drinking and other acts of bad conduct have played a part in Mr. Alligood's death?' The community caught that, as I went from church to church with it.

"As I've said, I knew it would be an uphill fight to weld the community of Washington into a workable support group, and it became hard even in the churches. On that Sunday I went to the Mount Hebron Baptist Church, the church where the Little family was registered as members, and asked the pastor if I could speak to the congregation. He refused me, saying that he was concerned about discussing crime from the pulpit. You see the community had moved thumbs down on Joan because of her previous record, her breaking and entering into a mobile home of a black person, see—she was ripping off black folks! They had known her since she was a child, when she had her little discotheque, her little shop on Fourth Street, riding around in cars, the fancy way she dressed.

"But when this broke, the community still could accept that Joan had a right to defend herself in that jail, even to escape. Being a backward place, with no black leadership, they would not organize themselves, but when someone came to them, they would help. In fact, the community's actions fit the pattern of the old Underground Railroad before the Civil War, when the slaves hid under the bushes, or in the hay in wagons. Joan, with her wit as a black person, skipped around hedges, hid behind buildings, until she could get into the black community where she could feel safe.

"You see, I believe this girl, with all her faults, was designated by God to raise these issues at this time, as

---

and (b) if the defendant was over sixteen and the victim had resisted, was overcome by a deadly weapon, or serious bodily harm was inflicted.

we approach the twenty-first century: she was designated to be the instrument by which women would
propel themselves forward, for we could not go into
the next century the way it was in this one. I can hear
that voice saying to her as she enters the black area,

" 'Not here. You got to go farther.'

"She went to one house, the house of her aunt and
uncle, the Cobbs, and they turned her away. They
were thinking,

" 'The people who are after you are my tormentors
too. The people who are after you are after me too. So
you go away from my door, because I don't want no
trouble.'

"She went to another house and was turned away
and then another, and the voice said,

" 'Move on down the street.'

"And there in front of that falling-down old gray
building, an old man was sitting out on his porch. It
was like Paul and Ananias.

Acts 9:11: And the Lord said unto him, Arise
and go into the street which is called Straight,
and inquire in the house of Judas for one called
Saul, of Tarsus. . . .

Then Ananias answered, Lord, I have heard by
many of this man, how much evil he hath done to
thy saints at Jerusalem. . . .

But the Lord said unto him, Go thy way: for he
is a chosen vessel unto me, to bear my name before the Gentiles, and kings, and the children of
Israel:

For I will show him how great things he must
suffer for my name's sake.

"So Paps Barnes kept her hidden, and the police
searched for her in the house and she lay hidden
under that bumpy, raggedy old mattress. If she had

sneezed when the policeman sat on top of her, that would have been all she wrote. But, like Martin Luther King, she kept her sneeze well dampened. You remember Dr. King was stabbed in a department store in Harlem after the Montgomery bus boycott, and the knife lay on an artery by the heart, and the doctor told him later that, had he sneezed, he would have drowned in his own blood, but he kept his sneeze well dampened. If Joan had sneezed, she would have drowned in bullets.

"After I was turned away from Joan Little's church on Sunday, I returned to the motel which had become our headquarters. Things were on the hum that afternoon. People were coming in from all directions: from New York, Philadelphia, Connecticut, and other places in North Carolina. Mr. James Speller, SCLC's top troubleshooter, had come in from New York. We rented two more rooms; one became our briefing room and was kept very secret, and I kept the key in my pocket at all times. We had a map of Washington on the wall, and Mr. Barrow had put red and yellow stickers on it to mark the police positions in the town. You see, they had police on all the dirt streets of Washington at this time.

"As the staff grew to fourteen and later to twenty-two, I had to be concerned with plants. That day, I received a call that we could pick up Joan Little at a certain time at the South of the Border compound in South Carolina, and even though I was very suspicious of the call I drove down there. When the information proved false—and it was very costly, because it lost us time—I became very concerned that some people on the staff were working a little too closely with local officials, that there was some hanky-panky going on. At another point, a black man came to me, said,

" 'Oh, you got to leave this town. I fear for your life.

The Citizen's Council is comin', and we don't know what's going to happen.'

" 'Well, what are you telling me that for?' I asked. 'You're a black man, and you got to live for something. So why don't you be out there guarding me, rather than telling me to run? We got a sister somewhere in this area, somewhere in these United States, and we got to save her life, because we can't build a movement around a dead person, and you most certainly can't do nothing with me dead.'

"When they plant someone, they become a part. They participate, and that's the danger. Two or three days after Joan's surrender, we were having a briefing, and we were really in it hot. I was telling the staff what it takes to be a leader: the thanklessness, how people would jump all over you, but you got to keep working, because Joan must be saved. And out of the cold blue, this truck driver arrived, with an empty truck, and started taking a big part in the discussion, distorting what I was trying to say. We knew he was a plant. So we stopped the meeting, and I served lemonade or whatever we had, and there was no more meeting that night. So we lost nine hours getting rid of him.

"Sunday was a day of calls and more calls—to black radio, to newsmen—and strategy sessions with the staff. In many ways, the day was reminiscent of the movement time in the 1960s. There was profound concern for the safety of Joan, but many of the staff wanted to jump ahead to the moral issue of the rights of black women in the jails of Eastern North Carolina. I urged the staff to stick to the immediate issue of saving the girl, that this was the best way to muster support. Some of the staff thought this was stupid, for they had very little confidence in local officials, feeling that we were up against a well-organized posse of racist whites—and they had very little respect for local black leadership. But there was a sense of real urgency, for we knew by this time that Joan was still in Washington, that on Tuesday the courts would be back in session, and that some judge would likely be asked to declare Joan an outlaw and that her chances of surviving were becoming more doubtful by the minute. We could already sense the frustration of the local officials.

"In the afternoon, I put in a call to Charles Dunn, the director of the State Bureau of Investigation. I had known Mr. Dunn over the years, and we had a relationship of sorts. I knew that if I was ever going to get a favor, it was at this juncture of history, because a life was at stake. I thought he would listen if I explained the absolute necessity of the girl being surrendered peacefully, so that justice would be done. He said he would call me back in an hour and a half. When he did call back, he said he wanted to trust me, that he was sticking his neck way out. I was to have Joan at his office at eleven A.M., Tuesday. He agreed that she could make a press statement before she surrendered, but that once she entered his office, she had to have a lawyer. So we worked out the arrangements, and he sent two SBI agents over to the motel to confirm the details.

"At that point the police pressure relaxed, and it was a good thing, because it would have been very difficult to meet the deadline the following day otherwise. Suddenly, the police cars on all the direct streets miraculously disappeared and pulled back to the Shell service station across from our motel. Still we did not relax, because we were sure that Sheriff Davis would arrest her—or worse—if he caught her in Washington, for he had his warrant. Even with the pullback, there was a police car stationed about fifty yards from the house where Joan hid, and beyond that, we did not know who the lookout man for the police on Seventh Street might be.

"At seven P.M. Margie Wright, who was by then the

contact with Joan, called me to the back of the motel
and told me that Joan was in a hysterical state of
mind and that she was talking suicide.

" 'What in the hell is she saying that for?' I asked
Margie. 'You go right back to her wherever she is—
and tell her I've worked out a plan with high state
law officials for a safe surrender, and that she will be
out of here by midnight.' I did not know exactly
where she was, nor had I asked. I left that to Margie
and Mr. Barrow. Later I learned that Joan had written a confession letter to me when she was in that
state of mind, but that Margie Wright and Joan's
mother had burned it up. [Jerry Paul insists that
Frinks had received the letter, and that *he*, Frinks,
had burned it.]

"I then put a call through to Attorney Paul at his
home in Chapel Hill and asked him if he could come
to Washington, and that he should be there by midnight. I did not tell him that we had located Miss
Little—simply that I had a 'big package' for him.
Meanwhile, I began to work on the transfer plan.

"We had seven cars and at this point, about thirty-
five people, including Joan's mother and sisters. I decided that the transfer would be made at Mr. Ed's, a
restaurant outside of town on Highway 264. I had the
driving time to Mr. Ed's place clocked, and we determined that the operation would take twelve minutes,
with all cars driving no faster than twenty miles per
hour. Mr. Speller's car, with its New York plates, was
designated as the pickup car, because we figured that
the police would not be interested in a New York car
no way. We sat back and waited for Attorney Paul to
arrive.

"At eleven P.M. he came, bringing with him a doctor, Dr. Arthur Finn. I took him to the briefing room,
explained to him the transfer plans, and also the
arrangements I had made with the director of the

State Bureau of Investigation. That done, we gathered the staff together for a final briefing, and we even had prayer. Mr. Barrow went out, and made a final check of police positions. He returned and reported to me.

" 'All is well, sir,' he said. That was the code phrase. 'All is well, sir.'

"The seven cars were loaded, five to a car, except for Mr. Speller's New York car. It had Marjorie Wright, wearing a wig and a coat, another girl, and Miss Wright's boy friend. Jerry Paul pulled out—that started the twelve minutes ticking. We knew it would take him two and one-half minutes to get to Mr. Ed's. The others followed, all going in different directions, one toward the project, another downtown to pull the police into the center of town away from the highway, the others to their respective homes, as if we were breaking up for the night. I left last, alone, in my car, driving out into the country toward the racetrack, farther to the airport, and pulled several police cars with me. I made a large circle, and when I returned a half hour later, all the cars had returned.

" 'She's gone,' Barrow told me. 'She was reluctant to get into the lawyer's car at first at Mr. Ed's. Nothing open, not even the bars, and a car with two strange white men. But eventually she did, and they rode off into the night.

" 'Well, Golden,' he continued, 'you've got Joan free. Now you've got to keep her free. But you know, I keep wondering if the police knew all along that she was in Paps Barnes's house.'

"Very early the next morning, Monday, Labor Day, I drove to Chapel Hill to Attorney Paul's house. Jerry was not there when I arrived, but I did see Dr. Finn. He said Joan was not eating, and I told him not to worry, that she would eat before the day was over.

Jerry and I talked by phone, and he said that the surrender time had been put back to three P.M., Tuesday. For most of the day, I lounged around Jerry Paul's house, waiting for him to return. Mrs. Paul said that she and her husband had talked about having a few friends over that evening to meet Joan, and she asked me what I thought of the idea. In fact, I did not like the idea at all, for I felt that the legal arm was encroaching on the political arm by such an action; but I told Lou Paul that if that was going to happen, I was going to stay right there.

"The guests began to arrive near nine o'clock, and shortly thereafter Jerry arrived with Joan. I had never seen her in my life but I was moved to say to her right off,

" 'Chile, you did not kill that man, did you? You're too small.'

"She replied with her eyes, and mumbled,

" 'He was alive when I left, calling to me to come back or else they would get me for escape.'

" 'You'll have to be strong and you'll have to trust me,' I told her. 'If you'll ever be free, I said, black folks will have to free you.' Sitting down in that living room in that university town, beside that black sister, I realized it was time for me to open my eyes, for in that group of twenty guests only three were black. I heard such words as,

" 'This is the first time in North Carolina that a person accused of murder is able to sit and tell about it while still a fugitive from justice.'

"This upset me tremendously. SCLC is a nonviolent organization, and I could not condone murder no way. I told the group that Mr. Alligood had been wrong by coming back there. That if Joan was guilty we would help her get a fair trial. If she was not, so much the better. I told the sister to go ahead and tell the group what happened. She started to talk, and then she started to cry. I scolded her for this, saying, 'Stop crying, Joan, you can cry tomorrow.' I held her hand and put my body close to hers to comfort her, as she told her story: how she did not have privacy in the cell, how her linens were never changed, but I never did hear her say that she killed the jailer. I heard her repeat over and over: 'I'm sorry he's dead.'

"The meeting did not last long, and Jerry announced that he was going to take Joan for some rest. But downstairs he told me in confidence that he was taking her to another meeting! I argued with him fiercely about this, saying these were not the right people for Joan to get involved with. But I finally acceded, and we drove to a house outside Durham that belonged to Celine Chenier. There, a group of sisters had assembled, all black—I don't know if they were lesbians or what—but I knew most of them. They rushed up to Joan, kissed her and hugged her. Some were crying. Someone said,

" 'Oh, sister, you have done a beautiful thing.'

"This upset me even more. But anyway, I was getting hugs and handshakes, and so did Jerry. Some wanted to know why I didn't just take Joan away and not turn her in. They said she'd be charged with murder, and that the State of North Carolina would never give justice to Joan—in fact, to no blacks who are accused of killing whites. It was better for her to surrender, I replied; we would raise some questions through the courts. Joan talked briefly, and again I put my body very close to her. Again she broke down crying. It was about three-fifteen A.M. when Joan left with Attorney Paul. I announced a rally in Washington, North Carolina, for the coming Sunday and I drove off east.

"Later that week I held a press conference, where I went out with my suicide theory. I argued that Alligood had committed a simple hara-kiri . . . there he was locked in her cell, naked like a banana, knowing his fellow officers were coming, semen all over the place. How was he going to explain it? So he scratched himself up a little bit, and then put one blow to his heart. He did fall to the side where the fatal wound was, and he was holding the icepick. And that Sunday we had our march in Washington, and do you know, none of the women that were at Celine Chenier's came to my march!

"You see, in the time that followed her surrender, Joan's lawyers grilled that girl till she was weak, until they'd brainwashed her. They made her agree that she committed a crime in self-defense, but the self-defense issue really didn't arrive until six or eight weeks after the surrender, and Ms. Karen Galloway was responsible for that. If the girl would really tell the truth, she didn't kill nobody. Self-defense started to dominate when the legal forces came together and cut out the movement.

"I suppose I worked harder in those days to save Joan Little than any time in my twenty years of civil rights—no sleep, taping, briefing, running—and yet, once I had delivered my big package to Jerry Paul and Karen Galloway, they cut me out completely—gave me no credit, made me a nobody, and that's probably why I became so alienated later. The agreements were very clear in that meeting in the motel, when Jessie Ruth asked Jerry would he defend her daughter. I asked Jerry how much he thought it would take to defend Joan Little and his reply was twenty thousand dollars. I said, all right, SCLC will hire you for twenty thousand dollars. You'll be guaranteed that. I'll take thirty percent of what we can raise: that was to get me some cowbells and mules and wagons and go from town to town in North Carolina talking about the abuses in the jails, how we were going to correct them once and for all.

"But the lawyers took over, and they took the case

out of Eastern North Carolina, and that was the worst
thing they could have done. For I wanted Washington, North Carolina, to pay for the wrongs that Mr.
Alligood did. Taking the case away meant that we
could not build a movement, and now that the case is
over, it has changed nothing. They've got the same
crew down at that jail, except Alligood, the same
sheriff and tired prosecutor, the same old antiquated
law. They removed that constitutional right: that
Joan have a trial by her peers. No jury with vege-
tarian-restaurant girls is a jury of Joan's peers. So you
see why I say, Jerry jumped the fence. He thought he
was true blue for black people, but he got carried
away.

"I used to talk about the walls of the house: mine
are rough and raggedy, and yours are smooth. And
that lets you think a little better. You're drinking the
milk, while I'm drinking the clabber. You're living in
that white house on the hill, and I'm down here in
Black Bottom. You are better off economically and
become more educationally wise. Joan got caught up
in your world and turned her back on her own. She's
up now, but she will soon drift off into the wild blue
yonder.

"She's the symbol. She's designated all right, chosen
to raise the level of womanhood, like Esther was
chosen. In the Book of Esther, you remember, the
King Ahasuerus had a feast and had his officers tend
to 'every man's pleasure' while the Queen Vashti was
having her own party. The wine flowed at the King's
party and everyone got soused. On the seventh day of
the party the King called for Vashti, who was very
beautiful, to dance in front of the men to show her
beauty, but she didn't want to do that. You can't
blame her. But a woman is not supposed to disobey
her husband, especially if he is king, and the King's
advisors told him,

" 'For this deed of the Queen shall come abroad

unto all women, so that they shall despise their hus-
bands in their eyes, when it shall be reported. . . .
Thus shall there arise too much contempt and wrath.'

"So the King got rid of Vashti, said 'Every man shall
bear rule in his own house,' but he needed a new
queen, and from all the fair virgins in the land, he
picked Esther, a Jew and niece of Mordecai. Mordecai
disobeyed Haman, the enemy of the Jews, and Haman
got the king to decree that all the Jews would be
destroyed. But Esther came to the rescue. She got all
dressed up in her royal clothes, and she sidled up to the
king, even though it was not her time to come to him;
she pleased him, and he asked her what she wanted,
and she said she wanted to give a banquet for the
King and the wicked Haman. At the banquet the
King asked again what Esther's request was, and Esther named Haman as the wicked man who would
destroy her people, the Jews. And the King became
angry and he went out into the palace garden to think
it over, and as he did so, Haman went to the queen,
scared for his life.

" 'Then the king returned out of the palace garden
into the place of the banquet of wine, and Haman was
fallen upon the bed whereon Esther was. Then said
the king, "*Will he force the queen also before me?*" '
Rape, see.

"And so Haman was hanged, and Esther's uncle,
Mordecai the Jew, took his place of influence in the
court, and Esther again went to the king, fell at his
feet, pleaded again with tears for the king to reverse
his order, Haman's work, to destroy the Jews. The
king could not reverse his own order, but he issued
another order that the Jews should sharpen their
knives and defend themselves against their enemies.

" 'Thus the Jews smote all their enemies with the
stroke of the sword, and slaughter, and destruction,
and did what they would unto those that hated them.'

"And the King went again to Esther to see if she was satisfied and she asked that Haman's ten sons also be hanged. This was done, along with another five thousand enemies slain. And so this is how Esther became a Jewish heroine.

"Joan Little won't be able to exert the authority that Esther did. She will fade away. In a few years, people will look at her family and not even know them as they walk down the street. They will not even know that her mama was responsible for borning this girl—with all her faults—who would be the symbol of true jail reform."

CHAPTER 4

JERRY PAUL (I)

*This is because mystery has energy. It pours energy into who-
ever seeks the answer to it. If you disclose the solution to
the mystery, you are simply depriving the other seekers of an
important source of energy.*

John Fowles, *The Magus*

"THE people of Little Washington think I'm on some
kind of vendetta against them, coming from their
midst as I did and making my law practice defending
blacks in Eastern North Carolina, but they've got to
explain my actions in their own terms, in terms they
can understand. I know these people. I know what
they are. I didn't really set out to be a rebel. I set out
just to be a lawyer. At one time I was as well known
in that town as anybody, but as a football player, not
as a lawyer. I won't say I was as well liked as anybody,
but I had my place, and it was a comfortable place.

"I am a country boy. I grew up with a lot of violence, from football to loading cucumbers in the
summer, hurting so much after a day of lifting those
crates that I knew I didn't want to spend my life
doing that. In the 1960s these upper-class kids would
talk to me about violence, about getting guns, blowing up the system, and I knew they had never seen
violence, because there's nothing pretty about it. Those

others, who were really good at violence, ended up so
screwed up in the head that it was easy for me to come
to a position of nonviolence. Still I never really slept
well in Chapel Hill, never felt entirely comfortable
standing around with a drink in my hand talking to
university professors. It makes me tense. I gain strength
when I come back here. Once when the white busi-
nessmen of the town turned out in force to give me
the finger, I knew I was generating more energy in
that town than they had had for years."

They were on their way to Washington to find Paps
Barnes, the author driving Paul's Cadillac, because
the lawyer was having pain from a prostate infection
that had gotten out of hand during Joan Little's trial.
The reporters had made a great deal of Paul's Cadillac during the year, always calling it his "golden
Cadillac," a gratuitous swipe, supposedly showing the
hypocrisy of this crusader for poor blacks. But the car
was actually a fading maroon; it had over 200,000
miles on it, and the reporters had never bothered to
point out that it had been given Paul by his father,
just as a large house in Chapel Hill, which they also
made fun of, had been largely paid for by his family.
But Paul had never complained about the obvious
distortions. It was part of the game, and if the Cadillac was to be part of his "image," so be it.

The trip from Chapel Hill to Washington would be
interrupted twice. The first time was in the town of
Wilson, in its Back of Town, where they stopped for
dinner at the house of a black family who always fed
Paul on these trips. Chicken and pastry were served in
healthy portions along with collards, which Paul
found "tender," and there was much talk about this
case or that where the lawyer had helped someone in
trouble. It was the week after the story had appeared
in *The New York Times* in which Jerry Paul was
quoted as saying, "I bought justice in the Joan Little

case," and the beefy woman standing over her pot had read the story.

"I said to my daughter, there's that bad Jerry Paul talkin' junk again." They all laughed, and more chicken and pastry were heaped on their plates. As they pulled out, Paul talked about the early days of his practice when he had traded his legal skills for these meals and a bed, as he traveled the eastern part of the state. The second stop was in Greenville, again in the black section, at a place called R. B. Jr.'s Bar and Grill, and as the lawyer walked down the crowded street toward the "bistro," there were shouts of greetings and congratulations and excitement. Paul was pulled aside several times to hear some whispered story. Later, on the way east to Washington, Paul speculated—unabashedly—that perhaps to these people he *was* the "great white hope."

Jerry Paul was used to living with pain. The prostate had been added to a chronic problem of migraine headaches, and when the judge in the Little trial sent him off to jail for contempt of court minutes after Joan Little was acquitted, Paul's only request to the judge was to insure in open court that he would have his medicine while he pulled his two weeks. He had seen enough cases in his own practice where inmates had not been given proper medicine in prison, including Joan Little, who had been denied pills for her thyroid condition when she was in the Beaufort County Jail. ("We never had any complaints from her," Red Davis said. "She even fattened up when she was in jail.") But Paul's physical problems paled next to the worst pain of all; that week in October 1975, his eleven-year-old son, David, had had a relapse—leukemia—and the question in his father's mind as they drove east was whether David would achieve remission this time. "David got dealt a bum hand," he said, as he slouched his huge frame deeper in the cushy seat.

(A year and a half later, during an evening at Paul's house, the author would watch in agony as David Paul swore at how bored he was, confined to the house. Couldn't perhaps he go back to school just one day a week? It was three weeks before the boy died. C. T. Vivian, a minister who had been with Martin Luther King at Selma in 1965, would say at David Paul's crowded wake that it was not the number of years, making up the dash between the birth and death years on a tombstone that counted, but the quality of the dash.)

The burdens of this thirty-three-year-old show. They show in his slow, lumbering walk and in his steel-blue, sleepy eyes whose focus on a listener seemed to fade in and out. He talks in a soft, intimate tone, almost a whisper, until he latches onto a political theme, and then the decibels climb and the words become sharp and clipped and gutteral.

"But I didn't like the idea of being known just as a football player. I'd walk down Main Street, and people would speak to me only because I played football. I'd mutter, 'If I wasn't a football player, sons of bitches wouldn't give me the damn time of day.' These old men used to hang around the locker room in Little Washington all the time, trying to give me money. I'd call 'em 'jock-sniffers,' just hanging around because you might have played a good game that day, damn bunch of phonies. If you lost you didn't see 'em. We might get in the state playoffs, one of them would come around and say, 'I told you I was going to get you boys into the playoffs,' and, hell, he hadn't done a damn thing. Players out there sweating and bleeding, and he's on the sidelines hollering. He hadn't got the courage or the guts to get out there himself.

"I probably had better black friends than white when I was growing up. In the old segregated situation people might say something to you about it. But there wasn't too many people who would say anything to me about *anything*, because I was mean as a damn snake. In high school we'd have parties and have black bands, you know, and I'd go dance with a black girl, everybody'd say, 'Oh, Jerry's gone crazy again.' They'd send a committee to see me. They couldn't come themselves.

"I was just a loudmouth, braggart, hell-raiser when I was growing up. I just assumed everything went before me. Just live rough. Washington, like any small country town, is a very physical place. I told one of those jock-sniffers one time, 'Don't ever get around me, I don't like you. I don't ever want to see ya.' And he had to come up to me again at one of our drinking places, and I threw him across the room. 'I warned you,' I told him. Hell, I even got in a fight one time with an ABC (Alcoholic Beverage Control) officer and a chief of police. We were down at the beach having a party, and they drove up. They'd been drinking, see, said, 'We hear there's a party in here, and we're comin' in.' Couple of dirty old men, trying to get in on some teen-age fun. I went to the door, said, 'You ain't comin' in here, Jack, I told you that.' He said, 'I'm an ABC officer, and I'm comin' in.' He started pushin' his way past me, and I knocked him down, told him to get back in his car. As he was leaving, he said,

" 'You might be the boss down here, Jerry, but we'll get you when you come home.'

" 'You watch out for me, 'cause I'll be back,' I shouted back at him, and when I got home I sat out across from his house, drank beer, and threw beer cans in his yard. I've calmed down some since then.

"Of course, in a little place like Washington there's absolutely no form of entertainment. You work all day. Don't have a television; no country club to go to. The only form of entertainment was drinking and fighting and maybe a little whoring. I used to hear 'em in the working places, bragging about how they got some pussy the night before, and always the question would come up,

" 'Was it white or black?'

" 'Oh, it was black,' someone would say. 'Picked up this nigger walking on the road . . .' That's why I know what their attitude towards Joan is. They figure Alligood was just having a little fun. It's completely accepted. They're used to that.

"There used to be a place out in the country, a cinderblock house, a juke box, and mattresses on the dirt floor. The guy had his house in the back, sold bootleg liquor. I used to watch women bringing their daughters, and I'd watch these old men feeling up these girls, and I'd say, 'What in the hell is that woman bringing her daughter in there for that kind of treatment?' So I got to talking to some of those mothers. The best answer I could get was that there were enough instances of old men taking these girls and giving 'em work that the mothers thought this might be a way out for their daughters, a way that a mother could get her daughter out of her situation. I was good friends with one family who'd done that and they were very proud of their daughter. Oh, they'd seen her the weekend before, working behind a bar someplace. The guy had bought her some new clothes, and how nice she looked . . .

"White woman on a pedestal? Naw, she's a chattel. They might put her on a pedestal when they're talking about her. That might be the dream. That's why you hear of men beating the hell out of their women, because she wore her dress too short—even though that might have been what attracted him to her in the first place. A man makes a hit with a woman, and the first thing he wants her to do is lower her hemline. She doesn't fulfill her role properly, and he gets pissed off, gives her no individuality at all. So I don't think it's accurate to say that the white woman's on a pedestal in the South and the black woman's a sexual object. They're both sexual objects, but in different ways. The black woman is not regarded as human—she's somewhere between the animal and the human.

"Let me tell you a strange story I think will illustrate all of this. One night I was sitting in a motel room with Golden Frinks. Now, I've learned a lot from Golden. He taught me confrontation politics. He taught me that in a confrontation you reap a whirlwind of confusion, and it hurt me later that Golden could not be a part of the Joan Little confusion that we wrought. Anyway, on the TV movie that night was *The Sand Pebbles*, and if you remember the movie they auction off a Chinese girl at one point. So outside the door, suddenly there's a racket, and I go out. There's a drunk trying to get his key in the door and cussing at it. So I offer to help him, and he says, in a gruff voice,

" 'You got a drink in there?' So I invite him in and give him a drink. He's talking about what a big name he is in the area, and how he and his girl friend are right next door, and then he wants to know who I am. I tell him, and he jumps up.

" 'God damn, son of a bitch, I'm gettin' outta here,' he says.

"And I say, 'Sit down, Jack. Relax.'

" 'Listen,' he says, 'you're a dirty son of a bitch. Me 'n some other buddies were goin to kill you one night. We went out, running around in a car looking for you. But you ain't all that bad. Listen, if I stay here, you won't hurt me, will you?'

"I told him, no, I wasn't going to hurt him. Then he found out that Golden was with me, and that excited him even further, and said,

" 'You know, won't anybody believe I'm sitting here talkin' to you all, and you ain't hurtin' me. I've got to have a witness.'

"So he calls up his girl friend, says, 'Honey, you asleep? I want you to know who I'm in this motel room with, right next door. It ain't good enough for you to hear it on the telephone. You got to come around here 'n' see it.'

"He hangs up and proceeds to pass out on the bed, sound asleep. So in a little while there's a knock on the door, and I answer it, say,

" 'Lady, look, I didn't ask you to come out here. I don't want to offend ya, I don't want to put you in an embarrassing situation. Your boy friend's here passed out on the bed. I'm not going to hurt him. I'll take care of him . . .'

"She waves her hand, 'Don't worry about it,' and she comes on in, wakes him up. They start talking, and suddenly, he jerks up her dress, says,

" 'You ever seen a thigh like that?'

"I said, 'Man, don't do that shit. Ain't no call for that.'

"He pulls open her blouse and flops her titty out, and I'm thinkin', This is *The Sand Pebbles.* He's talkin' about how much he lo-o-o-oves her, what a fine woman she is, and she's standing there, looking a little embarrassed, but she's puttin' up with it. Well, he passes out again, and I say to the woman,

" 'Look, lady, you can leave if you want to. I ain't saying you got to leave, but I didn't bring you out here to go through this kind of treatment.'

"So I went down to the manager and rented another motel room, and I'm carrying him down to this other room when he wakes up again, and starts telling me about his problems with his wife! Wants to know, will I represent him in a divorce proceeding? So we get down to the room, and I put him down on the bed, and he looks at me all sincere like.

" 'Let me ask you a question,' he says. 'I hear you mess around with niggers.'

"I said, 'I got a lot of friends who're black, yeah.'

" 'You ever had sex with one of 'em?'

"Now that's a bad question. If you say no, then immediately he says 'I knew he was that way; he's just like us all along.' If you say yes, that brings in an area of disrespect. I said,

" 'I ain't gettin' into that with you, Jack.'

" 'Well, I'm a deacon in the church,' he says, 'and I want to talk to you about the mo-rals behind what you're doing. Don't you know that what you're doing is mo-rally wrong?'

"I said, 'Wait a minute. You come in here drunk; you bring in your girl friend and start floppin' her titty out, and you're going to talk to *me* about what's morally right and wrong?' And he became offended!

"That's the kind of crossed-up thinking that's down here. *I'm* the moral degenerate. They attach morality to it: it's *morally* wrong to defend blacks; it's *morally* wrong for blacks to go to school with whites. My mother used to write me, 'You've become a traitor to your race. You've turned your back on God. Do you ever go to church anymore? If anybody ever asks you, don't ever tell 'em you're kin to us.' Well, that's easy because I'm an adopted child, but I think they're probably typical of the area.

"I had a case where seventeen whites attacked a black kid in a high school, and they charged the black with assault with a deadly weapon with intent to kill! So we go to trial. The white kids are so confident that nothing's going to happen to them, they get up on the stand and tell the truth.

" 'Yeah, we attacked him. We planned it.'

" 'Well, didn't you think you'd get in trouble for doing that?' I asked 'em.

" 'Naw, we ain't goin to get in no damn trouble for doin' that.'

" 'Didn't the principal do something about it?'

" 'Naw, the principal's not gonna do nothing.'

"I got the kid off, but here's my father-in-law ranting and raving about blacks always attacking whites in the schools, and I say, 'What about this case?' and show him the transcript. He says,

" 'Oh well, there's always exceptions.'

"They're racists in Eastern North Carolina, and they know they're racists, but in 1975 it may not be a good thing to admit you're a racist. They have the notion now that the nation comes down on you if you're that way, and you won't get industry in your town. They're programmed, and if you know someone's programmed, you can manipulate them.

"I had this dope case: the guy was caught with hash, LSD, and two bags of marijuana on his table. The SBI burst in on him, and he's sitting there rolling a joint. SBI picks up one bag, says,

" 'This stuff doesn't look as good as this other stuff.'

" 'That's right,' my guy says, 'That's my stuff in the good bag. I only sell good stuff. I'm doing a service to the community by only providing good dope!'

"I'm thinking about this, say to myself, 'This kid is an extremist,' and if you're an extremist about one thing you'll be an extremist about another. So I hook him up with a religious group, and they save him. I knew he'd get saved. So we go to trial and pick the jury. We get a lot of holiness people, fundamentalists on the jury. Don't even bother to put him on the stand. I put on this woman from the country-club set. She speaks in tongues. She's been saved.

" 'What do you know about this young man?' I ask her on the stand.

" 'Well, I know he's come to Christ. He's been saved.'

"Now the State can't object to that, because if they object to God, then that's bad for 'em. Meanwhile, the sheriff's over there snickering—which I point out to the jury. So we try the case, and the jury finds him not guilty, and a woman on the jury comes up to me afterwards, a tear running down her cheek, says,

" 'Oh, Mr. Paul, I knew a young man who had taken Christ into his heart couldn't be guilty of what the Gestapo says he's guilty of.'

"The first call about Joan Little came from Margie Wright, when I was in Edenton, having just gotten Golden Frinks out of jail. I was exhausted; I'd been trying cases at night, and trying to get Golden out, but I agreed to meet Margie and Joan's mother in Golden's motel room in Washington on the way home to Chapel Hill. Now, I'd known Margie Wright since we were teenagers together in Washington, and sometime in the course of that meeting in Golden's room we went into the bathroom together, and she told me she knew where Joan was hiding. She had not told Golden this: she did not trust him—or she *did* trust me. Anyway, Margie and I agreed to let Joan stay where she was for a while, while I made some arrangements. 'Tell Joan just to sit tight and not get scared,' I told Margie, and after the meeting I drove on home.

"Golden stayed there, making a big call for Joan to surrender herself, and I just let him go ahead with it. I try not to get mixed up in movement matters. Golden can lead. I'm not interested in leading. You couldn't stop him anyway, and why not? His posturing created a diversion. The local people were worried about Golden, and it kept everybody happy, doing something. In order to stop him, you'd have to get into an argument with him—and why?

"I tried to get Charles Dunn, the director of the SBI, the next day, Sunday, but he was not home, so when Golden called that night, while we were having a dinner party, I wasn't ready to get her out of Beaufort County. I had made none of the arrangements, but Golden was insistent.

" 'You got to come. She's going to commit suicide,' he said, and so I agreed.

"Daniel Pollitt, a professor at UNC Law School, was at the dinner party, and he advised me to turn Joan in to the Governor, and make a big deal about the stupidity of the outlaw statute. I didn't want to ride to Washington alone, so Dr. Arthur Finn, who was also at the party, and who is a professor in the Medical School here [Chapel Hill] agreed to go with me.

"When we got there, Golden didn't know where she was. He couldn't tell me who had told him that Joan was going to commit suicide. He didn't even know why he'd called me: sometimes he calls me to come down, just so he can play games. What he was really interested in that night was chasing a young girl, and trying to get her mother away from the motel. James Barrow, the SCLC coordinator in Washington, probably did know where she was, but he was drunk. So I sent someone to try to find Margie Wright. In about an hour and a half they finally found her, and she came in—with a wig on, and drunk too—not stone drunk, but she'd been drinking. So I got her back in the bathroom again, and told her I'd come for Joan.

" 'Why?' she asked. 'I thought you weren't going to get her for a while.'

"I told her go to find Elizabeth Hines, a young girl they called Sissy, who lives two doors from Margie, but first I had Margie sit down for a while to sober up. Now Sissy is a highly nervous person, and when she got to the motel she was having a fit. So I got them both back in the bathroom, calmed Sissy down, and we decided how we would do it. Margie's boy friend was to drive the car: they were going to the house where Joan was. Sissy was to wear the wig in, have

Joan put on her wig and change into her clothes. Then Sissy was to stay at Paps's house while Joan got into the car in her place, and then they were to come to Mr. Ed's, a restaurant outside of Washington where I would be waiting.

"That settled, I went out and woke up James Barrow, told him to drive the girl Golden was chasing to Chocowinity, four miles out of town, and told Golden, Why didn't he go out and drive around a little? I figured he would follow Barrow and the girl. Others were to drive in different directions. Then I got to thinking, and I called Sissy and Margie back into the bathroom and asked 'em if they had any marijuana on them. I could just see the cops stopping the getaway car and busting them for possessing grass, and that would mess everything up. Sure enough, I took an ounce of marijuana off them, and I stuck it up behind the light in Golden's bathroom—figured, Golden's doing all this talking; if anybody's going to get busted tonight, let it be him, or let him talk his way out of it.

"So they all pulled out, and I went to Mr. Ed's and waited by the phone. Soon enough, they drove up, and there was Sissy in the car as well as Joan and Margie! I thought, that dumb ass Sissy forgot to change clothes and came out with Joan, but at least they had remembered to put the wig on Joan. There was a difficult moment, because Joan wanted Margie to get in my car with her, but I blocked that. Joan got in, and when she saw me, she sighed with relief.

" 'What's the matter, Joan?' I asked her.

" 'I could only see the back of your head, Jerry,' she said. 'You looked like a policeman to me.' I had represented her before, when she was a juvenile. She'd seen me in Greenville and Ayden demonstrations, and I'd gotten her out of jail once in Chapel Hill when she'd had a fight. We'd talked then about coming from the same hometown. Margie came up to the car.

" 'Gimme the wig,' she said to Joan.

" 'Get the shit back in your damn car, Margie,' I said to her.

" 'I'm gonna get my wig.'

" 'I'm gonna *keep* the wig,' Joan said.

"So I flew mad. 'God damn it, Margie, get back in the damn car and get the hell out of here.' I even offered to buy it from her and fumbled around for some money. I could envision us getting busted as Margie argued about her damn wig.

"As we were pulling away from Mr. Ed's, there was a full moon out to my right. It was a chilly night. I was fortunate that I knew the area, because I wanted to drive west on back roads without going through any towns. I'm well enough known in the East, and I knew that the police constantly kept surveillance on me when I was in the area. I thought it was very possible that they would put two and two together. It would have been stupid for them not to. They had been hunting her with helicopters. I knew these people were very excitable. Some of the officers in Beaufort County would have shot her; some like Sheriff Red Davis would not have. It depends on the individual. I think one of the officers saw her at Paps's and intended to come back and kill her. The officer who looked under the mattress had to have seen her. He picked up the mattress, so Joan said, and shined the light right in her face. I bet that was Peachey. How Peachey missed her, I don't know, unless . . .

"There on those back roads, with that full moon, and the chilliness, you could almost visualize the underground railroad in slavery times, when they were hauling the blacks out of the South. The slaves were underneath the wagon, and the white driving the wagon. What I felt that night, getting Joan out of

Beaufort County, must have been what the white wagon driver felt. For that moment I captured a piece of history. Perhaps I'm programmed to think that way now.

"To get across the top of this state, from Washington to Chapel Hill, you need to go through either Wilson or Rocky Mount. So I went above Wilson, around by Pinetops, and came into the rich white section of town. I didn't think they'd be looking for me there. It was three-thirty or four A.M. by this time. So we were riding through the rich section with my window cracked open, and all of a sudden something hits the side of the car. WHAM! I thought we'd been shot. I felt this viscous stuff running down the side of my head; it felt warm, and I was warm, and I was sure it was blood. Joan jumped down on the floor of the car, when it hit. Then she looked at me.

" 'Jerry, that was an egg.'

I glanced in the rear-view mirror, and there's this kid in the bushes, egging cars. I said to myself,

" 'Here I am, in the rich white section of town, with Joan Little, and one of those motherfuckin' brats is out here eggin' cars.' For a moment I considered going back and kicking his ass, and then I said to myself, 'Now I go back there and spank him; his mama calls the police; the police come investigating and they got me.' The damn egg is all in my hair and running down my face. It's splattered all over the back of the seat. But I drove all the way back to Chapel Hill without washing it off, and it got all sticky and smelly by the time we got home.

"Labor Day, September 2, 1974, was the crucial day in that initial period. I left Joan at Dr. Finn's house, where she slept most of the day. I went to Raleigh to negotiate the surrender with Charles Dunn. Dunn is a political creature, diplomatic, personable, an ex-newspaperman, one who understands public relations, and I had known him for some time. One time we were having a demonstration in Raleigh in support of the Tuscarora Indians, and Dunn was furious at the Governor for the way he was handling the situation. He came to me, said,

" 'Jerry, what can I do to get the ox out of the ditch? If you would tell me how I can diplomatically get us out of this situation, I'll be so grateful to you.'

"So we get along fine, and I often ride with the SBI in civil-rights protests; it's the best vantage point if there should be trouble.

"I presented Dunn with four demands for her surrender:

"One, that she be surrendered to the SBI in Raleigh.

"Two, that she not be returned to Beaufort County.

"Three, that an aide from the Governor's office be present at the surrender.

"Four, that there be an early preliminary hearing to hear the evidence against her and motion for bond.

"As it turned out, the State breached the fourth condition immediately to deny me a forum, and the third condition was meaningless, because the Governor's man was a numb-nuts; he just sat there and said nothing. Sometimes I wonder why we go through these motions with the Governor. Those people have never been responsive, and in this situation it was obvious that the Governor couldn't care less if some 'nigger bitch' was turning herself in.

"The negotiations with Dunn were mostly stumbling and fumbling. I had to fool him, making him think that Joan was still in Beaufort County, because I didn't want him to turn around and start looking for her in Chapel Hill. To my conditions, Dunn said, 'Cool. I'll see what I can do,' but he cautioned,

" 'Jerry, I cannot help you as long as she's in that area. You'll have to get her out of Beaufort County on

your own, and then I can help. . . . I have no control over
the local officials, and I have no influence with them.'

"You see, Dunn is very sensitive about local rela-
tionships. Some of those eastern counties view Raleigh
as Raleigh views Washington, D.C. They resent intru-
sions into their affairs, and I'm sure Sheriff Davis still
suspects that some secret, mysterious deal was made
and that it's going to come back on Charles Dunn.
William Griffin, the prosecutor, refers to Dunn as an
'incompetent newspaperman.'

"I negotiated with Dunn from eleven A.M. to four
P.M. that day, and the deal was struck that she would
be surrendered at three P.M. the following day.
Meanwhile, Golden had arrived at my house looking
for Joan. He'd realized that he'd make a mistake: he'd
lost her, and she was under my control now. He'd
realized that he didn't really want to turn her in. But
the die was cast. If you didn't turn her in, you were
harboring a fugitive, and nothing would go smoothly.
The longer she stayed out, the more it would look as
if she turned herself in because Golden asked her to,
rather than because she wanted to, and that would
make a jury view her differently. So I told my wife not
to let Golden know where she was.

"He would see her for the first time ever that night
when I brought her home, where my wife had gathered some twenty friends from Chapel Hill to meet
her. In introducing her to university people, I
achieved several things. These were the people who
had the money and the ability to put together the
program I wanted and who were people I could call
on later to do all sorts of things. I was introducing her
to them in a dramatic way, a way they were not likely
to forget. I could test out her story on them, see if they
believed her, how they reacted to her generally, and I
could test what issues in her case would float. Beyond
that, I was giving her experience at talking to groups.

This was Joan Little's first public, and it was a sympathetic audience. Hard as it was, she had to begin then, even though it was soon after the incident happened, because I knew she wouldn't be out long. She had to begin to develop her style, and her deliverance. [Did he mean 'delivery'? Both words would fit.] That first night was when she began to practice sitting on the witness stand.

"You have to understand how she first looked to me. She was a raw little country girl. She couldn't talk. She couldn't verbalize her thoughts. She had a negative appearance. You can't change those things overnight. You change those things by experience. Yet she couldn't be too fine, too nice, or she wouldn't have been as easy to sell. Her looks were part of her salability. She had to develop some dignity, but not too much.

"So I watched how she handled herself that night. I had told her not to go into the details of what happened in that jail cell—and that became the rule from then on. She was not to tell *anyone* what happened, including me, until I told her to, and I did not know the details of her story until ten months later, and even then it took four hours to get it out of her. She could say simply that advances were made, and that she tried to defend herself. So she began to talk, and she got right up to the point where Alligood came back to her cell, and she broke down crying. The group was impressed with this, and Dr. Finn said later that you could not help believing her, when you watched her struggle that night. I took her back in the bedroom, and talked to her awhile, and she told me that she wanted to tell the group one thing: that she did not go off and leave a dying man, that had she known he was dying, she would have stayed.

"I was also watching Golden, and how he got along both with the group and with Joan. She didn't like him at all. He was trying to put words in her mouth, about how she did not kill him, and he even had the gall to say that she had had prior sexual relations with Alligood. You see, Golden himself is a victim of racism. He never understood rape. He never understood that rape is not a crime of lust, but a crime of degradation, humiliation, and violence. In many ways, he looks at the black woman in the same way the white racist does: he, like Beaufort County whites, was programmed to believe that Joan Little lured Alligood in there.

"I watched Golden's performance that night, and how *he* turned the group off. When she cried, he told her to 'shut up' and 'be strong' and he would pat her on the knee. As we were walking out of the house, Golden came up behind her, said,

" 'I got to talk to you about your story. Remember, you didn't kill that man . . .'

" 'I did,' she said.

"And I turned on him. 'Look, Golden,' I said, 'you've got to understand that the truth is going to win this case. Don't make up a story. You've got to believe this girl. She's got a good story. Don't try to mess it up.'

"Joan would be free only that night, so there was not much time. The two quickest meetings I could throw together was the one at my house with the university crowd and the later one at Celine Chenier's house in Durham with a group of black women. Celine was active in prison reform, and she knew the black community in Durham, which is large, wealthy, and well organized. I knew that Celine would be going over to the prison and seeing Joan. Later Celine became a member of the Joan Little Defense Committee, Incorporated, and was very active in the rebellion at the Women's Prison in Raleigh a month before the trial began, but in that riot she allowed herself to come under the influence of Larry Little, the Black Panther leader in North Carolina, who kept urging that the protesters move from the women's prison and burn down Raleigh.

"At Celine's, a woman in an African outfit offered to get Joan out of the country, and this offer was repeated the next day, before the surrender, by some-one else. This was useful to me as well, because it tested Joan's commitment to go through with the long, difficult process ahead. She refused these offers, insisting that she wanted to turn herself in and tell her story in court. Joan began to relax some at Ce-line's even though she broke down again when she got up to the point of Alligood entering the cell, and that told me that I must expose her more to women, for she was more comfortable with them. I let the meeting go on longer for this reason, until about three A.M., and Golden once again got Joan mad at him. He could see her being drawn away from him even far-ther, and he did not like those women anyway. Some of them were lesbians.

"The following day, about an hour before the sur-render, I took Joan aside.

" 'Now, we're going to turn you in,' I told her. 'There are going to be men in Dunn's office you won't know. A man from the Governor's office will be there, and press. You're going to be scared. You're going to walk in,' and I told her how to walk in. 'When you walk by the press, say just one thing: that you acted in self-defense. Nothing else. And when you get into the office of the SBI, say: "I committed no crime. I acted in self-defense. I was concerned about my safety, and I'm asking you to ensure my safety now, to see that I get to trial to tell my story." '

"I made her repeat it.

"Then I continued: 'Now, Joan, you're going to jail. You'll be there three to six months. You'll be scared, and you'll grow tired of it. But I promise you I'll get you out, and when I do, it will be the first time you'll know I can deliver on my promises. So be patient with me. People will criticize you, and they'll criticize me. And you're going to get depressed. But if you stick with me, I promise you'll never serve a day on this charge. It's going to be very hard, but you'll live to laugh at this day.' "

CHAPTER 5

CELINE CHENIER

Dark flying rune against the western glow—
It tells the sweep and loneliness of things,
Symbol of Autumns vanished long ago.
Symbol of coming Springs!

Frederick Peterson, *Wild Geese*

SHE is also known as Tamu Amaka Emodi, or, to inmates, just Tamu. In Nigerian that means "beautiful
one," and it fits her fine features, sensitive hands, intense face, deeply circled eyes. What a fine choice of
names, to be known in this world either as Celine or
Tamu! Her apartment in Durham was decorated with
amateurish inmate "art," mostly splashes of black, red,
and green, some of which attempted an idealization of
Joan Little; a rifle lay beneath the wall decorations.
She said it was because the FBI was harassing her so
much, and "if they want to come in, that door won't
stop 'em." But Celine was seldom at home and when
she was, another woman was often there, an ex-
inmate, who would slip away into the back room as
she sat down to talk about Joan Little. She said she
was nearly going crazy for not being able to find a job.
It had been nearly a year since she'd had one, since
she'd been fired from the Carolina Friends School—
fired, she said, because she had appeared on a tele-

vision show with Karen Galloway, the defense lawyer, pleading for support for Joan Little. That had seemed strange, because Quakers, even in the South, are not normally intolerant, and, indeed, the principal of the Friends School had said there were other reasons having nothing to do with Celine's support of Joan Little. Still, she sustained herself on the few dollars that inmates sent her from time to time, but if something didn't turn up, she felt she would have to leave Durham, go to New York or California, but not back to New Orleans, because her family had warned her that if she came back home, she would have to "leave the civil-rights work behind in Durham," and that was impossible.

"I resent the label of 'outside agitator,' " she began. "I am no radical. It has never been my intent to cause dissension, never, never. I'm not that kind of person—too sensitive to be good at it, probably. I set out as a good Catholic in New Orleans to be a singer, a singer of liturgical music; and I was never exposed to prejudice as a child, except between blacks and Creoles. Oh, I can remember once on a bus when a black woman sat down next to a white woman who was holding her breviary beads, and the good Catholic white woman got up and moved, but that was about it.

"So I grew up black, Creole, and very Catholic. My father was a dark-skinned black, and the only reason that he was accepted among the Creoles was that he had been to Notre Dame and had his master's degree in social work. He used to take me every Sunday to the Saint Louis Cathedral for mass and communion, and his sister was a mother superior in the French Quarter. I almost became a nun myself once—later when I was living in New York and teaching at the John F. Kennedy Child Study Center. My mother was

an octoroon, and she was very prejudiced against
blacks, with the exception of my father. In those days
a good Creole woman didn't need an education—my
mother had only been to high school—she only had to
look pretty and have straight hair. The Creole prejudice against ordinary blacks went back to the Mandingo tradition, where the Creoles were valued highly
and sold more expensively than the pure Africans.
The light-skinned and the straight-haired were the
house niggers. They would never put a Mandingo in
the field; they were considered much too delicate for
that. When I was seven years old, my grandmother on
my mother's side told me,

" 'When you marry, don't darken the room, en-
lighten it,' and I knew what she meant. So my first
experience with prejudice was black against black,
and my first boy friend, approved by my family, was
white.

"For seven years I worked with heroin addicts in
New York, before Dr. James Carter, the only black
psychiatrist in North Carolina, brought me down. We
set up a therapeutic community for addicts, and it was
through this work that I began to work with female
inmates and began to worry about prison conditions.
In New York we had inmates paroled to our program
and some of them had been off drugs for five or six
years. They didn't want to talk about drugs, but
about conditions in the prisons, and that is how I
became involved. Of course, inmates could get more
drugs inside the prison up there than on the outside,
and when we came down here we found that it was
the same thing, only by the time the drug gets down
here it's not so strong—it's garbage.

"Even without Joan Little, I'm sure I would have
been involved in the prison struggle, but perhaps the
issue would not have interested the public as much.
There have been changes in the last year, and there

will be more. How important the Joan Little case was to these changes, what the effect of our demonstrations in November 1974 at the Women's Prison in Raleigh were, or the violence there in June 1975—the 'prison riot,' the press called it—I do not know. But in September 1975 the laundry there was finally condemned by the Department of Labor—the place where the temperature could reach a hundred and twenty degrees, where there was always water on the floor. The women in that prison were forced to wash the clothes not only for the entire North Carolina Correctional System, but for local hospitals, whose laundry included isolation bags and germs, and many inmates developed rashes from this work. That's what you call institutional sexism. And it was in that laundry that sister Marie Hill worked for the years she was on death row, and because of the conditions she had to have two toes amputated.

"So when Joan Little was brought to my house on the night of September 2, 1974, in flight from Beaufort County, I felt her plight deeply. You see, through my work I receive letters from many inmates, and I knew of many who had been raped and who never came forward, because—who would believe it? They were black, they were inmates, and they were women. I have personal friends who were raped in prison, but who were ashamed to admit it. They held back before, but Joan's courage has inspired people to come forward now.

"I don't think it's going to be that easy to rape anybody anymore—in prisons or out. Joan Little has inspired me and countless other women to deal with any rapist, be he black or white, *as she dealt, as she dealt.* The courts see they can't railroad blacks anymore. Yes, Power to the Icepick.

"After Joan was released on bond in March '75, she took me down to Beaufort County. She showed me that jail. We just parked in the lot behind the courthouse, and she described the jail and the conditions—guarded always by a male guard—having to ask a male guard for sanitary napkins. Listen, once she asked for a Kotex and a radio operator, Lee Houston, came back with a tampon. Joan said she could not use a tampon because they gave her problems, but the radio operator said there was no money allocated to buy Joan Little anything special. So three days later Joan called the radio operator back to show her what the tampons had done to her, actually showed her three pieces of skin about the size of a thumbnail. And if this wasn't bad enough, a few days after that, this was told to the defense by Lee Houston, she asked Clarence Alligood how Joan was getting along with her problem. Alligood asked, 'What problem?' and Lee Houston explained it to him.

"That's one thing. Another is that in the eighty-one days that Joan Little was held in the Beaufort County jail, twice a policeman called Miller came back to the women's section and urinated in front of the women prisoners. Once he urinated in Joan Little's toilet in her cell, with her in it: that cell is only about four feet by seven feet. Another inmate, Ramona Markarain, testified to that at the trial.

"Anyway, Joan showed me where she grew up—on this dirt street in the black section, an old wood house, falling down; she told me about how she had to earn a living—priming tobacco, doing construction work. It was pretty much the story of a typical black woman growing up in a small town, in a racist town. I tell you, I've never been in a town like that in my life. And then she took me to see her great-great-grandmother, who's in her nineties. Her father had been a slave. The old women did not say much, but she would look down at Joan as if to say,

" 'Child, why are they bringing you to trial?' She, more than anybody, understood.

"That first night I saw Joan Little as myself, as did

most of the black women who were there. After all, we've had four hundred years of being raped by white men. Self-defense by a woman under attack *was* most definitely raised on that first night, regardless of what Golden Frinks says. Of course, Golden has his own way of operating in political situations, his own tactics, his own way of organizing, but there was no indication of a split on September second. The people in that room were all of one mind: we were overjoyed that Joan was alive, for we knew that they were after her with rifles and shotguns, that they had no plans to capture her, but to kill her. So we were most concerned with her safety.

"Jerry Paul, who was my attorney at the time, had called that day—September second, I'll never forget it, because it was my birthday, my thirty-seventh—and asked me to gather together some people who might be part of a Joan Little Defense Committee. About eleven people were there, about half men and half women, and Golden. I don't recall vividly my first glimpse of Joan because I didn't know who she was, but Jerry introduced her, and we rushed to her, hugging and kissing her, for we were so happy to see that she was alive, and we all felt that she had done what she had to do: she had defended herself! She had protected her womanhood! I don't remember anyone saying, as Golden claims, 'Oh, sister, you have done a beautiful thing,' but we greeted her very, very cordially.

"Joan seemed overwhelmed by the people there. I don't think she expected it, and she seemed shocked at what she saw. All that support already! I think she knew that my house was still not her final destination. After all that running and hiding, the fear and the shock, and the fatigue, this new situation, new strange people hugging her, people caring enough to want to protect her, well, she was overpowered by it. She sat down by the fireplace, she just sat there, while we did our best to put her at ease.

"I remember the people wanting to know the facts. They would ask her questions, and she would respond, sometimes only with a word or two. She explained the incident only in the vaguest terms—that advances were made—but she really did not get into it too much, and we did not press her on the details, for we could see that the meeting was very taxing for her. She did not *have* to get into the details, anyway. She really didn't have to, because we understood. When she got to the part about the struggle for the icepick, she broke down, just as she would later at her trial, and she could not continue. Jerry took her to a back room and tried to calm her down, and after a while they left. She did not come back to talk to us anymore.

"As I said, I was thinking that night, Joan Little is me, could be me, and I remember saying at the meeting that I would have done what Joan did. Later, when I would go around and make speeches, trying to educate the people about her case, I would ask, 'What would you have done if you had been in Joan's position? What would you do?' Women understand about rape. I'm not saying men don't understand rape, but women feel it. Women are the victims.

"It's no mystery why Karen Galloway, a black woman attorney, was the most effective, the most persuasive, of all the defense lawyers in the summations. She could make the jury feel the situation.

" 'Put yourself in Joan's situation and in Alligood's situation,' she asked the jury. 'You're a young black woman. You don't have any control over what happens to you. No keys; they control your life. You're lonely. You have different thoughts on different days . . . And you're Alligood, sixty-two, white. You've got the keys. You've got the control. You tell the inmates what to do. What can they do in return? Nothing . . .

And one night he comes back to your cell. Nothing unusual for him. He broke the rules all the time. He had no respect for her. She's just an inmate. She's an animal to him. And you're Joan, and he comes at you. What are you going to do? Give him a karate chop? You're scared. You stand there. It's not humiliating enough that he feels your breasts, that he puts his hand between your legs. He says,

" ' "I want you to suck my penis."

" 'Don't you feel good if you're Alligood? All that control. You've got her there sucking your penis. You're in charge.'

"You see, Karen understood, and she made that jury understand. Later, after she described the struggle with Alligood, Karen said,

" 'She [Joan] runs out of the cell. She runs out the moment he released her. She dresses quickly, and she grabs her pocketbook. Women understand that. And she slams the door on him. "This is a man I trusted, and there's a possibility that he might hurt me some more." Use your common sense: was it cold-blooded or was it common sense to slam that door? The State says, "Why didn't you bite his penis?" They make it out almost that she enjoyed it. Put yourself in her position. Can you enjoy that?'

"Sometimes I think it was probably ordained that I be fired from that Quaker school, because I went to work full time on the Joan Little Defense Committee afterwards. The debate at my house on September second on how to proceed with the Joan Little movement was a kind of mishmash, but in the days that followed, I knew what my immediate goal was: to see that she did not get the gas chamber, to see that she was not penalized for protecting her womanhood. I took many speaking engagements: Philadelphia, New York, talking with groups in the Raleigh-Durham area. Yes, I missed Golden's march in Little Washington on September ninth, because I couldn't get transportation, but there was so much to be done here.

"Joan was indicted for first-degree murder on September ninth, and from then on, the death penalty hung over the whole case. This State has forty percent of the death-row population in the nation. Does it have forty percent of the violent murderers? Do you know what I heard recently: that they have worked out a system at Central Prison whereby inmates would drop the pill and receive gain time on their prison terms for doing so . . . Not just one inmate, but ten, see, with ten buttons, only one of which would release the pellet of cyanide. Beyond that, Marie Hill had told me that in 1969, on the day she was supposed to be executed, she had met her executioner. So you see, Joan's fate was on my mind constantly."

The report that Marie Hill had talked to her executioner fascinated the author. It was plausible enough, for he had heard the warden of Central Prison, where the death chamber was located, prevaricate on who would actually drop the pill. The general statutes governing execution stipulate that a guard or "other person or persons designated by the warden" shall cause the condemned to be asphyxiated by lethal gas. So why not have ten inmates, say, with the least capacity for guilt lined up by ten buttons, as Celine suggested, only one of which would actually release the pill, and let each receive gain time on his or her sentence for performing an unpleasant duty as prescribed by law?

Marie Hill is a short, rotund woman of twenty-five years, with a low, modulated voice and a pleasant smile. Her crime was vicious: she had hit a sixty-five-year-old white store owner with a fire poker, shot him, dragged him to the cash register, shot him again before leaving with his cash and his wallet. She had been seventeen when that happened in Rocky Mount, and the all-male jury recommended no mercy when they convicted her on December 20, 1968. The amputation of her toes had not restricted her walking or even her running, but people would tell her that she had a tendency to rock like a penguin. She missed Celine Chenier's Sunday visits, which had been shut off after the riot in Women's Prison in June 1975.

The conversation with the executioner had taken place on January 3, 1969, she said, the day she was supposed to be gassed. She was awakened from sleep and taken to a large room, where she was introduced to the Governor amid a handful of men. The Governor asked if she knew that the appointed day had come for her execution, and she replied affirmatively. But the date had been postponed, the Governor informed her, and asked if she was happy to hear that. She did not remember her answer. She would now go onto death row to await the appeal process to complete itself. From then on she would be unable to mingle with other prisoners; she would be guarded by a male at all times, and she would have to "make the best of it."

The Governor had a few people he wanted her to meet, men who would have carried out the execution, and he introduced a white prisoner, in his late twenties or early thirties. The prisoner had nine life sentences against him, and had been promised that his time would be cut by performing the execution. Since there had been no woman executed since 1952, Marie Hill asked the prisoner what he felt about doing such a thing, and he replied that if it was his own mother he would do it, just to reduce his time in prison.

"I thought he was cold-hearted," Marie Hill said. "I could understand about wanting to reduce his time, but not his own mother! No, I couldn't do that."

Was this story true, or was it a delusion, bred of two and a half years on death row in isolation? The effects of the pariah treatment of death-row prisoners have never been studied—their mental health does not seem the main issue of prison officials—and their efforts to maintain their sanity are not always successful. Once when the author had been on death row at Raleigh's Central Prison with a television crew, one death row inmate had gone to the back of his cell and hid his face in the corner, while the crew filmed. And Jesse Fowler—whose case, some thought, in the spring of 1975 when Justice Douglas was still on the Supreme Court, might lead to the elimination of the death sentence—had an unusual mental-exercise solution. He would play chess with friends in the cells far above him, by shouting his moves to them at the top of his lungs. Fowler also played chess with a newsman who had taken an interest in him, by sending his moves through the mails, and finally won the match six months later. Winning had been important to Fowler.

Prison officials denied Marie Hill's story about the Governor introducing her to her executioner, and they denied any plans to use inmates for executions. "Of course, you can get inmates to do just about anything," said Juanita Baker, who had been the head of Women's Prison in 1969. "The talk about ethics in executions usually centers on the situation of the *guard* who has to drop the pill, and I'd have to think a bit more about using inmates." And it does seem unlikely that the Governor was at the prison on the day Marie Hill cited. He was Governor Robert Scott, and on January 3, 1969, the day Marie Hill was to be gassed, he was being inaugurated with bands, parades, and speeches. So it's doubtful that he slipped away from his fancy-dress ball to introduce the condemned to her executioner. But, delusion or fact, even if on a different date, it did not seem to matter.

Marie Hill had been technically right that no woman had been executed since 1952, but only technically. In 1954 there had been Eleanor Rush. The eighteen-year-old black woman was unruly, probably criminally insane, and for nearly a week in August 1954 she had screamed obscenities from her isolation cell, and there had been complaints from sick prisoners in the sick bay next door. On August 20, Superintendent Ivan Hinton and three guards went to her cell, had his men restrain her with medieval iron claws and tie her down with leather straps, and then, as Hinton was stuffing two hand towels down her throat as a gag, to silence her, Eleanor Rush's neck snapped, and she died instantly.

In the days that followed, North Carolina newspapers were filled with the details of the case. The language of the news stories was interesting: that Eleanor Rush had been "discovered" sprawled half on and half off the mattress of her tiny cell, her hands bound with leather cuffs, her mouth crammed with towels. Editorials lamented the "tragedy." On September 8, 1954, the coroner's jury met and heard sixty-four witnesses. On September 9, it handed down its verdict:

"Eleanor Rush was definitely incorrigible and very difficult to control. Her conduct caused her to be placed in confinement many times. On the night of August 20, 1954, her behavior was such that it was necessary to restrain her for the benefit of inmates in the building and also herself.

"We find that Eleanor Rush came to her death due to her violent efforts against necessary restraints while they were being applied and in her subsequent struggle to remove them."

Superintendent Hinton called the verdict "as fair, just, and straightforward as it could possibly be," but the State Director of Prisons cautioned that the case might "reveal administrative deficiencies requiring correction."

What then might have happened if Clarence Alligood had prevailed in the scramble for the icepick and Joan Little had been found dead in her cell? The Eleanor Rush case provided a script.

"So after Joan Little surrendered," Celine continued, "we formed a board of directors—the Joan Little Defense Fund—and became incorporated. We set up offices in Jerry Paul's law firm and began an educational campaign. We began to leaflet, trying to start a chain of events that would expand into a nationwide campaign. We knew it would take on a life of its own, simply by the mere facts of the case, for they were so sensational. There were ten members on the board, half men, half women, half and half black-white.

"The Board would discuss tactics at its meetings, but it would also discuss the nature of the case itself, and in that context the case of Inez Garcia came up. I became aware of Inez through the underground press, and later through talking to members of the Inez Garcia Defense Fund and to Angela Davis. Jerry Paul felt that the Joan Little case was much better than Inez's because Joan had to protect herself immediately —she had killed her attacker on the spot—whereas Inez had killed one of her attackers seventeen minutes after the rape. But Inez was held down and raped, then set free, went home and got a gun, and returned to kill one of the two rapists. The court could then say her act was premeditated, but I see no difference between the two cases: both were rape. Again I have to ask myself: what would I have done? I wouldn't just let it pass. I wouldn't have gone to the police—any minority person knows that's no use. She should never have been prosecuted, and it was an awful shame that she got five years.*

* Inez Garcia was sentenced to five-years-to-life imprisonment for second degree murder, but the conviction was later overturned on a technicality.

"Inez's lawyer, Charles Garry, argued in that case that self-defense should not be limited to the time of the rape, but should extend for a broad time afterwards, and I agree with that. But the judge in Inez's case—and this was true in Joan's trial also—would not even admit into evidence expert testimony on the nature of rape! Jurors in that case later said that they weren't swayed by Inez's story of the rape because they believed the rape testimony was not part of the evidence. When the judge sentenced her, he refused to allow her to remain free on bail pending appeal. He [Judge Stanley Lawson] said,

" 'I think this woman is dangerous, frankly.'

"If he feels that way, then I guess we're all dangerous. Yet people who know Inez Garcia say she is a gentle, soft-spoken woman, and even prison officials at the Frontera prison where she is being held want her released. They said,

" 'Further institutional incarceration [of Inez Garcia] is not deemed necessary as there is minimal indication that she is violence-prone' (Dr. Beatrice Franklin, prison psychiatrist at Frontera, and Mary Grace Dick, assistant superintendent).

"One juror even admitted afterwards that the verdict in the Garcia case would make men feel safer to rape women.

"People have said that Inez lost her own case by her foul-mouthed outburst from the stand and that her statements were playing to her feminist gallery, but I'm not so sure. She said things like,

" 'I killed the fuckin' guy, because he raped me.'

" 'You want me to tell you what happened after that? He fucked me, the creep. What else do you want me to tell you?'

" 'I killed him, and I'm not sorry I did it. I'm only sorry I missed Luis [Luis Castillo, the other attacker].'

"But I can see these statements being made, and she

said that they were in response to the judge's hostility. I probably would say the same thing. To say something like that in a court of law, knowing that she's probably putting her life away for five or ten years for just one sentence, well, she must have been very angry. She probably didn't mean half the things she said, but probably thought to herself,

" 'I'm a Chicano. I'm going to jail anyway, I might as well let it all hang out.'

"America is not used to hearing blatant truth in the courtroom. We've been bound and gagged, so that we can't speak out in court. But Inez did it. Ruchell (Cinque) Magee, Angela Davis's co-defendant, did it; of course, he's still in jail, and that's one of the reasons the people have turned against Angela, because she allowed her case to be severed from his. She got out, and he's still in there . . . I think a lot more will speak out. If you're not even going to admit testimony in these cases about the rage and emotional trauma that a woman experiences with rape, what do you expect? Joan Little is just as quick-tempered as Inez Garcia, I'm sure. I've seen Joan angry, and you know just to leave her alone. She had to contain herself very much on the stand, and of course she had been prepped by her lawyers to cool it, but it was hard for Joan, very hard.

"One real difference between Inez Garcia and Joan Little was that Inez was Catholic, and that presented her with a special set of problems about rape that I can appreciate. We were really brainwashed in the Catholic Church. Catholic priests have a way of finding evil where no evil exists. We were taught never to wear patent-leather shoes, lest the boys would look up our dresses through the reflection. I was made to feel guilty if I wore a dress that was cut too short. It was supposed to be a mortal sin to go to another church, and yet, as a black, I wanted to go to a black church where they still shouted out their faith and used tambourines, but my parents would not permit it. Premarital sex was taboo, because of course you saved sex for marriage. You were taught to keep your panties up and your hemline down, and a good Catholic woman would never put herself in a position where she could be raped.

"A Catholic priest testified at the trial of Inez Garcia that for a devout Catholic what was worse than rape was that Inez did not die fighting off her attackers. He was undoubtedly thinking about Saint Maria Goretti, a martyr in the Catholic Church who was beatified in 1950 before a crowd of a quarter of a million people. Saint Maria, like Inez Garcia, was unable to read and write, and she came from poor peasant parents in Italy. When she was eleven years old a nineteen-year-old boy entered her home. She was alone. He put a dagger to her neck and tried to rape her. She fought him, saying, according to the story, 'No, God does not wish it. It is a sin. You will go to hell for it,' and she died, trying to fight him off. The majority of Creoles have children named Maria, and if it hadn't been for a relative who already had the name, I would have been Celine Maria Chenier.

"Still, I can't believe that Inez Garcia was a devout Catholic, a disgusted Catholic perhaps, because a devout Catholic would never have picked up that gun. She did tell the prosecution psychiatrist that she feared God would punish her for her act, and for a woman with a primitive faith, that's plausible. Her lawyer, Charles Garry, tried to get her to say this in court, but she replied,

" 'Charles wanted me to say I'm sorry, but I'm not. And I've never said I was.'

"Still I bet she did feel guilt over the killing, and, for a Catholic, the choice of submitting to rape or killing the attacker is a profound dilemma.

"In the fall of 1974, while we were organizing for her case, Joan was being held on a hundred-fifteen-thousand-dollar bond in Dorm C at Women's Prison in Raleigh. Dorm C is the section of the prison for 'safekeepers,' the ones who are simply awaiting trial, and the safekeepers are treated worse there than the admitted felons and murderers in the other dorms. She was kept in virtual solitary confinement from September '74 until March '75, when she was released on bond. If she wanted to communicate with an inmate in a different dorm, like Sister Marie Hill, she had to write to her, mail it to the outside, and have it come back in. One night she called me after I hadn't heard from her for a while and said it would be her last call for a while: they were cutting off her phone privileges because she attempted to *speak* to another inmate in Dorm C. And yet the district attorney at her trial tried to plant the idea in the jury's mind that she had a lover, a Linda Jones, in Women's Prison. Joan was open-minded about homosexuality. She understood how it happens in prison. They give dances at Women's Prison, for example, knowing that no males will be present, knowing that the women will get emotionally involved and sexually excited, and yet when they get too close, guards separate them. It's like taking away a husband, just when a couple is ready to make love. It's cruel. But to my knowledge Joan had no lover in prison. She could barely talk to anyone else. We corresponded intimately during her incarceration, and I would have known about it if she had taken a lover.

"In November '74, I called a rally at the Women's Prison in Raleigh. It was to be a mixture of issues: to free Joan Little and to protest generally about the conditions in the prison. I went to the warden, Juanita Baker, and told her that we would demonstrate not to demean what the prison was doing as much as call attention to prison needs: to improve conditions in the laundry, or, hopefully, have it eliminated altogether, and to get adequate medical care. Ms. Baker herself had been trying to get the Legislature to provide better facilities since 1972, but her pleas had gone unheeded. They had inmates doing vaginal and rectal searches, who were not qualified medically to do this. One of the women had hemorrhaged profusely after one of these searches.

"About one hundred people came to the November rally and many had made their own Free Joan Little signs. There were chants about Joan, but she never heard them because they had taken her to a different facility that day. There was some publicity about the rally, but the most important thing that came out of it was the formation of a group we called Action for Forgotten Women. These women in prison had literally been forgotten, and this is true nationwide. Because there are so many fewer female prisoners than male, women's prisons are always the last to get good facilities or adequate rehabilitation programs.

"In the months that followed, I became a community volunteer at Women's Prison, able to take inmates out for a few hours three times a week. I would tell them,

" 'Don't fight each other. That's what they want you to do,' and those women started to unite, started to call one another sisters, and the prison officials began to complain that I had too much influence over the inmates. When the violence broke out in June of 1975, a month before Joan's trial, they tried to make me a scapegoat.

"In mid-June, an inmate called me, said, 'Celine, we're human beings. Just because we committed a crime, that's no reason to be treated like a beast,' and she said that they were going to have a peaceful sitdown protest and simply refuse to be locked up for the night. They wanted spectators, because they anticipated that they would be hurt.

"On June 15 they assembled themselves in a circle outside, placing the pregnant women in the middle, because they knew what was waiting for them. They had no weapons, only blankets and pillows. The police came, dressed in riot gear, with helmets, tear gas, and Mace. The women sat peacefully; some even went to sleep. In fact, at five A.M., when the police descended upon them, only about fifteen were awake. The spectators urged them not to struggle, to go limp. The police tried to get them to go to the gym, but they refused, because they knew what that would mean. So the police began to carry them away. One policeman yanked a woman's arm behind her. She struggled to free it, so she could be carried properly, and he hit her with his billy club. Another woman tried to prevent him from beating her, and that's when the swinging of the billies really started. They started herding the women into the gym, now by any means necessary. Those they could not carry, who were too heavy or too fat, they hit with their clubs— unarmed women. Marie Hill somehow got out, and ran to me at the fence,

" 'Celine,' she cried, 'they're beating them down there.' They were not supposed to do that. They were not supposed to do that.

"In the chaos, a woman kicked in the gym door to let the women out, and the inmates came out of there any way they could, through the door, through the small slit windows—however. Many inmates were injured in that protest. One almost died. The newspapers later, in calling it a riot, said that the women threw rocks and bricks. But I was there, and that is not true. I was in on the negotiations—until I collapsed from exhaustion a week later.

"Two weeks before her trial, Joan Little and I appeared on the same platform before four hundred people at the University of North Carolina. Joan had not planned to be there, but when she heard I was going to speak about the disturbance she came, because she felt so strongly about the conditions in Dorm C. On that platform, it was clear how much she had grown since Alligood's attack, intellectually and from experience. She had acquired a political awareness, and she speaks now as if she has been at it for years. She will sit back and listen to you, taking it all in and siphoning out that which she can put to her own use. She's got the potential, and she's come a long way on her own capabilities.

"A while back, Angela Davis and I were quite close, and I had been urging her to write to both Joan Little and Marie Hill—these two women about whom Angela was doing a lot of speaking around the country but whom she had never contacted. Now I'm not a member of the Communist Party, never have been, and never will be. Angela and I would discuss Communism relative to black liberation, but I couldn't see its feasibility at all, and we drifted apart. I'm inclined to think that she's simply recruiting for the party now, rather than dealing for her people. Anyway, Angela and Joan finally did meet in Washington, D.C., at a Free Joan Little rally. Later, Angela attended Joan's trial. I really feared that Joan would get sucked in by Angela, but she wasn't. She has publicly split with Angela now, and publicly denounced the Communist Party.

"This is what I mean about Joan's political education. Here's a black woman, who fought back, who spoke out, who won her case, and continues to fight for those who're left behind. I really respect that. I hope she lives a long, long time, but I'm not very optimistic. Now that she's beaten the murder charge, some of the sisters in prison don't think she's dealing for them, so if you see Joan, tell her to be in touch with me, because she's still got seven to ten years on the breaking-and-entering charge, and when she goes back in there, I wouldn't want anything to happen to her. If I tell the inmates she's cool, it will be OK."

CHAPTER 6

JERRY PAUL (II)

Socrates: And when men are deceived and their notions are at variance with realities, is it clear that error slips in through resemblances?
Phaedrus: Yes, that is the way.
Socrates: Then, he who would be the master of the art must understand the real nature of everything; or he will never know either how to make the gradual departure from truth into the opposite of truth which is effected by the help of resemblances, or how to avoid it?
Phaedrus: He will not.

Plato: *Phaedrus*

His house in Chapel Hill is not the retreat of a private man. Situated in fashionable Lake Forest, modern in design, it has great sheets of glass surrounding the living room and the front stairwell, so that one feels out of doors indoors, but also knows from some distance if the Pauls are at home. Six weeks after the trial Jerry Paul was seldom at home. He had become a bona fide celebrity, constantly moving to lectures before college audiences—"They all want to hear that the Joan Little case proves that the system works, and they get uncomfortable when I say I tricked the system into working"—negotiating movie rights with the likes of Dustin Hoffman, appearing on *Black Journal* with Golden Frinks as an authority on racism and Southern justice. His reference point had suddenly become William Kunstler, who took two or three cases a year and spent the rest of the time lecturing, and Paul had even told one reporter that he had become bored with the law.

That was the bluster of his public side, the side that scandalized some and bored others, but the warmth of his private side was also at work. That week Joan Little had fled back to him from the Black Panthers. She had been in their tow ever since the acquittal, traveling around the country saying silly things. But after a television show in which she failed to be uncomplimentary to Jerry Paul, there had been a tussle with Larry Little, the North Carolina Black Panther leader. Celine Chenier had said:

"The Panthers have a way of dealing with you if you're a woman."

Paul sat on his living room couch, "the very couch," he said, where he had done most of the preening of Joan Little for her deliverance, where he had planned her wardrobe, "the very couch" where only six weeks before her trial she had told him for the first time what really happened in that cell on August 27, 1974.

"At the very beginning—even on the trip under the moonlight from Little Washington to Chapel Hill—I realized that this was the case I'd been looking for. It had all the issues—civil rights, women's rights, prison reform, and later capital punishment—and I realized that right away. I've tried so many cases that if I hadn't recognized its potential immediately, I'd be very poor. But the question was which of the issues would float. I also knew immediately that if I was to get Joan Little free, I'd have to do some things that you don't ordinarily do in a case. I had to get it out of Washington. I had to have money, and I had to create a big public interest. Without these three things, I'd never win it. A large part of my preliminary planning was done on that trip back. I suppose I was already programmed to act as I did. It was a case of preparation meeting opportunity.

"But my mind was also on the system that we were up against. You've got more prisoners per capita in this state than anywhere else in the nation. In one eastern county, Jones County, one person in ten is in jail. You've got more young people in jail than anywhere else, and I had defended many of them. The system is so repressive that it is making the young frustrated and forcing them to do irrational things, trying to fight back. The overcrowding of the jails is the nation's worst, and you've got a prison commissioner, David Jones, who advocates public executions and is a potential candidate for Governor. In one judicial district consisting of two rural eastern counties, a prosecutor has put twelve people on death row in the last two years—that's more than the entire death-row population of twenty-four out of the thirty-four states which have the death penalty.

"Still, the courtroom is the worst place to raise political issues. The state is in control. The court is the instrument of social control. Yet the public seems to be attracted to court cases, and historically, the movement or the Left has used the courtroom to demonstrate abuses. I had spent ten years of my practice doing that. Also, Watergate was on my mind, where Mitchell and the others had spent hundreds of thousands of dollars on their defense. You see, people wanted to believe after Watergate that the system worked. The system didn't work. Look, I had defended kids who had done much less than the Watergate figures had, and yet they got much, much longer sentences. So, the question to me, riding back to Chapel Hill, was: Could a poor person get the same kind of defense that Mitchell got? If the least really are judged equally with the best, why can't the least go up there and be the least?

"I could not sell Joan with her negative side coming out. She has that basic personality flaw that her environment created in her, and it's still there. She's not an honest person. She's not a kind person. She's a violent person. That doesn't mean she committed this crime. It only means she's a product of her environment. Beyond that, Joan is an actor, a mimic, an impersonator. The psychiatrist to whom I later referred her told me,

" 'Joan Little is not a real person.'

"So I decided early that I had to create her totally. She could not carry the character alone unless you gave it to her. You could let people see only so much of her. If they saw too much, the mask would slip away. You walk a double line here. You've got to have the publicity, so she's got to be seen, but you run the risk of creating a person whom a prospective juror will not like. So I maintained a strict control on everything. If I had let her say publicly before the trial some of the things she said afterwards, she would have lost.

"To be really good on the stand, the client must be an extension of her lawyer. The client literally must *be* her lawyer in that chair. You must be able to control —by eye contact, by body movement, by inflection of words. She must know what I want her to do in every situation. Joan's training in this began that first night in this house. That night, and from then on, I would sit at an angle from her when she talked in public, so she could watch me out of the corner of her eye. She could glance at me for approval of what she was saying.

"She had to take the approach: 'I don't like to kill people. I don't believe in capital punishment. I don't believe in killing. Maybe I shouldn't be punished in court for killing this person, but I still have to suffer with it.' You see, Inez Garcia was stupid. I went to California after the verdict, and these feminists would come up to me, say,

" 'If only you had argued the Little case in the way we did the Inez Garcia case, then we would have *really* had a victory,' and there was Inez Garcia rotting in jail on a five-years-to-life for a second-degree!

"If I had tried to sell Joan with the stance: 'I did a brave thing, I killed the old lecher and I'm glad of it,' I'd have blown it. Because if you can't sell your theory to the public, you can't sell it to a jury. Still, once I made up my mind to take the case, all the ideology goes out the window, and there's only one consideration: winning.

"A case like this attracts a lot of immature people who want their presuppositions to be worked out in fact. The feminists wanted Joan Little to be a goddess on a pedestal, and when she didn't act like one, they got so disillusioned that they missed the real issues. For instance, when the riot happened at Women's Prison, one of 'em asked Joan what she thought about it, expecting a political pronouncement, and Joan said, 'That's what happens when you get a bunch of horny women together.' So they couldn't see the real human being who was suffering, the human being who couldn't get along in society, who couldn't stay out of jail, because her talents never were encouraged. The feminists were trying to create an illusion for Joan that she couldn't deal with, and because I became responsible for her, almost a father to her, I wasn't about to give her anything but a realistic starting point.

"In the first week, I brought my colleague, Karen Galloway, in on the case. I already anticipated problems down the line with Golden Frinks, although I needed him at first for publicity. Karen was the only black person I had. Her participation would negate actions by Golden, and I surmised that he would not be effective in his attacks on me if he had to attack Karen at the same time. Beyond that, Karen was just starting out: she passed the North Carolina Bar a week after this case fell on us. She had been with me since her junior year in college, so I knew she would be more willing to put up with my antics than the other lawyers in the firm. The other partners had a more conservative and traditional view of the law. They didn't like publicity. They were very concerned at first with how much money we were going to get out of the case, and urged that we not take it unless the Little family could come up with so much money at the outset. I told them,

" 'We're going to take the case for nothing.'

"Joan is a lower-class black. Karen is a middle-class black. I'm watching the favorable reaction of white women to Karen, and I figure if they'll accept Karen, if she comes off well, she'll drag Joan along with her. They'll never look at Joan. I've got to give them an image of what Joan can be . . . and maybe is.

"In the week of Joan's surrender I started a technique that was later to become an oft-used strategy: of filing appeals and motions by the pound and attaching information to them as exhibits that I wanted to make public. Later we would use this strategy to buy time. On Thursday of that week, we attached the autopsy report to a motion that had nothing to do with the report, and then called a press conference. This was the only way the autopsy could be made part of the public record. It happened this way:

"I received a call from Dr. Page Hudson, the State Medical Examiner. He told me that information in the autopsy report indicated a different picture of what had happened in the Beaufort County Jail than the one being painted by public officials. He invited me to come over to his office and damned if the report did not fit with the story Joan had told me! When I told Dr. Hudson what she had said, he replied, " 'I'm reasonably certain she's telling you the truth.'

"It was not the first time that medical people had been helpful. In the few days after the killing, when Joan was still at large and Sheriff Davis was talking about making her an outlaw and the local newspaper was editorializing about what a 'good man' Alligood was—one who had died 'in the line of duty'—Dr. Harry Carpenter, who did the autopsy, went to a Washington lawyer and told him that if Sheriff Davis didn't quit talking about the outlaw statute, he, Dr. Carpenter, was going to go to the local TV station and tell them what he had found. That scared Red Davis so bad, he straightened up some.

"In a general discussion with Dr. Hudson that followed, we talked about how the public generally feels that medical examiners as state officials work only for the prosecution, and he told me a story of a murder case in Smithfield, North Carolina, where the medical people had evidence of the innocence of the defendant, but the defense attorney had never asked the examiners any questions. This was when I first saw the possibility of using Dr. Hudson and his colleagues, and I invited Hudson to correct the public's impression by attending our press conference. I knew the press wouldn't pay a bit of attention to the intricate details of the autopsy, but I felt that the mere presence of the doctors would have an effect. It turned out better than I could have hoped.

"The press conference was held at a community church in Chapel Hill, and the autopsy report and the motion were released. Karen and Celine were there, along with Dr. Neil Hoffman from the Medical Examiner's office. Hoffman read out a carefully prepared statement and the press paid no more attention to it than I expected. But someone asked him,

" 'Where are the pants?' referring to Alligood's pants.

" 'I don't know where the pants are,' Dr. Hoffman replied.

" 'Are you saying that your investigation is not complete until you find the pants?'

" 'Well, yes, that's right.'

" 'Are you also saying that this autopsy report raises doubts as to whether Joan Little killed the jailer?'

" 'It raises some doubts in my mind.'

"The next day the papers carried the headlines, STATE MEDICAL EXAMINER THROWS DOUBT ON LITTLE'S GUILT, and I figured that was the last time I'd ever get a medical examiner to a press conference. You know, it's a damn shame that you've got to trick public officials into telling the truth. If I had been the medical examiner, I would have stood up there and said, 'They've hidden the pants. This report raises doubt about her guilt, and what're people hollering about making her an outlaw for anyway?' but no, you've got to trick 'em to say that, and that's a sad commentary on the system.

"A newspaper story like that starts you, but of course it does not make a national case, and in September I began to work with the underground press. Now the underground press will print. You've got to give them the whole story. You've almost got to write it for them. But they will print. *WIN* magazine came in and did a story, and I started to get letters from all over the country. Later, *Great Speckled Bird, Rage, Rising Up Angry, Off Our Backs* ran stories. Meanwhile, I contacted Marvin Miller, an attorney in Washington, D.C., who had good contacts in the underground up there, and who had worked with the Attica cases. This was a period of kicking around ideas and sizing up the situation, and I was thinking about bringing Marvin in on the case. Having an out-of-stater—a so-called foreign attorney—on a case gives it a little more appeal, and Marvin could help get the word around. But I made no firm commitments to him yet.

"In October 1974 the case took off, and it did so in Washington, D.C. Four years before, I had done some work on an NBC White Paper on the black exodus from Eastern North Carolina and collaborated with Nancy Mills, who is with the Institute for Corporate Responsibility. I called her up, told her I had this case, and asked how I could get some national publicity for it. We talked about it some, and she told me to make a trip up there and promised to set me up with some women's groups.

" 'You do all the organizing,' she said. 'I know you're going to do it anyway. But remember, let Karen do the talking, and you keep your mouth shut. They don't want to hear from you anyway.'

"At that point we had about six hundred dollars in the Joan Little Defense Fund. I took two hundred fifty of it for the trip, took Karen with me, and before it was over we had raised twenty thousand dollars in Washington, D.C., alone. We talked to several women's groups, with me pushing Karen out there. They put us on the radio, made tapes of what we had said, and sent them all over the country. A TV station got interested, and sent a woman down to do an interview with Joan, Karen beside her, in Women's Prison. I went back up several weeks later, and Nancy told me,

" 'You've got the biggest case in this town.'

"We sold the Joan Little case in Washington, D.C. All the women's groups started to pick it up, and if I learned one thing in this whole business, it was that you've got to have the women in any political movement. They've got the time and the intelligence and they'll work hard for you.

"Meanwhile, I knew that the case *had to be delayed*. You can not try a case effectively with the defendant still in jail. The trial was set for November 18, and I had to get her out, because I had not put my strategy together yet. I had not put my publicity together . . . the publicity was still not great enough so that local officials would feel that everybody was watching. With what we had then, they still would not feel that they had to project at least the appearance of fairness.

"Beyond that, I had realized on September 19, 1974, that the prosecution had the evidence to convict Joan Little on first-degree murder. Perhaps it was not the 'smoking gun,' but it could be made to look like it. I realized what they had the first time I went through the evidence, and I had to keep them from noticing it somehow. But I ran scared about that from September 19, 1974, until August 15, 1975. It was sitting right under their noses that whole time, and they never saw it.

"I figured if I kept Billy Griffin, the prosecutor, mad all the time, he'd never come up with the answer. I had had one case with him before, a labor case, and I knew his temper. In that case, the officers could not identify the black defendants, and so I put other blacks at the defense table to demonstrate this. Griffin got mad, threw one of his famous temper tantrums, insisted that the defendants sit in prescribed seats, and answer the calendar when their names were called. He got his way. The judge even made the defendants stand when their names were called, and the officers took notes on where they were sitting. That was illegal and unethical as hell.

"Later I could make Griffin mad at a moment's notice, and he'd go off and pout, but in the fall of 1974 I had to have that continuance, so I was being nice to him. We had a lunch at the Poet's Corner in Chapel Hill in early November, and I brought along my partner Jim Rowan. Rowan is polished and cosmo-

politan, and he came at Griffin with his style, and I
came at him with mine. I had to neutralize Griffin,
and I did so by telling him some things I knew he
didn't know: about a heroin ring in one of his counties
in which some sheriff's deputies were participating. I
told him how they operated, and let him visualize
himself busting it up, and getting a big reputation.
I'm laughing with him. He really hates Golden
Frinks, so I feed his ego a little on that. I want him
relaxed. I'm not ready to jump him yet. We're dealing, but he doesn't realize what we're dealing for.

"Down here, you've got to hustle solicitors. Later
on, when Morris Dees joined our defense team, he'd
go to Griffin, say,

" 'We'll take a dismissal. We're going to win this
case,' and that would piss Billy off. That's nutsy. You
can't get nothin' out of him when you do that. So I'd
use this on him, say,

" 'Billy, I apologize to you about Morris. But I can't
control him. He's so damn crazy; he's liable to do
anything.'

" 'Yeah, I know the problem,' Griffin would reply.

" 'I know John [Wilkinson] is treating you the
same way.'

" 'I didn't say that,' he snapped back.

"I know I have to make an ogre out of Griffin
eventually, but it's not time to do that yet. I want him
relaxed, so I can get my continuance. Griffin's not easy
to paint as a villain. He's stupid, but he's not an ogre.
That's why later I was so happy that they brought in
Wilkinson, because John's so much easier to portray as
an ogre.

"You can not create a national case like Joan Little's without a fool. About a year before this case, I
read *Selma 1965*, and in that book the author made
the point that without Jim Clark there would never
have been a Selma. Without Bull Connor, there never

would have been a Birmingham. In every big case
you've got to have one who'll act the fool for you, and
Billy Griffin always acted the fool for me time and
again. Once he said to a reporter,
  " 'I've had a bellyful of you bastards.' I couldn't
have paid him to say a thing like that! So I played on
it.
  " 'Billy, I'm going to make a hero out of you. I'm
going to put you on national TV.'
  " 'I'm not talking to anybody,' he'd quip.
  " 'Aw, I know you want to talk to these people,
Billy. You know you're seeking this publicity. You
want to run for judge.'
  " 'I don't want to run for nothin'.'
  " 'I'm going to make you a state senator, Billy. I'm
going to send a reporter from *Time* magazine down to
see you next week.'
  " 'Don't you send no damn reporter down here.'
  "That used to tickle the dickens out of me.
  "So you've got to know how people are programmed. We were getting all that publicity in the
Joan Little case by accusing people in the east of
being rednecks, and they're scared of that. If they're
scared of that, that's their program. They've got to
prove they're not. They're on the defensive. Griffin
played right into our hands time after time. He's a
fascist, you know. Fascists don't come across as ogres.
They don't run around with swastikas on, but if you
read the diaries and letters that people in Nazi Ger-
many wrote, it's the same line: how the law must be
preserved, fighting for freedom, that kind of thing.
  "What worries you in a trial like this is a line of
questioning like,
  " 'Miss Little, aren't you a prostitute?'
  "She says no, and there's never been any evidence of
that. But the jury goes into their room and says,
'That's the district attorney talking. He must have

some information. She must be a prostitute who lured Alligood into her cell.'

"You see, simply by asking the question, the district attorney testified to that, even though there is no such evidence. But if the solicitor comes out bad in all the pretrial publicity, and he asks that question in court, the jury's going to go back into their room and say,

" 'The son of a bitch is railroading her. He must be one of those rednecks they've been talking about. We're not rednecks. We're going to prove we're not by finding her not guilty!' "

CHAPTER 7

WILLIAM GRIFFIN

OF all the principals in the Joan Little affair, Bill Griffin had the toughest job. As the elected prosecutor for five counties, including Beaufort, he tries over eighty jury cases in a year and was trying different cases both the week before and the week after his six-week ordeal in Raleigh. He was the target of charges and innuendoes from all sides, even his own, and the persistence of both Jerry Paul and his own assistant prosecutor, John Wilkinson, in calling him "Billy" conveyed an element of disdain which went beyond quaint Southern colloquialism. Wilkinson maintained that because of political pressure from high state officials who felt that it was in the state's interest to have Joan Little acquitted, again an "image" question, Griffin had not been a free agent in handling the case since November 1974. In it all, Griffin had coined a new phrase: he wondered constantly if in the Joan Little case "the state could get a fair trial."

He works out of an office in an old two-story house in Williamston, twenty miles north of Washington and the county seat of adjoining Martin County, and it is a setting which would more appropriately be graced by a ruddy-faced, sixty-year-old prosecutor with rubber bands around his upper sleeves than this boyish thirty-two-year-old. Griffin operates between his modest office and his large, newly constructed, colonial-style house in the country outside of town.

"I like symmetry in my life," Griffin had said about the house, and he works hard in the summer to keep crabgrass from sneaking into his fescue in the expansive lawn around it. He likes his territory. Born and raised here, he speaks of how in the fall the sky gets black with the geese migrating south or heading for Lake Mattamuskeet to the east; how this is a sight we may not see in the United States much longer. And he jokes about holding court over in Hyde County: "It's so small that in the winter they stoke up some coals on the courthouse lawn, shovel some oysters onto them, and judge, jury, defendants, and lawyers gather around for lunch."

In the course of the Joan Little trial, Griffin's youthful looks had caused an odd television problem. As there could be no live television coverage of the proceedings (although the *Raleigh News and Observer* had editorialized that the trial should be televised to show the openness and fairness of the new Southern justice), the visuals were the province of the sketch artists. While the sketches of the portly, long-haired, overblown Jerry Paul or the jowly judge, or the defendant with her accentuated features had worked well for television sketch artists, the sketches of Griffin always seemed flat and grade-schoolish. His most identifiable mannerism was standing with his hands in his pockets (he rarely gesticulated), and this pose made strange television when the script for, say, the cross-examination of Joan Little had Griffin asking,

"How long did you maintain this position with him [Alligood] with his private parts in your mouth there?"

The week that Griffin and the author talked, a full-page ad had appeared in *The New York Times*, dominated by a letter signed by Joan Little, appealing for $50,000 to help Jerry Paul fight his fourteen-day contempt citation, pronounced by the judge immediately after the verdict. Griffin told of a conversation between himself and Susie Sharp, the Chief Justice of the North Carolina Supreme Court, who might later have been a candidate for the U.S. Supreme Court vacancy opened by Justice Douglas's resignation, if Betty Ford had gotten her way. Immediately before the trial, Griffin had sought yet another continuance of the trial, and Susie Sharp refused.

"Mr. Griffin," she told him on the phone, "this case must be tried. This albatross around the neck of North Carolina *must* be removed."

Griffin joked about sending the *Times* ad to the Chief Justice with the notation: "The albatross is still there," but he let it slide.

"This is a small place," he began. "I suppose in my solicitorial district there are no more than seventy-five thousand people. If the local bar and the district bar like you, then you get elected district attorney, and that's all there is to it. Even though this job is elective, I don't know of any district attorney who's ever run a contested campaign. It's still a region where people know one another; they know from word of mouth what's going on in the courthouse; they know the way you operate, and they know what to expect.

"I've made an effort since I took this job in 1969— when I was only twenty-five, just out of Rutgers Law School—to feed everyone from the same spoon. I don't keep statistics on my convictions—purposely don't keep 'em—because I don't think a fair, decent prosecution can be based on how many indictments and how many convictions a man can get. I've been guided by a simple philosophy: first, my business is not punishment; that's the judge's province, and I do not want to preempt him. Oh, I have to get into punishment problems, but I don't want to, so I have a real

problem with plea-bargaining. Second, I'll form an
opinion simply from the evidence, as to whether the
defendant is probably guilty.

"In these small places, you see the same people over
and over again, and I suppose that engenders an attitude in me that a certain segment of society just needs
to be kept out of circulation. It's a matter of protecting society from those members who can't conform. In
the past few years I've grown less and less interested in
what happens in the nation: I used to read both
weekly newsmagazines and several newspapers. Now
I'm more concerned with things I can do something
about, and I've developed an aversion to people whose
own lives are messed up, going around involving
themselves in other people's business. They're only
trying to solve their own emotional problems by losing themselves in someone else's business. Perhaps this
attitude comes from having several kids in school and
moving into my early thirties. Now I concentrate on
simple rules like 'stealing is wrong.' Kids nowadays get
no training in morality. They don't get it in the
schools or in the home. There was some discussion in
the Joan Little case about whether black women are
more promiscuous than white women; that may have
been true ten years ago, but I don't know if it's true
today.

"I've had my share of capital cases, and I tried my
best to treat the Little case like all the others, as just
an ordinary case. It was circumstantial, sure, but most
capital cases *are* circumstantial. *Your* witness is gone. I
can't say that the death penalty bothers me. In fact, I
have a man on death row now for first-degree rape,
George Vick, or I should say, Mr. Vick put himself on
death row. There was criticism of that case in the local
press because Vick was indicted, tried, convicted, and
sentenced to die in sixteen days back in December
1973. It's one of the speediest trials ever in a capital

case, but it happened that things just fell into place. The lawyer came to me, said, 'There's nothing to this case,' and so we just moved forward.

"At his trial, Vick's victim testified:

> I bit him and scratched him and I fighted him, the door was partly open and I was trying to get out, I went to the door and he grabbed me again, and he started ripping—pulling my pants off, and he threw me on the floor again. I don't remember where I bit him, I think along his shoulder. I pulled his hair and I scratched him I think but I don't remember where. I just know I was fighting. I was still fighting when he had me on the floor and he grabbed hold of my neck and said, 'Shirley I swear if you don't lay still, I'll kill you.' I was scared and I laid still and he went ahead and had intercourse.
>
> . . . I did not consent to the act of having intercourse with him. The reason I laid still when he told me to do so is because he started choking me, I thought he was going to kill me.

"But Ashley Futrell, the editor of the *Washington Daily News*, made a considerable fuss. He wrote an editorial entitled 'George Vick Should Not Die,' and I replied to the editorial in a letter:

> I am in a position in which I have had to make a decision about capital punishment, and I have made my decision after careful thought and deliberation. I believe it should be retained, not as a deterrent, but as punishment. Punishment is a basic principle of our system, from which we have strayed. Those who have difficulty making up their minds about it are those who have superimposed sociology on top of basic Christian ideals

and traditions which are reflected in our laws. It is interesting that the Bible not only required punishment for crimes. It demands it. And one of those punishments is execution. If your readers desire to explore the philosophy of crime and punishment, I suggest they consult the Bible, not the *Daily News*. [*Washington Daily News*, June 3,1974.]

"So I have no problem with capital punishment *per se*, but I think the Supreme Court is responsible for this state's high number on death row. They were trying to be helpful in their *Furman* vs. *Georgia* decision by taking the arbitrariness out of capital punishment. But by removing the power of the jury to recommend mercy, they've populated our death row. If juries could still recommend mercy in first-degree cases, we wouldn't have ten people on death row now.* We'd have only the felony murderers, like the three bank robbers who killed the state patrolmen which I tried in June, but certainly not Jesse Fowler, who killed a man after an argument for ten dollars in a crap game.

"Rape cases are the hardest cases of all to prosecute, because the public simply has a difficult time believing that rape is possible. I shouldn't put it so bluntly, but that's my experience especially when no violence, no terrible physical abuse like a beating accompanies

---

* The North Carolina capital punishment statute, under which the Joan Little case was tried, called for a mandatory death sentence for a first-degree murder conviction. A jury could not recommend mercy. The United States Supreme Court struck down this law as unconstitutional in 1976. Under a new provision passed by the North Carolina Legislature, which went into effect in June 1977, a jury could recommend mercy in a separate proceeding on punishment after a first-degree murder conviction.

the crime. When there are no bruises or scratches, the public puts the prosecuting witness on trial. It's a terrible situation, not only here, but universally. So when the defense is that the woman gave consent, a rape case is very difficult to prosecute. Still, in my seven years as district attorney, I've gone out of my way in rape cases. I've given law-enforcement officers hell for not adequately investigating rape complaints. Too often their attitude has been to tell the woman to go get a warrant, as if to say, 'don't bother me.'

"Sometimes you have doubts, sure, but I have ways that I satisfy myself. I had a rape case where two men were charged with raping a woman. All the parties were black, and the woman had two illegitimate children, and the defense argued that she consented. I'm sure I'm like your average person: when a woman has two illegitimate children, you have questions. That would influence anyone, and it influenced the jury in that case. But she was very convincing.

"The Joan Little case is the second case of interracial rape I've had. The other was a horrible thing. A fifteen-year-old black, Billy Ewing, crawled into the back seat of a woman's car when she was in a Washington shopping center. The victim had another person's small child with her. When she came out of the drug store and entered her car, Ewing rose up, put a knife to her throat, and forced her to drive to the outskirts of Washington. We went to trial on second-degree rape, because in this state the defendant must be over sixteen years of age to prosecute rape as a capital offense. Ewing got forty years. I wonder why there hasn't been more publicity about that case. Nobody paid much attention to it—in the nation *or* in Beaufort County.

"Jerry Paul made a lot of charges about racism in Eastern North Carolina, but I want to tell you something: there's less racism in the South than anywhere in the country. I've got more black neighbors than I have white. People who perceive racism, who bandy around the term, are the real racists. They're hypocrites, and there were a lot of hypocrites who took advantage of the Little situation. I got a little cynical in that case, I suppose, because I'm in the business of judging people's motives.

"Listen, when I'm trying a case involving blacks, I would *rather* have black jurors than white. A good black citizen makes the finest juror in the world, for the simple reason that he's closer to violence than your average white citizen. I had a double homicide case over here in Martin County; they took the jury from Bertie County, and I suppose the black population in Bertie is as high as any in the state. We went into jury selection—I tell ya, I'm getting disgusted with this jury-selection process—and there were seven or eight black jurors. Of course, I asked the Witherspoon question* and I let the last two—they were black women—sit, *even though* they had reservations about the death penalty. The jury was out fifteen minutes and came back with a conviction on first-degree murder, and they did not recommend mercy. So that proves two things to me: First, blacks make good jurors, and second, if they see a case that's bad enough, even though they have reservations about the death sentence, they may change their mind."

The courts have a term for picking a jury in a first-degree murder case. It is called: choosing a "death-qualified" jury. In seeking a "death-qualified" jury for Joan Little, the questioning followed a set pattern. For those who believed in the death sentence, the

* "Would you vote not guilty in a first-degree murder case *under any circumstances*, knowing that a conviction would mean the imposition of the death penalty?"

court had no problem. For them there would be no tough questions of conscience. Neither prosecution nor defense would ask why a person believed in the death spectacle. No true believer was ever asked if he had seen the gas chamber, seen the two wooden, straight-backed chairs, side by side in case of dual executions, in Central Prison in Raleigh, their thick leather straps dangling from the wooden arm rests, the little bucket underneath the chute down which the cyanide pellet rolled, or the control panel behind the glass and wire mesh, where, it was rumored, other inmates would press the release button and receive gain time on their own sentences.

The author had been there with a television crew in April 1975, when he did an interview with Jesse Fowler. Fowler had talked in the interview about watching from his cell as busloads of schoolchildren would drive up to Central Prison, coming to see the gas chamber as a school outing. As a joke, the crazy light man in the crew, a thirty-year-old hippie, had asked the guard to strap him in as it really happens, and then the cameraman shot a sequence of the light man acting out the struggle, eyes rolling back in his head, mouth open, gasping for oxygen. That had been for the amusement of editors back in the cutting room, but the cameraman had also tried another modern television trick. He had rubbed vaseline around the edges of his lens to produce an ethereal effect, and then shot a sequence of the gas chamber. But the producer in Washington, D.C., thought the stark reality of the chamber, without tricks, the more effective footage, and that had been used. Once in the three-minute story on Fowler they had used pictures of the condemned man sitting quietly on his death-row bunk, reading a book of writings by Malcolm X, and spliced in a "super" of the death chair, making it look as if Fowler was about to be gassed. Did it really have a shock effect, or did it excite a prurient impulse instead? To the producers in Washington such questions were uninteresting. They made good television; that was the point.

The "death-qualified" juror had to undergo no such interrogation. His opinion was certified by the court. It was the veniremen with reservations about the death penalty who underwent the grilling of conscience and were made to feel as if there was something loathsome about their opposition. The prosecution would begin with its stock question:

"If you were convinced that a woman was guilty of murder in the first degree, could you vote her guilty of first-degree murder, knowing that it would be the duty of the state to impose the death sentence?"

If the venireman answered, as a young broadcasting technician Gary T. Otto had, that he did not know if "his mind would be clear enough" to judge a case on its merits (Otto was struck off the jury), or as Pecola Jones, later empaneled, did, "Don't want nothin' on my conscience about the death penalty," the prosecutor would move to the Witherspoon question:

"Could you under *no* circumstances vote a verdict of guilty knowing that verdict would result in the death penalty? Would you *automatically* vote not guilty in that situation?"

With a venireman holding onto reservations, the burden would shift to Jerry Paul. He had a set situation. "What if there were three killers of children, one killer is caught, and then if by a guilty verdict and the sentence of death you could prevent further killing of children, would you support the death penalty?" Well, yes, who could be for the killing of children? Paul would then turn to the judge, saying, "You see, there *is* a circumstance in which this venireman would vote guilty."

So the judge would have his turn, reading from the Witherspoon decision.

"Is it your irrevocable belief that you could not and would not return a verdict of guilty under any circumstances, if that guilty verdict would mean that it was the duty of the State to pronounce the death penalty?"

By this time the venireman, particularly the less complicated ones like Pecola Jones, a 49-year-old black, female machinist was thoroughly confused, and usually mumbled something vague and incoherent, and the judge in his judicial discretion would pronounce the person either "death-qualified" or not.

Griffin continued:

"Jury selection here is less difficult than it is in other places, because you've got a panel sitting over there, and somebody in the courtroom usually knows the people. I depend a lot on the officers to assist me in this. If you've got a special venire with a jury from a different county, the sheriff usually accompanies them, and I can rely on him. The defense in the Little case made a big deal about 'racism in Eastern North Carolina,' but that was not the reason the case was moved. It was simply the type of case where you expect a change of venue. It happens all the time. I've got a case now with a highway-patrolman killing, and I called the defense lawyer last week to tell him to get his papers in order for a venue change. It's just that type of case.

"The character of the defendant on trial is extremely important as well, because the average juror looks very closely at the kind of person they're dealing with, not just their prior record. Like I said, it's a small place. It's a whole lot easier to know about a person than in a big city, and I know a whole lot more about Joan Little than simply her breaking-and-entering conviction—through information I've gathered, through prior contact. In fact, we had such a mass of negative information on Joan Little that it was almost impossible to marshal it all.

"There's a reason why this 'groundswell of interest' in her case didn't affect the people around here. The defense portrayed Little as the 'poor black girl, victim of the system, of white injustice,' and all that crap. And yet the black people in Washington were incensed that she was ripping off black people, that she was breaking into their homes and stealing their stuff. They'd tell you all about it privately, but not on the stand. They knew what she was. One black lady came in here, said,

"'Joan Little? Why, she ain't nothin but a whore.'

"I was in New Jersey, sitting on a dock with my feet hanging in the water, when Sheriff Davis called me in August. He gave the bare outline of what had happened, and my initial reaction was that if things like that are going to happen, they'll happen in Beaufort County. All the messy cases in my district seem to take place in Beaufort County. People are more litigious there, and the county has quite a few sorry folks, white and black. Anyway, I didn't think much about it, went and stuck my feet back in the water.

"I came back home on the Sunday before Labor Day, and went to Washington for discussions with Red Davis and SBI agents on the case. We discussed using the outlaw statute. I had used it once before, in the case of Sam Moore, who was convicted before I became district attorney. Moore escaped from Central Prison, and he had made threats against several attorneys in Washington. They came to me and asked for an outlaw petition, and it was done. Moore eventually gave himself up, but not for a long time, and in that case as well there were negotiations about surrender. The outlaw statute is no more than a tool to encourage a fugitive to give himself up. They claimed Joan Little would be shot on sight if she were found in

Beaufort County, but that is pure propaganda. How many people have you heard of who've been shot on sight down here? Name 'em. That was simply one of the many pieces of propaganda in this case.

"Red Davis and I both decided that the outlaw statute was not worth the effort. I have a recollection of saying it's not worth it or let's wait and see, and the next thing I remember Red was telling me that she was going to give herself up. A condition of her surrender was that she not be returned to Beaufort County Jail, and I prepared the safekeeping order that made it possible for her to be held in Raleigh. Then I put my mind to the indictment.

"I had a term of court in the week of September ninth and had already prepared bills of indictment for the grand jury. That grand jury, by the way, was thirty percent black, or exactly the percentage of the black population in Beaufort County. It was also half women, and, in fact, the Beaufort County Bar had been complaining recently that there were too many women appearing in the juries and not enough men. Yet the defense alleged that blacks and women were underrepresented. I don't know how you contend with blatantly false charges like that. I just kept my mouth shut.

"I decided to bypass the preliminary hearing in this case and go directly for an indictment on first-degree murder from the grand jury. There's nothing wrong with that. It's a usual thing to do in drug cases, for example, where you've got informants. But in this case, I had a different reason. I knew Jerry Paul's penchant for making big shows, and my purpose was to deny him a forum. I knew his reputation, and I had had one case with him before. It was a labor dispute at the Scovil plant, and there was a series of misdemeanors: puncturing tires, trespassing, that sort of thing. Paul pled them all guilty or *nolo contendere*, but in the process he'd pull stunts like getting out there on the picket lines and marching with them, or bringing three men to the bar, assuring the court that one of the three was the defendant. He was going to make the witnesses identify the real defendant—an adaptation of *To Tell the Truth* to the courtroom. So I knew what to expect.

"As a matter of course in any homicide case, I send a bill on first-degree murder. In this state, the lesser offenses are automatically subsumed under that charge. That way, you can worry about the degree later, when you have had a chance to look at the facts. I knew the case wasn't going to be tried that week. It was just a matter of getting an indictment. Later, I could actually go to trial on second-degree or manslaughter without having to worry about it. Getting an indictment is a fairly cut-and-dried proposition. The grand jury is only considering whether there is a scintilla of evidence that the defendant is probably guilty. I can remember only one time that I did not get an indictment from the grand jury that I asked for, and that was because of procedural difficulty.

"The grand jury, of course, is a secret meeting, and I'm forbidden by law to be present. All I do is send the bills of indictment. Willis Peachey, Red's investigative officer, and Agent William Slaughter of the SBI were the chief witnesses. The defense later charged that I had deliberately prevented the medical examiner, Dr. Harry Carpenter, from testifying before the grand jury about the sperm on the body, but the truth is that I did strike Dr. Carpenter's name from the grand-jury witness list after his secretary called to ask if his presence was really necessary. I knew the grand jury would have the autopsy report, in which it was stated clearly:

" 'Smears of the urethra were made and stained by the paps method. The smears were teeming with spermatozoa.'

"In a later hearing, a grand-jury member testified that Agent Slaughter actually read the autopsy report to them. And yet even after we got up to Raleigh, Paul was perpetuating that damn foolishness that the grand jury never had the autopsy report, and if Dr. Carpenter had testified before the grand jury, there never would have been an indictment. Hogwash.

"Anyway, the indictment came down on September ninth. The trial was set for November, and I began to put my mind to the evidence. If the case had been tried in November, it would have been entirely different both factually and from the standpoint of the law of self-defense. The chief difference in the factual case would have been the testimony of Terry Bell, the sixteen-year-old trusty, who was in the jail at the same time as Joan Little. The saga of Terry Bell is the strangest twist of events I've ever encountered in my law career. Alligood was like a father to Terry. He didn't have any family that amounted to anything. All he'd ever known was institutions, and Alligood had been very kind to him. At about ten-thirty on the night of August 26, Joan Little, Terry Bell, and Alligood were in the jailer's office, and Joan Little was on the telephone. A woman came in trying to find the magistrate, and Alligood offered to take her around to the magistrate's office, just down the hallway from the basement. He told Bell to watch Little while he did the errand. When he returned, the jailer said,

" 'C'mon, Terry, let's go back to your cell.'

"When Bell got up, he noticed that the second drawer of the jailer's desk was cracked open two or three inches, with the icepick lying there clearly visible. The icepick, by the way, was used by the jailers to clean out drains that were constantly getting clogged up by inmates' trash. Bell and Alligood went back to his cell, and they stayed there about five minutes, just talking. Alligood then locked the trusty up for the night. A few minutes later, the jailer came back to Bell's cell, said,

"'Joan wants some cigarettes.' Bell gave him three Marlboros. A few minutes later, back he came again, saying she needed a lighter. Alligood left once again and returned with the lighter. That was the last thing Terry Bell knew, until the following morning when he was awakened up from a deep sleep by Deputy Peachey. Peachey told him what had happened, and Terry Bell went into the classic case of shock, speechless, numb, staring, starting crying. After a period of time Peachey got him calmed down, and Bell told his story of the night before. He also told Peachey that when Joan was making her phone call, it was the first time he had ever seen her fully clothed in the jail. He was full of stories like that. He told Peachey and SBI Agent Slaughter further that a white female inmate called Neva Tetterton had told him that Joan Little would get visits from a 'white man from Tarboro, North Carolina,' every night when Alligood worked.

"We had intended to use Bell to prove that Joan Little was in the jailer's office alone, with the icepick visible in the drawer. That made him a very important witness in a circumstantial case, when the only living witness to the crime itself is the defendant herself. But Terry Bell ruined himself as a witness the following June, and was never called to the stand.

"Two other witnesses who were never called were Mr. and Mrs. Raymond Cobb. It was to their house that Joan came after the incident, and they turned her away, saying that they did not want any trouble with the law. At that time Joan told them she thought she had killed the jailer, that he had tried to make her have sex with him, had forced her to take her clothes off, and that when he, Alligood, *had started* to take his clothes off, she stabbed him.

"And finally, had the trial been in November instead of the following July, we could have called Anna Eubanks and her son Ervin, and I'm sure they would have told the truth. Anna Eubanks was a friend of Joan's from Chapel Hill, and it was she to whom Joan was talking on the phone at ten-thirty that night. In that conversation Joan told Anna Eubanks that she would see her on Friday, four days later, and that she was getting very tired of jail. Eubanks cautioned her not to do anything foolish.

"Then Anna Eubanks's son Bobby got on the phone, and he later told the SBI that Little had said.

" 'Do you know how I'm going to get out of jail?'

"Bobby Eubanks said no, and then said in his interrogation that he did not hear Little's response. Five hours later, at three-thirty A.M., the phone rang again at the Eubanks residence, and, once again, it was Joan Little. She talked this time to Ervin Eubanks, another son. This was the key phone call, because it was either immediately after or immediately before the killing. In that conversation Ervin Eubanks asked Little what she was doing, and she replied,

" '*Watching TV and having a good time.*'

"There is no commercial TV in that jail, nor is there any television programming that late at night in this state. The only TV that she could have been watching at that hour were the TV monitors in the jailer's office. If that call was made after the incident from the jailer's office, it meant that she was not in too big of a hurry to get out of there. Joan also asked Ervin Eubanks for the address of his sister in Durham.

"It was hard enough in September to get any of the Eubanks family to talk about those calls. In the case of Ervin Eubanks, the SBI and an Orange County deputy had to bring him into the sheriff's office and really put the screws to him. That deputy sheriff said to him,

" 'Looka here, boy, I'm gonna load your basket full of bricks, if you don't tell about that call.'

"He really threatened him. But with all the pressure and publicity after November, all the Eubankses turned extremely hostile. I had an inkling later that Anna Eubanks would testify that she was about to have a bond signed, that would release Joan from jail and that would have damaged the hell out of us. I tried to force the defense to call her, so that I could elicit information on cross examination, but you can't do that if she's your own witness. You can't impeach your own witness, barring a ruling by the court that she was a hostile witness, and to get that ruling is a very difficult, complicated procedure.

"None of the Eubanks family was ever called when the case finally came to trial, and we had to be content with the testimony of a phone operator who placed the three-thirty call from the Beaufort County jail to the Eubanks home. They managed to confuse this testimony by calling the operator a liar, and by trying to cast doubt on the symbols on the telephone records. But there's no doubt in the world that she made the call, and that she perjured herself about it on the stand.

"The law of self-defense was also entirely different in November 1974 and July 1975. Until June 9, 1975, the law in North Carolina and a number of other states was that the burden was on the defendant to show that she or he acted in self-defense. That gave the state a real card in this type of case. If the prosecutor can say to the jury,

" 'Look, the state presented evidence that this person was present at the scene, that the defendant killed the deceased, and it's up to the defendant to show that it was done in self-defense.'

"But on June 9, 1975, the U.S. Supreme Court in the *Mullaney* case reversed that concept: shifting the burden to the state to prove that the defendant *did not* act in self-defense in killing the victim. That was a profound change in the law; it's the most far-reaching decision of the Supreme Court in a long time, and few people realized it. You've got the only living witness standing there and claiming that she acted in self-defense, and the prosecution, under the *Mullaney* case, *has to prove that she didn't!* It's impossible! When I saw the *Mullaney* decision, I knew we were in an entirely different ball game."

[Jerry Paul had made a point of this in his summation: "Now, to tell you that you have to believe what Joan Little says is wrong. You don't have to believe what she says. You can disbelieve everything Joan Little says and still find her not guilty, and that is the law. Because the state must prove it was *not* self-defense beyond a reasonable doubt."]

"Also, Judge Hamilton Hobgood made a concession to publicity in his charge to the jury on August fifteenth, that another judge in a less publicized case in November would not have. He told them that the killing was excusable if the jury believed the defendant felt herself to be in danger of death *or of sexual assault*. That's not the law in this state, and it won't be the law in the next case. The law reads that killing is excusable only if the defendant believes herself to be in jeopardy of her life or of great bodily injury, period.

"Mind you, even though there were these differences, I still think a Beaufort County jury would have turned her loose in November under the old law and with all the material witnesses. As soon as it became known that the jailer's pants were off, the attitude in Beaufort County was that Alligood got what he deserved. People were saying, To hell with it. Neither race cared. I believe that Leroy Scott, the old pro who represented her in the breaking and entering case, could have disposed of the case without a tenth of this brouhaha. I've seen him do it too many times."

(But Leroy Scott had represented Joan Little in the original breaking and entering case, and the old pro did not even know the facts of the case on the morning he went to trial. In fact, he thought the charge against her was something entirely different and had not bothered to check. The basis of her appeal of the original charge, therefore, was on inadequate counsel.)

"In early November I got a call from Jerry Paul, asking if I would agree to a continuance of the case rather than go to trial as scheduled on November eighteenth. I told him no, that I was going to try the case and be done with it. He insisted that we talk about it, and on November seventh we had lunch at the Poet's Corner in Chapel Hill for two or three hours. Paul explained at that lunch that the reason he wanted a continuance was that they wanted time to take Joan Little's conviction in the breaking-and-entering charge up on appeal, that they felt sure that the verdict would be upheld, because the case was a clean, clean conviction. They would then, in all probability, plead her guilty to a lesser charge in the Alligood killing. He did not promise me that they would plead, I'm not saying that, but the implication was clear. I told Paul then that I would take a plea on a lesser charge, and I further offered to dismiss all the charges against Joan Little if she took a polygraph exam—and passed. But Jerry Paul would not agree to this offer, and when I renewed it in April 1975, he did not respond, so he must have been convinced of his client's inability to pass the test. She had ten years on the breaking-and-entering conviction, and second-degree murder carries thirty years. So if the two sentences ran concurrently, it didn't make a great deal of difference, when you figure in the parole time.

"But Paul insisted that he needed time to convince the Little family that a plea of guilty was in Joan's interest, and they needed time to deal with Golden Frinks, who was fomenting a lot of trouble at this time.

"That week of November seventh to fourteenth, Judge Joshua James was holding court in Martin County, adjoining Beaufort, and Jerry Paul had told him essentially the same thing as me about their intention to plead her guilty. He had also been to the Chief Justice of the North Carolina Supreme Court, then Justice Bobbitt, trying to get him to intervene and delay the case. Judge Henry McKinnon, who was assigned the Joan Little case at first, was also brought in on the discussions. There were phone calls backwards and forwards—James to McKinnon, McKinnon to Bobbitt, back to James, around and around, and, finally, Judge James said to me,

" 'If they're going to plead her guilty, hell, what's the use of bringing this special jury down here to Washington? If you're willing to take a plea of a lesser offense, let's give 'em the time they want, set it up and do it later.'

"Finally, I said, 'Well if that's what the judges want . . .' and I acquiesced in it. Shortly thereafter, this promotional sequence took place with the Julian Bond letter.

"If there is any truth anywhere in the entire Joan Little affair, I know one thing for certain: they wanted that continuance to promote the case nationwide. In December, it finally dawned on me why they were buying time, and I knew I'd been *had*."

It is well known among fund-raising experts that a direct-mail campaign soliciting contributions works best when a highly emotional issue, like Vietnam or rape, is involved. People simply give more to such efforts than to bland, do-good appeals. A solicitation must not be too abstract or philosophical; it should be narrow and about people rather than ideas. General mailings about the good works of an organization generally fail. It is in many ways a cynical process.

For the direct-mail solicitation in the Joan Little case, which is the most successful cause-mailing in history, the defense had the best in the business. Thirty-eight-year-old, beautifully tailored, multimillionaire Morris Dees was thought by a young female juror in the Little case to be "the next thing to Robert Redford." He had seen the possibilities of direct mail as a college student at the University of Alabama, when he made a deal with a local baker and mailed letters to the parents suggesting they send a birthday cake to their child on the happy day. Later in 1960, he used the mails to sell tractor cushions through the Future Farmers of America groups, and finally made his fortune selling cookbooks of all kinds. He lives on an expansive estate outside Montgomery, Alabama, where he runs the Southern Poverty Law Center. With his fortune secured, he has turned to the less fortunate. He sought damages for welfare mothers in a South Carolina sterilization case; handled the appeal of three blacks in Tarboro, North Carolina, convicted of raping a white woman; won a suit requiring the Alabama State Police to reach a quota of twenty-five percent black.

But also he became Mr. Direct Mail. He designed the five-page, single-spaced letter of George McGovern to John Q. Citizen, in which the candidate spoke seriously but simply to the voter, primarily the liberal voter, about the issues the liberal would care about. It was a departure from the vacuous, short political fund-raising letters of the past, and the Dees effort raised $26 million for the McGovern campaign. Fought for by the platoon of candidates in the 1976 presidential primaries, Dees ended up with Jimmy Carter, another millionaire Southern liberal, who was equally handsome, and after Carter's election, would turn down the offer of a high post in the new administration.

The Joan Little solicitation, which seemed to reach every liberal in America and some four times over, had four noteworthy qualities: (1) It was signed by Julian Bond, who had a high "recognition factor"; (2) it was a clever presentation of the facts, offering a quiet, shy defender of her black womanhood being rushed to the gas chamber; (3) the importance of the case was legitimized by the inclusion of a December 1 piece in the *New York Times,* and without this "objective" certification, as most fund-raisers know, people might not believe the facts as described in the letter—"the credibility factor"; and (4) a contribution was tax-deductible.

Dees had no time for a test mailing, for the Joan Little case was expected to go to trial soon. So using the 1972 McGovern list and the lists of organizations like the ACLU and publications like *Ms.* magazine, two million letters were mailed, costing the Southern Poverty Law Center a quarter of a million dollars. By March 1975, $150,000 poured in, and by the end of the trial the figure would be $350,000. It was this phenomenon more than any other that so amazed the townspeople of Washington, North Carolina.

"The case just doesn't seem that big," said one bewildered local.

An architect in Landenberg, Pennsylvania, offered his $20,000 life's savings for Joan Little's bond. Professors in Chapel Hill put their houses up as collateral to get the prisoner released from prison on $115,000 bond. A stirring appeal appeared in the *London Observer,* and money flew in from Britain.

The Reverend R. J. H. de Brett, a contributor from Somerset, England, wrote the author from his vicarage:

"It seemed to me, on the available evidence, that here was a clear case of prejudice versus justice. On the face of it, this poor girl was bound to go down simply because of the colour of her skin unless she were well-defended."

And another contributor, from San Jose, California, Christine Harris, wrote:

"I realize I can never understand what it is to be a black woman. I admire the black men and women for their strength, self-confidence, and the way they deal with reality. . . . The publicity aroused my emotions, and I saw great hope in this case where a black woman could come out on top for once."

A woman from Seattle, Washington, Ms. Marge Casey, wrote:

"God made all people!!! The color of the skin is only on the outside; it's whether or not a person is good *inward*: Joan is good! (Whitewashed not on the outside, but whitewashed on the inside too.)"

CHAPTER 8

JOHN A. WILKINSON

FIFTEEN miles east of Washington, in Beaufort County, is the tiny village of Bath, the oldest incorporated town in North Carolina and a state historical site. It is disappointing, as historic sites go—a few well-kept eighteenth-century houses, including one that "Blackbeard" lived in before he was killed on the Outer Banks, mixed in with the normal clapboard houses common to the area, and the oldest church in the state, St. Thomas Parish. But the mystery of Bath is that it never grew beyond its small cluster of houses.

For several centuries one explanation for Bath's stagnation has been the Whitefield legend, or the Whitefield curse, as it is known to a few local historians. The Reverend John Whitefield, a great Methodist pulpit orator and evangelist, is said to have come to the North Carolina wilds in search of sinners in 1738 and to have preached in the St. Thomas Parish. But when he railed against the misbehavior of the local citizens, he was unceremoniously escorted out of town—whether on a rail or not is unknown. In retaliation, so the story goes, the Reverend "shook the dust of Bath off his feet as a witness against this place" and prophesied that Bath would never prosper.

The Whitefield curse is not documented, and some feel that the real reason why Bath never grew was that in 1788 the sessions of the courts were moved away to Washington, where a new courthouse was built. This is lore John Wilkinson loves, and in years past, whenever the Bath Pageant took place, Wilkinson would act the part of Whitefield in the play and could put more than requisite emotion into the line about "shaking the dust," especially when a Democrat would play the part of the English Governor.

But the legend also gives Wilkinson a chance to speak of his family's roots in Beaufort County, going back two hundred years, and his pride in those roots made him the most contentious and effective respondent to those who would put a modern curse on Beaufort County, making it, too, stagnate at its present size: the curse of Joan Little.

At sixty-two, with a grainy voice and archaic turn of phrase, round, ruddy face and bulbous nose reminiscent of Burgess Meredith, a limp that one imagines came from action at El Alamein alongside Field Marshal Montgomery or from sailing the high seas shouting "Shiver me timbers," Wilkinson revels in the interest paid to his crusty attributes. Many think of him as the last of a dying breed, but Wilkinson waves aside such foolishness. To a reporter from the *Washington Star*, he said he often traveled to the Capital to buy fine, $40 brandies.

"Don't drink anything but fruit liquor," he confided. "The grain stuff can give you boils. Learned that years ago."

That quotation made everyone happy. The reporter got his lead, and Wilkinson got a profile of himself in the big-city newspapers, touting him as the prosecution's comic relief for the trial.

The author had gone to see Wilkinson on a stormy afternoon in October 1975, and instead of talking in his law office on Market Street, in Washington, they had piled into Wilkinson's Chrysler, baby blue and white, the colors of UNC, of which he is a trustee and active alumnus, and headed back to Raleigh. North Carolina would play North Carolina State in football the following day and lose by one point, when the official failed to penalize State for tackling a right end at the line of scrimmage on a two-point conversion play. Wilkinson always had a seat in the President's box, and the poor officiating for the State game would outrage his sense of fair play.

They took the back roads—switching back and forth until the author thought they had made a full circle, through Crisp and Conetoe, (the route Jerry Paul took on the night of the escape from Beaufort County,) and once they passed a vineyard where Wilkinson usually stopped to buy homemade wine, made on the QT, but it was too late in the season then, and the grapes were all gone.

"The breed of 'country lawyer' is an arbitrary and irrational classification, and I don't know exactly what's meant by it, but I do practice in a relatively small town, and, like most lawyers in a town like Washington, I'm a general practitioner. And, as with most general practitioners in small Southern towns, more than half my clients are black. I enjoy trial work. I'm naturally contentious. I've always liked public speaking, and I'm credited with a certain facility for words. In my forty years of practice I've been reasonably successful, but the success of a lawyer often depends on the nature of his competition. A person of mediocre talents may look good if everyone else around him is similarly limited, or even more so. It's an adaptation of the old saw, 'In the land of the blind, the one-eyed man is king.'

"I've won some cases, and I've lost some, and that reminds me of what my old friend Buss Hearn used to say. He was a great baseball pitcher for the New York Giants back in the twenties, and he was a better pitcher than conversationalist. When he went to coach

the baseball team at Carolina in 1931, somebody
asked him,

" 'Mr. Hearn, how's your ball club goin' to do?'

" 'We're going to win some, and we're going to lose
some,' Buss replied, 'and some of them're going to get
rained out.' Well, I'm glad the Joan Little case didn't
get rained out, because I couldn't stand a rematch.

"All my ancestors since 1708 have been born and
raised in Beaufort County. My father's side were
Republicans, before that, Whigs, and before that,
Federalists, but my mother's family were fanatical
Democrats, old Jefferson Davis types. So I had a choice
of political persuasion, and since 1936 I've operated in
an overwhelmingly Democratic area, as an active,
vigorous, and outspoken Republican at a time when
the party's strength was at its lowest ebb, here and in
the nation. I like to think of myself as a nineteenth-
century liberal and a Henry Clay Whig, meaning I
believe in a strong federal government with very strict
limitations, and I'm in very good company. When
Abraham Lincoln was asked once about his true political feelings, he replied,

" 'Scratch me, and you'll find an old Henry Clay
Whig.'

"Still, a Henry Clay Whig in today's parlance may
be an arch-conservative, and I do take a position directly opposed to the collectivist. But if I'm an arch-
conservative, Jerry Paul is a disciple of the Far Left.
He made a dramatic turn to the left in college, and I
heard his mother say that Jerry and his father had
such terrible arguments that they couldn't speak to
one another. Still I like Jerry, always have, and he
said at the Joan Little trial that I had been his inspiration for going into the law.

"People think he's just playing a good thing with
the Little case, but I don't think that does him justice.
He conceives of the case as fundamentally worthwhile,

one in which the good of mankind can be advanced. He would like to see the overthrow of the present system—I won't say by force, because that would make him guilty of treason. He's sharp as a butcher's cleaver. He knows exactly what he's doing, and if he chose at the trial to spend his full time plus fifteen minutes trying to throw racial prejudice in the minds of the blacks who sat on that jury, he did it because he thought it would work. But cases are supposed to be decided on facts. If in a jury box any other criterion can be inserted, then may God Almighty help us all, because if one time an appeal to black prejudice against white is introduced, the next time it will be white prejudice against black, or getting away from race, one time female prejudice against male, the next time the reverse, and there is no end. Like the horrid insects that flew out of Pandora's box in the ancient legend, the pestilence will swamp us all.

"But if Jerry thought the proper way to argue to that jury was to inflame race against race, then it was because he did not dare argue the evidence. Beyond that he argued divine inspiration, that God Almighty or some holy spirit guided him through this case and planned it all the way. I can't say that ain't so. As a poor, unworthy vessel, I'm frank to say I don't know. I've heard it said the Lord works in mysterious ways his wonders to perform, but I do recall that the last person of prominence who claimed to have personal contact with Almighty God, who had voices guiding him, was Adolf Hitler.

"Jerry is no Adolf; he's at the other end of the spectrum. But Jerry, old friend, whenever the Lord starts whispering to you, you'd better be certain it's not coming from the other end of the supernatural spectrum.

"If Jerry was right about divine inspiration, it would be a terrible indictment of Almighty God that in order to bring about social advance, He would cause a man to be killed—a gory, nasty killing—and so much money to be diverted into a trial, and so much hatred and passion and misunderstanding to be aroused. I said to him at the trial,

" 'Of course, you realize, Jerry, that your damn client is guilty, and a psychopath on top.' He just laughed.

"Even though I'm a rebel like him, my rebellion has been within the system. In 1936, right out of college, I ran for Congress on the Republican ticket. Of course, I was a sacrificial lamb; it was a bad Republican year. I got about the Republican average for the time, ten to sixteen percent of the vote. Again in 1940 I ran, unsuccessfully, for Congress, and in 1948 I was the Republican nominee for the U.S. Senate and led the Republican ticket in the state. I'm proud to say that I ran 25,000 votes ahead of the rest of the ticket, and it was due to tireless campaigning, because nobody knew anything about me. I ran no more until 1966, when I sought a seat in the Legislature, running against the strongest Democratic candidate available to the party in this area—the owner of the local television station —and I'm proud to say that I did carry Beaufort County.

"Of course, George Washington is the authority on the evil of unbalanced political parties, and Jefferson said he embraced the anti-Federalist position just to keep the Federalists from establishing a kingdom. For a hundred years in Beaufort County, the slogan of the hard-nosed Democrats has been,

" 'I'd vote for a yallar dog if he was a-runnin' on the Democrat ticket.'

"To which I'd always reply, 'Those who're willin' to vote for a yallar dog, if he's a-runnin' on the Democrat ticket, often get the opportunity.'

"There is an aristocracy of sorts in Beaufort County. At least, some folks like to think there is. But this county was never plantation Southern. There were some medium-sized plantations, and perhaps before the War ten or fifteen families owned as many as fifty slaves. One family, the Grists, were the only real plantation owners, and they probably had over a hundred slaves. The Grists are nearly all gone now, but their blood is around about. No, the prominent families owe their fortunes more to the shipping trade, sending pine-tar products to the West Indies as well as salt meat and salt fish, in return for rum and molasses. Before the war, 1830 to 1860, the county was Federalist and later Whig, and had it not been for Reconstruction, Beaufort County would be Republican today.

"Other than pine products, ours is a corn-and-hog county, rather than cotton, with the Grists as the reigning family. An old colored barber friend of mine has the best story on the point. He broke into his trade around the turn of the century, and one of his favorite customers years ago was old Judge Peoples from Northampton County up on the Virginia border, which is one of the few genuine plantation areas of North Carolina. Judge Peoples came down often to hold court in Beaufort County, and he usually employed young Price, as he was then, to rub him on the head for an hour after court. Late one afternoon, he slouched into Price's chair, said,

" 'Price, you can't rub me much today, damn it all. I've got to go to a damn soiree.'

" 'Soiree. Soiree. Soiree, hell,' Price replied. 'There ain't nothin' in Beaufort County but piney-woods folks and a few Grists.' I have a lot of fun telling that story to my friends who are proud of their family lineage.

"They could not pick a more unlikely character for sainthood than her. I should know. I represented her twice in shoplifting charges—both of which I won, by the way. I had represented her boy friend, Julius Rogers, about whom she was absolutely wild. She was crazy about Rogers. I've never seen a black woman so crazy about a man. Whenever she was in his presence, she gave him absolute rapt attention, and, in my opinion, her love for him was the motivation for this whole case.

"The seeds of the crime are in the crossword-puzzle books which she abandoned in her flight, in the notes in their margins:

"On page three, *Bell Crossword Puzzles*: 'This book belongs to Tarus [*sic*], a symbol, Miss Joan Little, age twenty, fifth month, Chocowinity, North Carolina. Today is August 22, 1974; time, ten-twenty-five P.M. Alligood just came on duty. I pray to God I be out very soon. To whom it may concern. She loves, she loves Mr. Julius Rogers. Cancer, June 4, 1935, Portsmouth, Virginia.'

"On page fifty-three: 'Roger, I love you honey, God bless you, our love.'

"On page thirty-seven, *Seek and Circle Word Game*: 'Friday, June 28, 1974. Just finished crying. I miss you so bad. If I don't see you soon, I think I will crack up.'

"On page thirteen, *Seek and Circle Word Game*: 'June, started twenty-ninth, finished, the thirtieth. Still got Roger on my mind, I really love you, the star in my heart. I love you no matter what you do, hope to see you real soon.'

"On page thirteen of *First Rate Crosswords*: 'Everyone is trying to reach Roger. I wonder myself what's happened. He must have found him somebody else.' That entry is undated, but the one on the following page is dated July 22, 1974.

"Now Rogers has more intelligence than the average of his race, with his education and his position. He's considerably sharper, has an IQ substantially above one hundred. He has skills as well—it was he for whom she worked in Chapel Hill as a sheetrock finisher and paper hanger. He had poise and know-how, was older, and had contacts outside of Beaufort County.

"In the winter of 1974, Rogers ran, for lack of a better word, a 'bistro' in Washington at Fourth and Gladden streets, which is, you might say, the Forty-second and Broadway of the black section of town. It was a little club, supposedly for membership, where the boys brought in their own bottles and put tags on them, drank while they shot pool. It was a colored version of our Brentwood Country Club, and I saw no reason why the blacks ought not to have 'em a little club if they wanted it. Didn't bother anybody. But he had some routine charges against him—selling liquor without a license, that sort of thing (for which I got him acquitted)—and he always came to me for help. The only thing he was really guilty of with his club was not paying his proper taxes, but it was *de minimus*.

"On March 18, 1974, his girl friend, Joan Little, was indicted along with her brother, Jerome Little, on three counts of breaking and entering, and larceny. Rogers came to me and asked me to represent her, and offered me a fee. But I had already been appointed by the court to represent her brother Jerome, and I told Rogers that I could not represent both brother and sister, especially because there was a conflict in their testimonies. So she retained Leroy Scott, who is considered, if not the best, at least as good as any criminal lawyer in the area.

"The situation was this: on January 14, 1974, three mobile homes belonging to black people were broken into, and goods including two TVs, a stereo component, a thirty-thirty Winchester rifle, clothes, vacuum cleaner, kitchenware, and a piggy bank with fifty dollars in it were taken. The combined value of the stolen goods was put at one thousand, three hundred and seventy-five dollars. One of the victims, Roland Rhodes, came home to find his trailer a shambles, and a pork chop that he had left on the table that morning half eaten. He went next door and talked with his neighbor, who said she'd seen three young people at his trailer about noon: two women and a man. The neighbor could not identify the people by face, but she did say one of the women was wearing a short fur coat. Rhodes knew Joan Little well, but not her brother Jerome, and he knew that coat. So he went down to Fourth Street to find her. When he found her, she was with her brother and his girl friend, Melinda Moore, aged fourteen, for whom the current rumor had it at the time, that she was a madam. Rhodes testified at the trial that when he found Joan Little,

" 'She was in a place that was kind of warm, so all she had on was a blouse.'

"After the conversation, Rhodes went to the sheriff's office, and with a deputy sheriff returned to the trailer court, where, God help him, young Jerome Little, my client, was just leaving. The deputy stopped Little, and there in the back seat was Rhodes's vacuum cleaner and shoes, along with the other loot. So they had Jerome cold turkey, and other stuff was later found in his trailer; his later statements indicated a degree of knowledge that implicated him of necessity as a principal, or at least an accessory before and after the fact. The question was: was he in on the break-in—a felony—or was he guilty only of receiving stolen goods—a misdemeanor? Jerome Little admitted to me that he knew the goods were stolen; he testified at the trial that he had told Rhodes how Joan and Julius Rogers had planned it out. But how exactly Joan got the goods, he did not know, did not want to know, and only wanted out of the whole mess.

"So I went to Billy Griffin before the trial, and said,

" 'This fellow is not guilty of breaking and entering, only receiving, and I'll plead him guilty to that, in return for a *nol pros* in the breaking-and-entering charge.'

"Griffin laughed at me. 'You must be out of your cotton-pickin' mind,' he said. 'I'm not going to do any such thing. No deal.'

" 'All right,' I replied. 'If you want war, war it is.'

"Griffin thought Jerome was a principal, but several days later he came back to me.

" 'I'm not going to let you plead him guilty to only the receiving charge, and you'll not get any cooperation from me. But plead him not guilty on both counts and let the chips fall where they may. If the jury finds him not guilty on the felony charge and guilty of the misdemeanor, I'll tell you what I'll do. I'll let you amend your plea after the verdict, and if he doesn't appeal, I'll recommend a suspended sentence to the judge. That will ensure that he'll serve some time, since he's already under a suspended sentence.' He had been convicted of a similar stealing deal before, and that's what he's now serving time for.

"So I fought it out on an adversary position, and midway in the trial Jerome Little did change his plea to guilty to receiving, but the jury was out of the room when he did so, and he was made no promises for doing so, other than the pretrial assurances. He then went on to testify about seeing the stolen goods in the possession of his sister and Julius Rogers, asking his sister whether the goods were stolen, to which she replied in the affirmative, and finding more goods in his trailer.

"So it is simply not true that Jerome Little changed

his plea midway in the trial at his sister's expense, that he sold his sister down the river. The basis of the state's case against Joan Little was her being identified at the scene of the crime by the fur coat she was wearing. The arrangements about the plea had been made beforehand, and I even argued to the jury that I would not quarrel with a verdict of guilty in the receiving charge against my client, but insisted that he was not guilty of the felony. Anyway, that's all water over the dam, because after the jury found her guilty of all the charges against her, and found her brother guilty only of receiving, she admitted it all."

It's doubtful that Wilkinson really expected to persuade his listener that Jerome Little had not sold his sister down the river. Without Jerome's testimony, the only evidence that connected Joan at the scene of the larceny was the identification of the fur coat. The neighbor of the victim Rhodes testified that the woman at Rhodes's trailer wore a "short black-and-white furry coat."

Prosecutor Sam Grimes asked Rhodes on the stand,

"Does Joan Little have any particular coat she customarily wears when you have seen her?"

Leroy Scott's object was overruled.

"Yes, it's a little white fur coat," Rhodes replied.

Scott's motion to strike was denied.

This interchange formed part of the defense appeal to the higher court, in which it was argued that the judge erred in allowing Rhodes to respond to the general question and that the jury may have been confused by the pattern of objections, thereby attaching more significance to the answer than it deserved. The defense brief to the appeals court read:

"The fact [that one of the girls outside the trailer] wore a fur coat . . . would not be substantial evidence of Joan's identity as one of the participants. The coat could easily have been borrowed by someone else, or the girl at the break-in could have worn a coat resembling Joan's."

Nor was Wilkinson's protestation that the jury had been out when Jerome Little changed his plea persuasive, for the U.S. Supreme Court requires that the jury be out during a change of plea.

Regardless of Joan Little's guilt in the stealing, which seemed undeniable, the author did not approve of trying a brother and sister jointly, particularly when their interests were contradictory, and saw no real difference between a brother testifying against a sister and a husband testifying against his wife—the latter being prohibited by law.

A later conversation with Prosecutor Sam Grimes bolstered his opinion. Grimes admitted that going into trial, the state had a strong case against the brother on the lesser charge, and a weak case against the sister on all charges, but,

"Joan was the one we were really after, and we would never have convicted her without him. . . . In fact, by the end of the trial, it was two prosecutors versus one defense lawyer—John Wilkinson and I against Leroy Scott."

The prosecution's hunch was that Julius Rogers was probably the man behind the stealing, but Grimes said,

"I never believed that he was completely the dominant force, because she was too alert, not dull-witted by any means."

Grimes had found Joan Little one of the most intractable witnesses he had ever examined, and so he was not surprised with her cool performance on the stand later in the murder trial. She had a native ability as a witness, he thought, even before Jerry Paul started coaching her.

"When I examined her, even after her brother testified against her, she had an answer for all the significant points. When I deliberately would ask her about points of lesser importance or even questionable relevance, just to see how she would respond, she either refused to answer or she would reply with her rehearsed answer on a significant point again. She is cunning, strong-willed, and reasonably intelligent."

Wilkinson pressed on with his narrative.

"After the verdict was brought in—*and sentence imposed*—I got up and said something for my client. I was anxious to keep his time in jail to a minimum. Then Leroy Scott said something. I don't remember what it was, some sort of routine jabber as mine had been—and suddenly Joan Little hopped up, said,

" 'I want to say something.'

"Scott conferred with her, and I could see him shaking his head, but she kept insisting, so he said, go ahead. And she said clearly to the open court,

" 'I committed perjury on the stand. I went in there.'

"That electrified everybody, and she turned to her brother and pointed at him.

" 'But he committed perjury too,' she exclaimed, 'he was right there with me. We went in there together.'

"The judge was astounded. 'Get the court reporter back in here,' he said.

"With the reporter back in, Joan Little admitted everything about the break-in, but implicated Jerome at the scene of the crime and said the stolen goods were taken directly to his trailer. But she also was very careful to say that Julius Rogers knew nothing about it. She even went on to say that *she* had a job in Chapel Hill where she could make a hundred and fifty dollars a week, and her brother could do nothing, so they ought to send him to jail instead of her.

"I turned to her brother, 'You see what this bitch is

doing, don't you? She's trying to put you behind bars for a very long time.'

" 'I see,' he replied, 'but I can't do anything about it.'

" 'Call your mama up here,' I told him.

"When their mother, Jessie Williams, got to the table she said to me, 'Rogers is your client. He's the one that got her in all this mess; she ain't had no sense ever since she's been going with him,' and that infuriated Joan Little at her mother. An argument ensued right there in the court, and I broke it up.

"I'm not interested in all this jazz. You can't do anything for yourself by jumping on your brother, but you can hurt him. The judge right now is considering issuing a bench warrant for perjury.'

"And he was, but I talked him out of it, said to him,

" 'What're ya going to do: issue a warrant for a man who the jury has just said they believed on the word of a woman the jury has said they didn't believe? She's saying, "He's the liar, and I'm not." '

" 'No,' the judge replied, 'I don't reckon I'll do that.'

"Anyway, Jessie Williams did take the stand.

" 'Julius Rogers is influencing my daughter,' she testified. 'He's the whole problem in all of this.'

" 'You think he's the one behind all of this?' the judge asked.

" 'Yes, sir.'

" 'These mothers know a lot about what's going on,' the judge said. 'Mr. Solicitor, do you want to ask her anything?'

"Under examination by the solicitor, Mrs. Williams told a story of how one night Joan had come to her house, driven by 'a man from New York,' and that while Joan changed clothes Mrs. Williams had tried to get a look at him.

" 'This man was from New York, and he was going

to pick up [stolen goods] from here and take them off—I think my daughter is trying to take all the blame and trying to take it off Julius.'

"After Mrs. Williams got down, Deputy Sheriff Sherwood Sawyer, the investigating officer, took the stand again. Under questioning by the judge, he testified:

" 'I know even the people on Fourth Street have come to me and said, "Why can't y'all put a stop to this Joan Little and Julius Rogers?" And, I asked them why and they said, "Well, man, I ain't telling you nothing," because they get scared then. She is believed to be combined in a ring where her and Julius Rogers are both the heads of it. She sends people out stealing for her, shoplifting, and then they bring it back and they get rid of it. And, she was back in, I can't remember exactly what date or month it was, but the little girl Melinda Moore took a rap for shoplifting here in Washington. She took the rap for Joan so that Joan wouldn't get in trouble. That's just about the reputation that she has.'

"Still Joan felt that the anger of the court was misdirected. She resented the brother being whitewashed, and her being made to appear the only villain. And she wagged her finger in my face, said,

" 'I'm pregnant by your client, Julius Rogers. And I don't intend to have my child in prison. I'm going to get out of here, one way or another.'

"That's the first thing that popped into my mind when I heard that Alligood had been killed. Only her mother, her brother, and I heard it. It was a lie—she wasn't pregnant at all—it was an invention to justify to her brother and her mama the necessity of getting out.

"So that is why I argued at the murder trial that her love for Rogers was the motivation for the Alligood killing. When she went to jail in June, he went back to Chapel Hill and forgot her. Oh, Rogers made a lame gesture to help Joan. He hired a young lawyer in Chapel Hill to represent her on her appeal of the breaking and entering, and this poor young lawyer, bless his heart, had spent his own money on the telephone calls, worked hard and faithfully in this case, and got not one cent from Rogers, not penny one. It reminds me of a joke about lawyers: it's said that lawyers start off in practice by doing five hundred dollars' worth of work and get five dollars, and after they become old and affluent, they do five dollars' worth of work and get five hundred.

"That's how much Julius loved her. He didn't spend a cotton-pickin' cent and left his attorney holding the bag. And there's poor Joan, eating her heart out in jail because that no-good Julius had taken up with somebody else.

"On page thirty-four of the novel *Ben Hur*, also found in her cell, dated August 1, 1974:

This is dedicated to the man I love, Mr. Julius Rogers. I don't know where you are since the last I heard from you, July 5. But I still love you and I am hoping and also praying that I will be able to see you soon if only to say goodbye forever. The love we shared was something beautiful, and I shall cherish it until the day I die, for it is something not to be easily forgotten. I wish things didn't have to turn out this way, but maybe it is for the best. Just writing these few lines to help express my inner thoughts and though it hurts all the time to say goodbye; long goodbye's hurt the most, so in this time if you have found someone to take my place, I wish you both the best of luck. God bless you both. But if you have not it would be the best that's ever happened to me at this point. I feel so alone. The thoughts of today,

Baby, if you aren't going away forever, hurry back and make it very soon.

Jo.

"So she knew Julius had him another baby doll, and she knew she had to get out of there. She knew only one way to get out, and she did it with her left hand. I don't know if she wanted out to get Julius back—or to do him in. But there's something to that saying,

" 'Hell hath no fury greater than the wrath of a woman scorned.' "

From the first suggestion in March 1975 that John A. Wilkinson would be hired by the Alligood family as a private prosecutor in the Joan Little murder trial, his participation in the case was challenged as unethical. The defense argued first at the preliminary hearing in April, later in the first days of the trial before jury selection, that Wilkinson's representation of Joan Little in two shoplifting cases had made him privy to confidences and secrets of his client, obtained in the privileged lawyer-client relationship. This seemed particularly apt in a circumstantial case, where, as it developed, the state's best hope for conviction seemed to be an assault on Joan Little's character, making her out to be an "evil woman," capable of the most ghastly crimes.

At the murder trial, Judge Hamilton Hobgood had solicited the advice of the North Carolina State Bar Association on the propriety of Wilkinson's involvement in the case, and the association, its concern for the rights of clients not noted, especially when they come into conflict with a lawyer's opportunity to make an even better living, responded:

"The two shoplifting cases in which Mr. Wilkinson

successfully defended Miss Little are totally unrelated
to the homicide case. They are completely ended . . .
and once a case, civil or criminal, is ended, a lawyer is
not prevented by the Code of Professional Responsibility from thereafter appearing against his former
client in an unrelated matter."

On the basis of this advice, Hobgood allowed John
Wilkinson to participate, even though the real secrets
that Wilkinson had learned about the Little family
came not from the routine shoplifting cases at all, but
from his informal prosecution of Joan Little in the
breaking-and-entering case. But Jerry Paul could not
let the issue drop. While he bluffed about how glad he
was that Wilkinson had been permitted to remain on
the case, because he was so much easier to paint as an
"ogre" than William Griffin, secretly he was much
concerned that this cagey old pro would discover the
evidence, there under the prosecution's nose, that
could convict her. So Paul kept the ethical issue alive,
and, in turn, kept Wilkinson mad even after Hobgood's ruling killed it. Midway in the trial, before
Wilkinson was about to cross-examine a key witness
and the jury was in the adjoining jury room, Jerry
Paul went near the door to the jury room and read in
a very loud voice from the North Carolina Code of
Professional Responsibility about a lawyer's duty to
protect a client's secrets and confidences unless the
client waives that right, which Joan Little had not.

"This duty outlasts the lawyer's employment," Paul
boomed through the wall. "A lawyer should not use
information acquired in the course of the representation of a client to the disadvantage of the client, and a
lawyer should not use, except with the consent of his
client after full disclosure, such information for his
own purposes."

But the Bar Association had said the other cases
were unrelated. Hobgood's ruling, coupled with the

fact that Griffin's other assistant prosecutor, Lester V. Chalmers, Jr., of the State Attorney General's office, had represented Grand Dragon Robert Shelton of the Ku Klux Klan before a 1965 hearing of the House Un-American Activities Committee, gave the prosecution a distinctly "bad image" before the trial began, and played nicely to the country's synthetic nostalgia for the old-style racist justice in the South. The case began to be called "the most important civil-rights case of the seventies."

"There are some seven hundred Alligoods in Beaufort County," Wilkinson picked up again. "They're all distantly related, having come from the stock of four Alligood brothers who came here in the 1850s, and they multiply like the green bay tree. But the Alligoods have quit claiming kin with one another for a long time, and most Alligoods hasten to say they are no kin to this particular Alligood family—although they are very respectable people. In the eastern part of Beaufort County, Clarence Alligood inherited a fifty-acre farm from his father. He added twenty acres to the property and cleared it with his own hands. For most of his life, he farmed, planted tobacco, corn, and soybeans, and sold his products on the local market. The farm was located out on Lizard Slip-It Road—a path of Carolina clay which, so the story goes, would get so slick when it rained that a lizard would slip off it.

"Don Alligood, one of Clarence Alligood's six children, became the spokesman for the immediate family through the entire ordeal, and he came to me around the first of the year [1975], saying that this case was getting out of control, that they were being pestered by news reporters and wondered if I would represent the family as a private prosecutor. Of course, I was interested. There was profound disgust in Beaufort

County for its portrayal in the national press as a bunch of intolerant, ignorant slobs like the characters of Caldwell's *Tobacco Road*. There was already a lot of pseudo-intellectual snobbery about this poor, benighted Southern town—with its racial overtones.

"I told Don that I worked for a living and named a figure that I would require. He did not think that the family could put that kind of money into it, and I heard no more from him until the spring. I would like to have been in on the case earlier, because I later discovered that the solicitor, Billy Griffin, to use his own words, had not been a 'free agent' in the matter since November. You see, it was desired by a segment of North Carolina government that this woman be acquitted, and there was continual interference in the case by people up the line. Billy Griffin allowed himself to be led and misdirected, for which, in view of his age, his situation, and the pressure he was under, he is at the very least excusable.

"Through February and March, some individuals in the county, highly connected, who wanted to see justice done, offered to pay me whatever I considered reasonable to join the case. I refused to do this, unless the Alligoods still wanted to employ me. So Don visited again, and we agreed on a fee approximately a fifth of the original figure, and Don said they could raise that. As a matter of fact, public subscriptions were taken up in Washington before the trial, and the Alligoods were recompensed for what they had paid me. The trial did not cost them a cent.

"As a private prosecutor, I am simply there as an assistant to the solicitor—it is false to imply that there is any 'revenge' motive in such a scheme—and I told the Alligoods that I would follow the trail wherever it led, regardless of what they thought of it, and they understood that. I wouldn't go into any private prosecution if I were representing anyone except the State of North Carolina. I was not there to try to retrieve Alligood's reputation. Naturally, I wanted to serve their interests as far as it was consistent with my dut- ies, and I did urge the family to attend the trial in Raleigh, to show the press that they weren't afraid to go up there.

"In my opinion, the Joan Little fiasco was a glaring miscarriage of justice, and it didn't happen by chance, but by design. How anyone could listen to her story on the stand of what went on in that cell and not conclude that it was a complete, but clumsy invention . . . Why, the whole damn thing is ridiculous on its face. It was a fairy tale. The proposition that a two-hundred-pound strong man would have gone in her cell with an icepick and threatened her—not even an imbecile would have done that! How in the world do you take off your pants, conceal an icepick, and put your hand on somebody else's breast all at the same time? You'd have to have more hands than the four-armed Greek god!

"Alligood was pictured as a monster, but it didn't make any more sense than the rest of the goulash that was thrown at the jury. If Alligood was a monster, why didn't she say so in her private notes? There was not a single bit of condemnation of Alligood, not a single word to show that Alligood was annoying her, not a single word to show that she did not enjoy those hamburgers and sandwiches that came in at two-thirty in the morning. Her only characterization of him in the notes was as a 'nice man.'

"What kind of a jerk was Alligood? Here's a white jailer, sixty-two years old, being paid a good salary [$6,000 a year], his only other income from a scratchy little farm, risking his job? How was he possibly going to stick her with the icepick? How would he explain that if she resisted? Oh, I can believe he found her attractive. Interracial sex is not a novelty, and it works both ways. But I can't believe that a sixty-two-year-old man would attempt to cross the racial barrier forcibly with someone in a position to cost him his job. Goddamn it, anyone who can swallow that story has parked his intelligence somewhere in left field.

"They operated by naked assertion, statements loosely made which, if they were made outside the shell of the lawsuit, would put a person in jeopardy of a civil suit for defamation of character. They accused the state of subverting the evidence, and Billy Griffin of framing the case. Why would anybody seek to subvert the evidence, to change it, when nobody could know exactly what happened—nobody that's alive, that is, nobody but her? How in the dickens would you know how to rig it till you knew what she was going to say happened?

"Yes, I argued against reducing the charge down from first- to second-degree murder, because I considered that if we didn't have a first-degree case, we didn't have any case. It was either first-degree or none. Our case was built on the proposition that she took the icepick in there. If *he* took it in, then she wasn't guilty of anything . . . oh, maybe manslaughter, but only on the theory that she used excessive force, that she didn't have to kill him to resist his attack. But if she carried it in there, it was for one purpose and one purpose only. The logic of that is clear and unmistakable.

"That logic was pitted against a clever, intensive, and even honest, well-intentioned defense, diverting the minds of the jury and the minds of the American people from the obvious facts. It would make them swallow the proposition that a hundred-pound wisp of a girl overcame a two-hundred-pound man, fled from one cell to another cell, dressed herself, walked by him, and he with a silly grin on his face, put her blood-stained fingers on the door of the cell and slammed it closed, made a telephone call, walked out to freedom, then to international notoriety. Her name will live forever in the annals of the criminal jurisprudence of this state and of the country.

"But the case should have been tried in November and tried on its merits. The national publicity introduced a whole lot of extraneous issues, all of which befogged the real issue: did she kill him? Why did she kill him? How did she kill him? But by June 1975 the state officials were refusing to cooperate. There was improper follow-up on leads by the State Bureau of Investigation, which, of course, is not an independent organization. It operates on orders. We had word, for example, from authentic sources in prison that she had boasted of killing Alligood with the help of a sixteen-year-old. There was only a half-handed effort to follow that up. It wasn't done properly or effectively, and by the time the SBI went after it, everybody had clammed up. It had become a great national issue by that time, and no black would have said anything under compulsion of death.

"This trial was a travesty, and it was especially infuriating to me, because after we got to Raleigh, I was helpless to do anything about it. The decisive move in the whole case was its completely illegal transfer out of Eastern North Carolina to Raleigh. In the pretrial hearing in April 1975, we won all the disputed points except one—the change-of-venue motion. We not only won them, we ravaged the opposition. They didn't come close to establishing a position. But they won on the motion to have the trial transferred and that was the decisive battle in the whole war. It was impossible to convict her in Raleigh! They won that motion on the basis of a phony memorandum from the State Attorney General's office, so if the Attorney General, Rufus Edmisten, says his office was not involved in this case from the beginning, he's either uninformed, or careless with the facts.

"When Judge Henry McKinnon used the Attorney General's memorandum to move the case beyond a county adjoining Beaufort, which was his only legal power, beyond to Raleigh, I told him,
" 'You've just acquitted her!'
"And so she was acquitted. In my summation to the jury I concluded with Shakespeare's precept from the *Merchant of Venice*: 'The quality of mercy is not strained. It droppeth as the gentle rain from heaven. Blessed alike him who receive and him who give (*sic*).'
"But in this case mercy never came into play, and for those philistines in the courtroom, I might as well have been quoting from Mother Goose."

CHAPTER 9

COURTNEY MULLIN AND
JUDGE HENRY McKINNON

In April 1975, a preliminary hearing in the case of the State of North Carolina versus Joan Little was held in the Beaufort County Courthouse. In style, it would be a proceeding which mixed the directness of the sixties with the cool sophistication of the seventies in a curious blend—a counterpoint marked by noisy ineffectiveness outside the courthouse and turgid success inside. In substance, it would be a hearing that very likely determined the verdict of innocent later, and very nearly resulted in a dismissal of the charges against Joan Little. It would last two weeks, and would focus on two crucial problems: (1) was the entire jury pool of Beaufort County racially discriminatory in its composition? and (2) where could Joan Little receive a fair trial? The proceeding would reduce to a minuet between a skilled social psychologist, Courtney Mullin, who would apply her techniques of social science in this new arena, and a superior jurist, Judge Henry K. McKinnon, whose mind could appreciate the nuances of Mullin's showings, but whose instincts were "country" and rooted in the rules. The two became kindred spirits.

April 14, the opening day of the preliminary hearing in the Joan Little case, brought busloads of youths from Winston-Salem and Fayetteville to the steps of the Beaufort County Courthouse. They formed a circle in a nostalgic way, chanting,

One, two, three,	JOAN LITTLE MUST BE SET FREE,
Four, five, six,	POWER TO THE ICEPICK,
Seven, eight, nine,	WE'RE GONNA BLOW YOUR MIND!

The protest was organized by Larry Little, the Black Panther head in North Carolina, and the black politics surrounding the event were almost more prominent than any effort at upbraiding the system. Divide and conquer, so the saying went. For Golden Frinks's frustrations had finally run away with him. In late winter, the Southern Christian Leadership Conference had proclaimed that it intended to have Resurrection City III in Washington, North Carolina, after number I in Washington, D.C., in 1968 and number II at the Republican National Convention in 1972. The tent city would open on April 4, the anniversary of Martin Luther King's assassination, and end April 18. So Ralph Abernathy began to make trips into the state and made some local people take notice when he said, "North Carolina is number one in basketball, and number one in the death penalty."

But on March 14, at a news conference at the Raleigh-Durham Airport, welcoming Abernathy on yet another visit, Golden Frinks suddenly charged that Joan Little was being held hostage by her lawyers, that she was being drugged, and was being encouraged to deny old friendships.

"I feel bad about Golden," Jerry Paul retorted condescendingly. "The man spent seventeen years in civil-rights work looking for a case that would propel him into national attention, and now he blows it."

But, privately, Paul conceded that "Golden is rippin' us up."

Claiming that Paul had agreed that the "movement" would get thirty percent of the funds collected in Joan Little's behalf, Frinks joined with Jessie Williams, Joan Little's mother—at that time mother and daughter weren't speaking to one another—in a suit in Federal Court to block the defense team from using any further money raised by the Southern Poverty Law Center. The figure raised by then was $150,000. The defense in turn released a letter signed by Joan Little accusing Frinks of trying to sabotage Little's defense, and using her mother for the purpose.

Frinks's poignant lashing out brought the whole case closer to the heart of darkness, which had drowned so many radical *causes célèbres* before it. The suit came to nothing, but in April the Panthers, in front of the court house, began to chant:

"Up with Joan Little, Down with Golden Frinks."

Standing in the middle of a dozen puptents in a mud-soaked, puddled lot at the corner of Fourth and Gladden streets, the ruins of Resurrection City III, Frinks responded,

"We're not down here for no nigger-and-honky stuff. All the demonstrations have done is demoralize the whole Joan Little movement." The following day, claiming that "white liberals" had undermined black leadership, Golden Frinks quit the case (although he did produce a few sign carriers on one day of the trial in July).

Meanwhile a journalist from Holland, for the Dutch publication *New Review* arrived on the edge of a crowd of reporters watching the demonstrations. Either from jet lag or unfamiliarity with this peculiar little place, the bona fide foreigner tapped a reporter politely on the shoulder,

"Golden Frinks?" he asked. "What is a Golden Frinks?"

On the other side of town, the white side, other problems were of concern—April Fool's problems. On April 6, 1975, the author's article on the Joan Little case appeared in the *New York Times Magazine*. It was a folksy sort of affair, introducing a highbrow audience to the luminaries of Little Washington: Mayor Max Roebuck and Councilman Louis Randolph got their pictures in the spread, Randolph standing in front of one of the $1,300 coffins, and later Mayor Max said that the writer had been "dad-burn fair to our little town."

But, as it always seems to happen in such enterprises when vulnerable people are involved, several local citizens were hurt by the piece. One was an automobile salesman, who was known around the coffee table at the Holiday Inn as a hardrock Wallacite—but that was no sin, for Beaufort County went seventy percent for Wallace in the 1972 presidential primary. This writer had been sipping coffee with David Milligan, the local editor, who had been doing his best to put a good face on the county, but when the salesman walked in, Milligan wiped his hand across his face.

"Oh, no, there goes my case," he said.

The dealer joined them for coffee, and they began talking about Joan Little, and the inevitable happened. On the subject of black morals versus his own, the salesman said,

"Hell, to them, fucking is like saying good morning or having a Pepsi-Cola."

The week after the article appeared, the dealer's world came apart. He was visited by four blacks, including a federal official from the Office of Civil Rights in Atlanta, demanding a written retraction in the paper or an explanation. Without a satisfactory explanation, the delegation threatened to begin picketing the dealership, and this, in turn, brought pressure from the district manager of the motor company, who threatened to fire the dealer if he could not take care of the matter. It was bad for the "image" of the car.

A frantic call was placed to the author, asking if he would say he had misquoted the salesman, and while he could not agree to that, he offered whatever help he could to save the dealer's job, for the opinion was widely held, North and South, urban and rural, and he saw no reason why the dealer alone should suffer for it. It made the author think that journalists talking to simple people should be forced to give them an equivalent of a Miranda warning: that anything you say may be held against you later.

Another victim was Hardy Henry, an executive of the National Spinning Company in Beaufort County, who had said offhandedly as he was leaving the coffee table at the Holiday Inn,

"I'll tell you one thing: she [Joan Little] wasn't defending her honor in that cell. She'd lost that years ago at Camp Lejeune" (referring to the rumor that Joan Little made a practice of taking girls to the military base for prostitution on paydays).

The week after April 6, the national headquarters of the National Spinning Company in New York sent an *investigator* to Washington, North Carolina. He interrogated Hardy Henry on whether he had actually said that—Henry denied it—and visited the other two people who had been at the table, demanding sworn statements from them that Henry had been misquoted. The investigator even went to the lengths of having the National Spinning Company lawyer in Raleigh draft a letter for the signature of editor Milligan to the effect that he too "was alarmed at the misquotation in *The New York Times*." Milligan signed the letter out of friendship for Hardy Henry, hoping it would save the executive's job, but later Milligan, who is a devout Catholic, told the author that his signature had caused him profound moral pain, because he knew Henry had not been misquoted. The author told Milligan to forget it. Nobody deserved to lose his job over a crack like that, regardless of what "damage" it might have done to the "reputation" of the National Spinning Company.

One of her experts in court had described Courtney Mullin as "that hippie-looking girl without the hippie mind," but actually, despite her love for jeans, her long amber hair, and her Oscar de la Renta glasses that covered half her face, she was the mother of three, married to a computer expert for furniture manufacturers, and a highly competent professional. Despite her retiring, sometimes embarrassed, manner with the press and her occasional difficulty in making abstruse statistical theory comprehensible to the layman, she may have been more important to Joan Little's victory than anyone. For, after the whole process was over, the self-satisfied saw among lawyers became, "Any lawyer in North Carolina could have gotten Joan Little acquitted, *as long as he got the trial out of Beaufort County*"—and Courtney Mullin had been responsible for that.

"The Joan Little case was unique," she began, "because it combined so many different areas of prejudice toward one person: it was a rape case, and there is lots of prejudice against women who say they have been raped; it was a racial case; it was a 'cop-killing'; all together, it was a black woman who said she'd been raped by a white law-enforcement officer, and that combination of factors was just incredible to me.

"From the beginning I followed the case from a very academic point of view. I'd done research on minority discrimination, and on rape victims, for which I won a prize. The rape study proved that people believe a rape victim's story in relation to how they view her 'respectability.' If a victim is viewed as 'respectable,' her rendition of the facts is more likely to be believed; the rape is thought to have happened by chance; she was in the wrong place at the wrong time; and the crime said nothing about her as a person. But if the victim is viewed as 'disrespectable,' she is likely to be blamed for bringing the rape on herself, and a black woman would be considered disrespectable. So people reserve some blame for the victim. Translated into the legal area, this means higher sentences for rapists of 'respectable women,' and the reverse of that is the common practice of a rapist's defender talking about how the woman was dressed that night, so as to prove enticement.

"In psychology there is a theory called the 'just world theory,' the widely held supposition that good things happen to good people, and bad things happen to bad people. Human beings want to believe that God is just, rewarding the righteous and punishing the wicked. When a bad accident happens, people want to understand why. They want to see the hand of reason in what is often senseless, and so they make 'attributions of cause.'

"In October 1974 I noticed in the papers that the defense lawyers in the Little case made a motion to the court for funds to hire a criminologist to do a survey, and that the motion was denied. I sensed that they needed help, so I called them up, said that as a social psychologist I would be willing to donate my efforts. They invited me over to talk, and at first they were skeptical, because a number of people had been offering free help to them at that time, and most had not come through. I talked with Karen Galloway, and we were groping for reasons to persuade the court to move the trial. Neither of us had a very clear idea of how to go about it.

"So I set about doing research. Some work had been done on prejudice in trials, about conviction-prone jurors, but there was very little in a practical sense. Usually the study was done with simulated jurors, usually college students—and college students do not transfer very well to the regional and race problems that this trial raised. I began to talk with survey specialists about how we could prove in court that the trial should be moved. The question was: What sort of research design would be needed?

"You must start with a hypothesis, and you must have some basis for making the hypothesis. Mine was that the levels of racism were measurably higher in Eastern North Carolina, given the makeup of the region: rural, homogeneous, inbred, having few large cities with few Northerners having infiltrated, and there were sociological studies that indicated that. The East would be compared with the Piedmont region of the state, which is more diverse and urban and where, I hypothesized, the prejudice would be less overt, more subtle. Prejudice, you see, is subtle by nature; it operates on the subconscious level, and it exists everywhere. [Dr. Robin Williams, a sociologist and defense witness at the preliminary hearing, would define prejudice as 'a prejudgment of a category or group of people in advance of particular acquaintance with an individual case at hand, a prejudgment which is categorical, which is held with feeling and which is defended in the face of evidence contradicting the belief.']

"I was not inductively saying that my hypothesis was true, and I will set out to prove it. Just because a person has a hypothesis is not to say that she is going to prove it true. In fact, every statistician begins with the proposition that the hypothesis is false. It's easy to assume all kinds of things, and that's why it's so important to be careful about methodology, to be very cautious scientifically, so that when you find differences in attitudes you can be absolutely sure that those differences occur in fact.

"As a scientist, I was separated from the defense. It is not proper for me to argue like a lawyer from an adversary position. I can suspect racism, but if I found none in a scientific study, I would have reported that.

"As my project developed, it was directed toward two motions that were finally considered by Judge Henry K. McKinnon in the preliminary hearing in April 1975. First, the motion challenging the jury pool in Beaufort County as deliberately excluding blacks, women, and young people. If the judge ruled in the defense's favor on that motion, the indictment of Joan Little would be declared invalid. And, second, the motion requesting the change of venue.

"With the compositional challenge to the jury pool in Beaufort County, we focused on two questions: First, were blacks, women, and young physically excluded from the jury pool, and second, were attitudes of these groups different toward a whole range of social issues, such as rape, law enforcement, and race? If it could be shown that attitudes were different, and that the three groups were underrepresented, then Joan Little could receive, not the justice of a cross-section of her community, not a jury of her peers, which is constitutionally guaranteed, but rather the justice of a middle-class, middle-aged white male segment only. If the jury pool was thus contaminated, her indictment would have to be quashed by law.

"So we conducted an area survey. To see how jurors were selected, we interviewed the jury commissioners and the clerks of court, first in Beaufort County, then in the entire twenty-three-county region of Eastern North Carolina, because we wanted to be prepared to make a showing about prejudice in any eastern county to which the judge might move the trial. Our basic method was the random selection of one hundred interviewees taken from the 1974–75 jury lists. This set number is statistically a sound and accepted method, and you can be sure, with that number, that if there are differences in your sample those differences will be large in the general population, whereas if more people were interviewed you could not judge whether differences found would be great or small. This is basically the same method used in polling presidential elections. By this sample survey we determined that in the Beaufort County jury pool, twelve percent were black, compared to their proportion in the county population of thirty percent. The percentage of males was fifty-three percent, compared to forty-six percent in the population, and females forty-seven percent, as compared to the overall fifty-four percent. Young people aged eighteen to twenty-one were represented less than one percent of the time, as compared with seven percent in the Beaufort County population.

[At the preliminary hearing, the prosecution responded with a study taken from summons lists, but not following consecutive summons periods, and estimated the black representation in the jury pool at twenty-two percent. This occasioned an actual count, which came out seventeen percent representation. The question for Judge McKinnon then became, Does eight percent or thirteen percent or eighteen percent underrepresentation constitute deliberate discrimination, or a 'contaminated jury pool?']

"To arrive at our figures comparing the population as a whole to the population of the jury pool, we used the chi-square test, which is extremely sensitive to sample size. The sample size is always one hundred people chosen randomly, and if the result of the random sample does not equal the expected result based on population ratio, then prejudice is shown. A statistical formula is used, and graphs are drawn, and by this method we were able to establish that the composition of the Beaufort County jury pool was racially contaminated.

"With physical exclusion of blacks established, we wanted to show that the attitudes within the excluded groups were unique, and thus that if you exclude them physically you exclude those attitudes from the deliberations within the jury room. If you have a jury pool made up primarily of white middle-class males, you have a homogeneous approach to problem-solving and judgment. But the law demands a cross-section of the community, and that means that the spectrum of attitudes and the spectrum of prejudice must be represented in order to render a fair verdict about a member of society.

"The question was how to conduct a poll of attitudes, first in Beaufort County and then in all twenty-three eastern counties. I called several reputable polling agencies for an estimate of the cost of a face-to-face attitudinal survey, and the figure of fifty to seventy-five thousand dollars for one county alone came back. So we had to undertake the project ourselves. We knew that it would be time-consuming—the agencies talked about a year to do the survey—and that it would be a tremendous amount of work. We ran an ad in the newspaper, and the interviewers we got as a result were scientifically neutral. They were not responding out of any loyalty to Joan Little, but because they needed a job.

"The attitudinal survey would apply both to the compositional challenge and also to the change-of-venue motion, and so almost from the beginning we polled attitudes in the entire twenty-three-county area. WATS lines were put in at a cost of ten thousand dollars, and at the peak there were over fifty people working on the project. Telephone interviewing is a lot cheaper than face-to-face interviewing, and each method has its pluses and minuses. A somewhat offensive question like 'Black women have lower moral standards than white women. Agree or Disagree' is apt to get a straighter answer in a telephone survey. Interviewing a person face to face has a larger experimental error because of the variable of the interviewer's personality.

"Beaufort County was the only one where we did face-to-face interviewing. We approached one hundred sixty-nine citizens there, and since the judge was only interested in different attitudes of black and white people, we concentrated on that. Our results were these."

RACE

	Whites	Blacks	Percentage Difference Between Blacks and Whites
Attitudes toward poor			
1. The federal government is too concerned with giving aid to minority groups.	39%=No	77%=No	38%
2. Mothers on welfare are cheating taxpayers out of their money.	45%=No	71%=No	26%
Capital punishment			
1. While capital punishment may be undesirable, it is necessary to prevent serious crime.	19%=No	72%=No	53%
2. Capital punishment should be used more often than it is.	25%=No	81%=No	56%
3. Capital punishment should never be used as punishment for any crime.	16%=Yes	55%=Yes	39%

RACE (*cont'd*)

	Whites	Blacks	Percentage Difference Between Blacks and Whites
Attitudes relevant to rape victims			
1. A black woman who is raped by a white man has probably tempted him into it.	58%=No	81%=No	23%
2. If a woman says she's been raped, that should be enough evidence that the rape has actually occurred.	15%=Yes	29%=Yes	14%
3. Black women have lower moral standards than white women.	49%=No	72%=No	23%
Attitudes about the Joan Little case			
1. Do you believe Joan Little killed Clarence Alligood in self-defense?	58%=No	1%=No	57%
2. From your knowledge of this area, do you believe Joan Little can get a fair trial in Beaufort County?	34%=No	86%=No	52%
Other attitudes			
1. Policemen spend too much time arresting kids for smoking marijuana.	17%=Yes	41%=Yes	24%
2. Police should not hesitate to use force to maintain order.	71%=Yes	59%=Yes	12%
3. People should support state authorities even when they feel they are wrong.	29%=Yes	43%=Yes	23%
4. White people are more greedy than black people.	27%=Yes	83%=Yes	56%

(A defense expert witness, Dr. Robin Williams, a sociologist from Cornell University, was to testify at the preliminary hearing about these results:

("When you get a difference of fifty-six percent between whites and blacks in responding to a question, 'Agree or disagree that capital punishment should be used more often than it is,' you are getting a really astonishing difference; that indicates a substantial bias in favor of severe punishment in the white population. The whites in this sample did have more punitive attitudes than black people, and it can be safely said that blacks seem to show a position more nearly like that called for in the traditional legal doctrine of a presumption of innocence until guilt has been proved. . . . With the question, 'Do you believe Joan Little killed Clarence Alligood in self defense?' the differences there are very, very great, with almost no black people saying no. I would take that to mean they are withholding judgment on that matter, whereas fifty-eight percent of whites said no, creating the presumption in my mind that they have already made up their minds."

(In general, Williams asserted that the defense's attitudinal survey showed a "prosecution orientation" among Beaufort County whites; William Griffin argued in response that all the survey did was "describe the human condition.")

The argument over the composition of the Beaufort County jury pool took seven court days. Jerry Paul argued that the verdicts were predictable in Beaufort County with the underrepresentation of blacks, and elicited from Bessie Cherry, the clerk of court, the admission that one all-black precinct and one predominately black township were excluded from jury participation. Paul submitted to the court that if the county had really wanted a cross-section represented on the juries, the jury commissioners would have supplemented the tax lists and voter lists with a third list: welfare roles, high-school graduating lists, or even telephone-book lists. He cast the struggle in court as a conflict between the "new abolitionists and those who would fight change and progress."

William Griffin responded with equal passion. "I hold up Beaufort County before God and the world as blameless," he said. "The defense used innuendo, assertion, and pseudo-science. . . . There's no deliberate discrimination if the jury is fairly drawn in a systematic fashion from the best sources available. That's where the experts are confounded. They are missing the point by ignoring the practical problems. It's impossible to get an exact cross-section of the population for a jury." Griffin made much of the actual grand jury that had indicted Joan Little: four out of sixteen black, or twenty-five percent; eight women, or fifty percent. "If there was ever a cross-section of Beaufort County, that grand jury was it."

John Wilkinson called the scientific showing by the defense a journey of "Alice in Wonderland," and thought that "trying to balance prejudice on juries is a low star to shoot at, if you're looking for justice in the courtman." If the jury pool were ruled improper, he argued, "attorneys would be flocking to the court pell-mell to get rehearings for their clients."

On April 22, 1975, Judge Henry McKinnon ruled that there was "no systematic exclusion of blacks" on Beaufort County juries and denied the motion to quash. The challenge to the jury, he felt, was technically the most important because the defense was assaulting the very basis for the prosecution, but he did not find the defense position truly scientific and did not feel that a jury must be a one-hundred-percent reflection of the population as a whole. So long as the jury commissioners were doing their best in good faith from the best available list of the population— the voter and tax lists—McKinnon was satisfied.

"The defense raised interesting questions, I will say, possibly close questions. Had I accepted the twelve percent figure, as compared with twenty-nine percent population figure, that would have been enough to shift the burden to the prosecution to show that there had *not* been systematic discrimination. But while there were technical errors shown in the Beaufort County selection process, I saw no evidence of systematic, intentional exclusion."

Judge McKinnon was never told (during the preliminary hearing), that the defense jury project had made an actual nose count of the Beaufort County 1974–75 lists and had found an actual figure of seventeen percent black representation on juries. Jerry Paul apparently felt that he was close to winning the compositional challenge on the statistical showing derived from the chi-square test, and did not want to undermine the validity of the statistical sample. Courtney Mullin, however, was to feel in retrospect that this had been a mistake, that Judge McKinnon was conversant enough with statistics, and that had the actual figure, rather than the competing estimates of twelve percent and twenty-two percent, been before him, he might have ruled in favor of the defense.

John Wilkinson gloated at the prosecution victory. "The charges against Beaufort County have been dismissed," he said. And William Griffin said, "There are two things to remember when you go fishing. You've got to have bait, and you've got to have fish."

Meanwhile, Paul was making news differently. As McKinnon was weighing his decision, Paul scandalized the local citizens in a Washington shopping center by having himself wheeled around in a baby stroller by his mixed entourage. Once, in the course of the frolic, he stretched out on the floor in a department-store shoe department.

"I've always been a clown," he told reporters. "I was tired, and there was nowhere else to sit. I like to cut up, and it just messes these people up to see blacks and whites having a good time together."

The Panthers had not been seen since the first day of the hearing, and the twelve tents of Resurrection City III had been folded up long ago. The national press had left, for demonstrations, not statistics, made news. The nation was concerned about other events elsewhere.

Saigon was on the verge of collapse and surrendered April 28. On the day of the collapse, the North Carolina House voted to repeal the outlaw statute, but two months later, the state Senate acted to keep the law.

On April 16, after a switch of votes by three legislators, the ERA failed in the Legislature, 62–57.

But most importantly, on April 21, the U.S. Supreme Court heard arguments over the death penalty in the case of *North Carolina* vs. *Fowler,* the capital punishment case. Fowler's crime was a "garden-variety killing," according to the Attorney General of North Carolina: the inmate had had an argument with one John Griffin in a crap game over $10; later in the day, Griffin and Fowler had a fight, and Griffin broke Fowler's nose; and two hours after that, Fowler shot Griffin dead in a housing project. The case was tried before Judge Henry K. McKinnon.

"It was insignificant at the time," Judge McKinnon said. "Of course, it was a capital case, and we went through the formalities of picking a jury for first degree, but no one really thought it was going to be a capital verdict. The more predictable verdict from the factual situation would have been second-degree murder. If you accepted the state's version, the evidence had every legal element of first degree, though the defendant's version did raise an element of provocation. But the jury said what the facts were and applied the law. They did not exercise sympathetic discretion to reduce the charge from first to second degree, just because there were a lot of other murders just like this one."

How odd that potentially the most important capital verdict in history should be one arrived at almost offhandedly! How large would the national death-row figure be if juries for all "garden-variety" killings said what the facts were and applied the law?

In the arguments in the Supreme Court on the Fowler case, Justice Thurgood Marshall rhetorically took on the entire North Carolina criminal-justice system. He asked the Assistant North Carolina Attorney General, Jean Benoy, if a black had *ever* had his sentence commuted in North Carolina. Benoy could not recall one. With a total black population in the state of twenty percent, Marshall wanted ot know the percentage of blacks on death row. Answer: fifty percent.

"That does not give a problem?" Justice Marshall asked. Benoy replied that it did not.

Were there any elected black prosecutors? Benoy did not know of any. How about judges? There was one "Negro woman—a Negress," Benoy replied; an odd turn of phrase for a top state law-enforcement officer to use in 1975.

Elsewhere in the country, there was some refreshing enlightment on the issue. On April 28, the Governor of Massachusetts, Michael Dukakis, vetoed a bill to restore the death penalty that had passed his state legislature. "I do not believe that this commonwealth has the moral authority to execute human beings," he said. "I cannot reconcile the willful taking of a human life by the state with my own moral and ethical beliefs."

This contrasted with views of the North Carolina Attorney General, Rufus Edmisten, who said during the Fowler arguments: "I have religious scruples against the death penalty myself. You're not going to catch me pulling switches or dropping the pill, and

I've got more important things to do than have my lawyers up here all the time arguing the death penalty." Edmisten would say later that he was the chief law-enforcement officer of the state and as long as the North Carolina Legislature did not overturn the death sentence, his lawyers would argue the state's case with all the fervor they possessed.

And in a letter to the Governor of North Carolina the same week, Charles Dunn, the director of the State Bureau of Investigation, warned "of a growing potential for violence if you decide not to pardon or commute the sentences of those on death row." The death-row figure then was sixty-seven, and by the end of 1975 it would be over one hundred.

Courtney Mullin turned her attention to the change-of-venue motion, which Judge McKinnon felt was the most significant legal element of the entire Joan Little affair.

"From the very beginning of the pretrial hearings," she said, "it was quite clear that the trial would be moved out of Beaufort County, and technically the judge only had the power to move it to one of the adjoining counties. The prosecution said publicly on April 14 that the trial should be moved due to 'deliberate and excessive' publicity, and Judge McKinnon let it be known that the trial would be held in adjoining Pitt County, unless he could be shown that the attitudes and publicity in Pitt County made a fair trial impossible there as well. He gave us a couple of days to make our showing, and it was the most exhausting period of my life, made worse by the fact that the needs of the lawyers seemed to change from moment to moment.

"To prove the hypothesis that the level of overt prejudice was higher in Pitt County than in Piedmont North Carolina, we had to have a comparative county, and Jerry Paul wanted Orange County. I argued against that, saying that the public would dismiss the comparison. Of course, you chose Orange County, people would say, the liberal seat of North Carolina, one of only three counties which went for George McGovern in the 1972 election, the home of Chapel Hill. I wanted Mecklenburg County, which contains Charlotte, and which in fact is far more liberal than basically rural Orange County, which years ago had one of the strongest chapters of the Ku Klux Klan in the state. Still, Jerry was the boss, and Orange it became. There was no real difference between the populations or the jury pools in both counties: both rural, with one middle-sized university town in both—Greenville in Pitt and Chapel Hill in Orange. But there were enormous differences in attitudes toward all the issues raised by our attitudinal survey, except one: how much they had heard about the Joan Little case. That was identical.

"We had prepared a questionnaire with the help of the National Jury Project and of Jay Shulman, in New York, who had worked with the Attica, Berrigan, and Gainesville-Eight juries. The questionnaire had sixty-five questions, and combined attitudes toward blacks, women, and authority. No particular question was more important than any other, for it was the constellation of responses that showed the attitude and influenced the ability to judge Joan Little. Still, some of the comparative responses were as follows:

- Obedience and respect for authority are the most important virtues children should learn. Pitt 85% agree; Orange 60% agree.
- Killing a law-enforcement officer is the worst kind of crime. Pitt 66% agree; Orange 46% agree.
- Black women have lower moral standards than white women. Pitt 45% agree; Orange 16% agree.

- When ex-convicts are accused of another crime, they're probably guilty. Pitt 28% agree; Orange 16% agree. (This question, the experts argued, showed the attitude toward presumption of innocence.)
- If the prosecution goes to the trouble of bringing someone to trial, they're probably guilty. Pitt 30% agree; Orange 18% agree.
- If a person flees the scene of a crime, then other people can pretty much assume they're guilty of the crime. Pitt 39% agree; Orange 19% agree.
- Most women who are raped have brought it on themselves. Pitt 41% agree; Orange 16% agree.

"The overall conclusions of the comparison were that Pitt County believed more in racial stereotypes than Orange, favored capital punishment more, had more conservative viewpoints on rape, adhered more to traditional viewpoints toward women and authority, but that there was no statistical difference in the amount of publicity in the two places. But the Judge seemed most interested in the results of these five questions:

- Do you believe that Joan Little tempted Clarence Alligood into her cell in order to escape? Pitt 23% agree; Orange 7% agree.
- Do you believe that Clarence Alligood did in fact try to rape Joan Little? Pitt 41% agree; Orange 68% agree.
- Do you believe that Joan Little killed Clarence Alligood in self-defense? Pitt 56% agree; Orange 72% agree.
- Do you believe Joan Little ran because she was afraid? Pitt 76% agree; Orange 87% agree.
- Do you believe Joan Little ran because that was part of her plan to escape? Pit 32% agree; Orange 11% agree.

"The fact that the population of Eastern North Carolina is cohesive and homogeneous is partly responsible for these results, but that is not all of it. Those people really were besieged in the Joan Little case. People were talking about them as if they were the scum of the earth; it was terrible for them, and I felt truly sorry for them. They had the eyes of the world on them, and their county was being called the most bigoted in the country. That was unfair. The publicity intensified the discomfort, and the local citizens would go around wondering why everybody was saying all those bad things about them. It got very intense. Their 'dissonance' was aroused. They were forced to make a decision about how the incident happened, and the enticement theory was the choice that eased their anxiety the most. The choice was to grind down Joan Little or to face up to the guilt of what was happening in their jail. The more the publicity, the firmer their belief became. But I do not consider the results a condemnation of Pitt County. It was simply a description of the circumstances at the time of the Joan Little proceedings."

For an analysis of the press coverage of the Joan Little trial, Courtney Mullin relied on Dr. Paul Brandes, a professor in the Speech Division at the University of North Carolina. Brandes's studies of bias in oral and written communication date back to 1935, and he once directed a "Persuasion Laboratory" at Ohio University. Comparing coverage in Piedmont North Carolina with Eastern North Carolina, Brandes conducted "content analysis" of selected newspapers. He identified "clusters of words" favorable to Joan Little and unfavorable to her, and, if favorable and unfavorable clusters appeared in the same news item, he considered the stories neutral. The unfavorable cluster was "the icepick stabbing" and the favorable cluster referred to the condition in which Alligood's body was found: "nude from the waist down."

This is known as the "key-word method" of content analysis. Its data can be computerized, and one such MIT computer study claimed to have unraveled the mystery over which numbers of *The Federalist* were written by Madison and which by Hamilton, by identifying consistent differences in the use of prepositions. Another study found new themes in *Hamlet* by discovering a pattern in the use of paternal words in the play.

Dr. Brandes found that of twenty-three stories on the Joan Little case in the Raleigh *News and Observer* between February 15, 1975, and April 26, 1975, only ten paired the phrases "icepick stabbing" with "nude from the waist down," and the remaining stories were unfavorable to Joan Little. A story in the *Daily Reflector*, the newspaper for Greenville, in Pitt County, as late as March 28, 1975, still used the description: "Miss Little, a twenty-year-old black, is charged with first-degree murder in the icepick slaying of a white Beaufort County jailer. She claims the jailer was trying to rape her and that she acted in self-defense." It made no mention of the condition of Alligood's body.

As an example of a favorable story, Brandes cited the February 27, 1975, coverage in the Raleigh *News and Observer* of her release from Women's Prison on $115,000 bond. A photograph showed her sobbing in her mother's arms as she was led to a waiting car, and the accompanying news story described her as "frightened by reporters and photographers." This, Brandes testified, could have had a "sleeper effect" on some citizens initially opposed to Miss Little, permitting "pity" to operate within them in Joan Little's favor. Still, Brandes estimated that only a minimal number of people were touched by the "sleeper effect."

Brandes found further that stories concerning the funds raised and spent in Joan Little's behalf never contained balancing information on how much the prosecution, both public and private, was spending to convict her. His overall judgment was that unfavorable coverage exceeded the favorable or neutral coverage, and lamented that he had not had time to put his data on a computer so that he could present the court with a statistical number for the degree of unfavorableness.

Courtney Mullin nevertheless was to feel that Judge McKinnon's interest in the publicity angle of her showing avoided the main issue.

"When Judge McKinnon ruled to remove the trial to Raleigh in Wake County, it was essentially a cop-out. He latched onto the publicity in Pitt County as the reason for not having the trial there, and yet knowledge about the case was the *one factor that was identical* between the East and the Piedmont. I think the political pressures were enormous on Judge McKinnon. To rule that the people of Eastern North Carolina are prejudiced is simply not a politically expedient thing to do, and Judge McKinnon is a political man. So it required considerable evidence to overcome the political pressures, and he had an easy way out: to remove the trial to Pitt County and simply say that the statute did not give him authority to remove it any further. He did a courageous thing, and I admire him for it."

The author went to see Judge McKinnon one night in the fall of 1975 at his home in Lumberton, North Carolina, and down in his den, lined with law books, they talked. A tall, angular man with a thin face and prominent ears, his good sense and intelligence were evident in his first words. Sensational cases are not his cup of tea; he does not enjoy the presence of reporters or the clutter of television paraphernalia around the court house. The judge had set certain restrictions on the talk. "There are few things a judge can comment on that won't come back to haunt him at some time in the future, often in a case or situation that appears to have no connection with the subject of comment," the judge had written beforehand. "For this reason there are a number of things . . . that I am not likely to want to respond to in much depth if at all." The author took that to mean his suggestion that the judge speak to the question of the political pressures upon him.

"The statute in North Carolina covering a change of venue or a special venire, as it was written at the time of the preliminary hearing," he said, "enabled the trial judge to remove a trial to an adjacent county, or to bring in a special venire from the same or adjoining judicial district, and so, effectively, my choice under the statute was, one, to allow it to be tried in Beaufort County; two, to remove it to one of the six adjoining counties, or three, to bring in a special venire from one of the twenty-three counties in Eastern North Carolina. I assumed that the case would not be tried in Beaufort, and I would have found that it was impossible for Joan Little to have gotten a fair trial there, although most competent lawyers think she would have been acquitted everywhere in North Carolina, including Beaufort County. Before the preliminary hearing, the prosecution had agreed that the case should be removed, and had requested a removal to Pitt County, which was the largest county adjacent to Beaufort. Additionally, had the trial been in Beaufort County, the sheriff's department there would have been the security force for the court and the attendants to the jury. I didn't think they deserved that duty, or that it would look good to the public that the sheriff's department intimately involved in the case be the official court force. Beaufort County, for all practical purposes, was ruled out as the place of trial. However, if anybody deserved the trial, it was Beaufort County—it was their problem—and if Beaufort County didn't deserve it, nobody deserved it.

"Neither side requested a special jury panel from the twenty-three counties, and so a week before we began on April 14, I told both the prosecution and the defense that I had no plans to initiate a special venire on my own, and that it would be a question of removal. So no evidence of bias or prejudice was considered in any eastern county aside from Beaufort County and Pitt County, and neither my denial of the compositional challenge to Beaufort County nor my removal of the trial to Wake County was made on the basis of a persuasive showing of prejudice. I did not find or attempt to find that she couldn't get a fair trial in any of the twenty-three counties.

"Jerry Paul had told me that their studies showed that of the twenty-three counties in the East, Pitt County came out the best, and that if they had to have the trial in the East, Pitt was their preference, so I instructed both sides to direct their showings there.

"Now I had done some research on my own, and had had research done for me by a young lawyer in the state attorney general's office. I had formed the preliminary opinion that, under the constitutional right to a fair trial or, more particularly, under the idea that venue or the place of trial is waivable traditionally, it was within my legal power to remove the trial beyond the geographical limits set by the venue statute. So, if Joan Little knew what she was doing in asking that the trial be moved to the Piedmont, I concluded there would be nothing legally infirm about a trial in Raleigh.

"So both sides directed their showings to Pitt

County. I'll have to say that the validity of the defense showing was considerably undercut by picking Orange County as the comparison. Orange may be a norm of something, but it's not comparable to other counties in North Carolina. And indeed, the whole notion of a comparison, which the experts made so much of, really didn't get to me. I was looking at how Pitt was itself, and I paid more attention to the traditional questions on the evidence: how much had people heard about the case, had they formed an opinion on the evidence, what weight is given to opinions on the evidence. I let all sociological material in, and sifted it afterwards, and while I accepted the good faith of the statisticians who said that a sample size of one hundred was the most valid indicator of attitude, I can't help believing that a thousand opinions would be better than a hundred.

"Of course, the old country way of doing this would have been to call in, say, a newspaperman, a sheriff, and three or four others of standing in the community to give their "expert opinion" on what people are saying about the case. There have always been a lot of jokes about what an expert is in court, and while I accepted the credentials of the experts who testified, I considered their word neither gospel nor indisputable."

For courtroom jokes, the source had to be John Wilkinson, the best storyteller in the Joan Little drama. The "old chestnut" for this, Wilkinson said, was that "an expert in court is any son of a bitch with a briefcase from out of town," and "that," Wilkinson said, unable to resist a gratuitous aside, "applied to some of the jugheads the defense put up there [in the preliminary hearing]. I asked one of their 'experts' what experience he had had that didn't come out of a book. He said none, and I then asked him who wrote the book!"

The serious point was, however, that Jerry Paul had tried "the old country way" to secure a change of venue as early as September 18, 1974, three weeks after Alligood's death. The defense showed that newspaper coverage had been widespread and presented affidavits from local officials who would be in a position to describe the climate of public opinion. In good country fashion, Sheriff Davis had been called as an "expert," and William Griffin had asked,

"Do you feel it would be impossible to find twelve people in Beaufort County who could give the defendant a fair trial?"

"I think they could be found," Red Davis replied. "It might be a hard job, but I think they could be found."

But the judge for that hearing, Joshua Jones, would hear nothing of it and denied the motion for a change of venue.

"The country way," Paul said later, "was totally unsuccessful. So I knew then that I would have to build an ironclad case that would give them no choice but to remove the trial from Beaufort County."

"So," Judge McKinnon continued, "I was persuaded a little by the defense showing on the specific traditional evidence questions in Pitt County. In stages of relevance, the showing on publicity in Pitt County was more persuasive. The key-word method was certainly interesting, and then the affidavits the defense presented on the fixed nature of opinions about the case in Pitt helped. And I looked at the words of the statute: "A judge may remove if he is of the opinion that it is necessary in order to provide a fair trial." Well, *necessity* is a pretty absolute word. I never felt it was *necessary* to move it out of Eastern North Carolina. Rather, it was very much a matter of practicality with me, practicalities and probabilities. I was more practical than legal in my order, I reckon:

While much of the evidence offered by the defendant appears to be incompetent or irrelevant, it does appear that there had been substantial publicity about this case in the news media in Pitt County and that many people have formed fixed opinions about the case, and the court finds from the evidence that it would be difficult to obtain a fair and impartial jury in Pitt County without the calling and examination of a large number of jurors, and for those reasons there are probably grounds to believe that a fair and impartial trial could not be obtained in Pitt County without considerable time and expense. . . .

WHEREFORE, it is ORDERED that this case be removed for trial to Wake County, North Carolina. . . .

"Well, that's pretty weak. It really doesn't meet the language that the statute for removal calls for, even removing it one county, much less beyond the legal limits, or maybe even the language that the constitution calls for. When William Griffin appealed my order to the North Carolina Supreme Court, its response, as I read it in the newspapers, was in the nature of damning me with faint praise. They upheld the change of venue, but—I'm guessing now—their concern was that I did not make a positive finding of prejudice. The Supreme Court seemed to be saying, 'We'll let it go this one time to get this over with.' "

Jerry Paul was triumphant. At a news conference, he was outrageous as always. The change-of-venue order was, he said, one of three victories for the people that week: the other two had been in Vietnam and Cambodia, and he thanked the press.

"If it had not been for the press coverage, Joan Little would be in the gas chamber," he said.

Meanwhile, in New York City the same day, a judge dismissed rape charges against Martin Evans, thirty-seven, a cable-television personality. The charges had been brought by Beth Peterson, a native of Charlotte, North Carolina, a Wellesley student, who claimed that Evans picked her up at LaGuardia Airport, bought her drinks at a singles bar, and then attacked her back at his apartment. But Manhattan Supreme Court Justice Edward J. Greenfield found Miss Peterson "incredibly trusting, gullible, and naïve.

"The question in this case," the judge's ruling read, "is whether the sexual conquest by a predatory male of a resisting female constitutes rape or seduction. We recognize that there are situations that do not deserve extreme penalty, and in which the male objective was achieved through charm, guile, protestations of love, promises, and even deceit. This we label seduction, and society may condone it, even as we despair.

"Bachelors and other men on the make, fear not! It is still not illegal to feed a girl a line, to make promises that will not be kept, or to indulge in exaggerations and hyperbole, or to assure her, as in a fairy tale, that the ugly frog is a handsome prince."

PART 2

*"The horror!" . . . After all, this was the ex-
pression of some sort of belief; it had candor,
it had conviction, it had a vibrating note of
revolt in its whisper, it had the appalling
face of a glimpsed truth—the strange com-
mingling of desire and hate. And it is not
my own extremity I remember best—a vision
of grayness without form filled with physical
pain, and a careless contempt for the evan-
escence of all things—even of this pain itself.
No! It is his extremity that I seem to have
lived through. True, he had made that last
stride, he had stepped over the edge, while I
had been permitted to draw back my hesitat-
ing foot. And perhaps in this is the whole
difference; perhaps all the wisdom, and all
truth, and all sincerity are just compressed
into that inappreciable moment of time in
which we step over the threshold of the in-
visible. Perhaps! I like to think my sum-
ming-up would not have been a word of
careless contempt. Better his cry—much better. It was an affirmation, a moral victory
paid for by innumerable defeats, by abominable terrors, by abominable satisfactions. But
it was a victory!*

Joseph Conrad, *Heart of Darkness*

CHAPTER 10

TERRY BELL

IN the second week of June 1975, the newspapers in
North Carolina were replete with the details of the
riot—or the rebellion, as Celine Chenier preferred—at
the Women's Prison in Raleigh. But in Washington,
North Carolina, the investigation of the Joan Little
case was taking a confusing twist, and the key to its
unraveling to this day lies somewhere deep within the
mysteries of a seventeen-year-old psychopathic personality.

Bill Griffin was prosecuting three bank robbers in
the Beaufort County Courthouse that week, but his
mind was thrusting forward to the biggest prosecution
of his career. In the late spring he had received a call
from a source, "a responsible citizen," who told of
Joan Little boasting in Women's Prison that she had
"killed the son of a bitch, had had the help of a
sixteen-year-old boy, and she wasn't going to serve a
day for it." Griffin's source gave him a few names of
inmates, including Jacquatta Davis, who purportedly
would verify the statements.

Accompanied by SBI agents, Griffin went to see the
female inmates, and while he heard a number of juicy
prison stories in a two-hour interview—"People have
no idea of what goes on in those prisons," he mused—
he found no one who could directly confirm the Joan
Little statements. Jacquatta Davis remembered the

authorities as "really desperate that day." They attempted to provoke her into an incriminating statement about Joan Little, saying Joan had turned in Jacquatta Davis's name to the superintendent for having drugs when she was on lockup. The trick was an attempt to "bribe her," she said, but she hadn't fallen for it. The inmate also spoke of another prisoner who constantly said to Joan's face, "You killed that man in cold blood," inevitably leading to arguments and fights—an *agent provocateur*? According to Jacquatta Davis, Joan Little never talked about the case in prison other than to relate some of the bad dreams she was constantly having. One such dream had been that a grotesque "black figure just stood over her in the dream, and Joan had found it terrifying."

It was a small world, and Jerry Paul heard of Griffin going to see Jacquatta Davis. So he in turn sent a defense lawyer to see the inmate, just to determine what, if anything, she knew. If it turned out that she knew something damaging and was prepared to testify to it on the stand, Paul wanted her to know that he had a note, procured by Celine Chenier, in which Davis boasted of having "copped some coke" and in a search of her person, the "dummies" never thought to look . . . everywhere she might hide something. But the defense lawyer reported back that Davis didn't know anything damaging; she was never called to the stand, and that was the end of it.

Still Griffin was intrigued by the rumor of a sixteen-year-old accomplice, and the only sixteen-year-old in the jail on the night of Alligood's death was Terry Bell, a trusty who had been convicted of breaking-and-entering and sentenced to ten years. Bell, of course, was already vital to the prosecution case. For only he could testify that Joan Little had access to the icepick as she was making her phone call at 10:30 P.M. on August 26, five hours before the killing, and that Alligood left Joan alone in his office, where the weapon was in a drawer, when he took Bell back to his cell, spoke to him for five minutes, and then locked him up for the night. Looked at from the strictly legal viewpoint, the prosecution needed Bell's testimony on Joan Little's opportunity to lift the icepick at 10:30, for them to get beyond any defense motion for nonsuit.

So Griffin called for Bell on June 11 during a break in the court session, and the trusty told his original story of the 10:30 phone call, and of then having been awakened by Deputy Peachey the following morning with the news of Alligood's demise. But after the interview, Sheriff Davis talked with the trusty, and first thing the following day, collared Griffin in court.

"I think Bell's got something he wants to tell you," the sheriff said excitedly.

So Griffin went down to the sheriff's office and, as Griffin tells it, "that was when Bell told this incredible story about climbing up in the rafters of the jail, where he had been ordered to change light bulbs before, crawling along the steel beams in the ceiling across the women's section that night, and peering through a glass frame above Joan Little's bunk, witnessing the killing of Clarence Alligood.

" 'Help me,' Joan Little called out to Bell. 'Help me put him on the bunk, take his pants off, so it will look like rape.'

"He really went into detail."

Griffin returned to the court greatly excited. Bell had been an important witness before, but now he was suddenly Victory and Vindication personified. That afternoon, the prosecutor had a local lawyer, Ed Rodman, the chairman of the Ethics Committee of the North Carolina Bar Association, appointed as Bell's lawyer—after, of course, Bell's self-incriminating story had been told in full.

For two days in Rodman's office, Bell went through an extensive interrogation, and on the afternoon of June 13, Special Agent D. S. Keller of the State Bureau of Investigation administered a lie-detector test. It contained nine questions:

1. Did you aid Joan Little to escape?
2. Did you help Joan undress Mr. Alligood?
3. Did you help Joan kill Mr. Alligood?
4. Did Joan ask you to help her?
5. Did you place Mr. Alligood on the bed?
6. Did Joan ask you to remove Mr. Alligood's pants?
7. Did the icepick fall out while you were placing Mr. Alligood on the bed?
8. Have you given Joan's lawyers any of this information?
9. Did you ever have sexual relations with Joan Little?

Terry Bell answered "yes" to all questions.

William Griffin often used the polygraph test "to satisfy himself," even though, as nearly everyone, including Terry Bell, knows, its results are not admissible in court. But the validity of the Terry Bell polygraph was questionable even in a polygrapher's terms. For all the questions applied directly to the evidence. There were no "known-truth" questions in the test, and no control questions, which might apply to a subject's known criminal past, about which the subject was likely to lie. The point of having "known-truth" questions is to establish the subject's norm, and the point of the control questions, or the "cheat-and-steal" questions, as an expert calls them, is to show what the subject looks like when he or she lies.

John E. Reid, a polygraph expert in Chicago and coauthor of the book *Truth and Deception: The Polygraph Technique*, operates on the theory that if a subject responds to a greater degree to the control or "cheat-and-steal" questions than to the evidence questions, "and consistently does so," he reports that the subject is telling the truth. With the reverse—a greater response to the evidence questions than to the control questions—then he reports that the subject is lying. Blood pressure, pulse, respiration, and skin resistance to the small electrical waves sent through the fingers are the data for the test, and on June 27, 1975, John E. Reid's subject was to be Joan Little.

So when Special Agent Keller concluded on June 13, 1975, that Terry Bell was being "deceptive" in the answers to the nine questions, it is difficult to fathom how he knew. For he had established no norm for Bell, and had no idea what Bell's graph looked like when he lied. Beyond that, of the nine questions, only two, numbers 5 and 7, applied to Terry Bell's actions alone, while the others applied to his actions in concert with Joan Little, and no attempt was made to detect a deviation in the answers between the solo questions and the teamwork questions. But perhaps most important, Bell's history showed that he was not likely to find lying stressful. His junior-high-school principal, Shep Grist, one of the last of the Grist gentry in Beaufort County, was to say that Bell was the closest thing to a "person without a conscience" he had ever seen, and John Wilkinson wondered why the state fooled around with lie-detector tests, when Bell was "completely impervious" to them.

"Lie-detector tests did not have any more effect on him than showing him tea leaves," Wilkinson said.

Wilkinson had taken an interest in the boy several years before Bell became a shadowy figure in the Joan Little case. The lawyer had been appointed to represent Bell in "one piece of trouble after another," and once got the boy a job as a mechanic on a tugboat, only to watch him get married, quit the job, and re-

turn to Washington, where soon "his criminal proclivities took over again." Other Bells in Beaufort County
were "high-tone folks," Wilkinson called them. An
uncle, "Snooks" Bell, had been the jeweler and watch-
repairman in town (as well as an overt homosexual),
but Terry's father was a "monster" who had killed
another of his sons, called Dutchy, and served four to
six years on a manslaughter conviction for it. Mr. Bell
had been luckier years before, when his first wife had
been found in her front yard with her head blown off.
Townspeople politely refer to her death "under mysterious circumstances," but a local educator was sure
that the elder Bell killed the woman: "Everybody
knew it."

"He's a violent, dangerous man," Wilkinson said,
"but he's the best damn lawnmower mechanic in
town."

After the death of his first wife, by whom he had
had three children, Mr. Bell married a very young
woman, about fifteen years old. She was a "little sav-
age" and a "slut" to Wilkinson, but "some men like
that." Mr. Bell's problem was to keep his sons by his
first wife away from his second wife. Twice wife number two came to Wilkinson's office, terribly beaten,
asking him to prosecute her husband, and twice, before the judge, she lost her tongue and refused to say a
word. The third time she came in in the same condition, Wilkinson turned her out of his office and told
her never to come back. Before she ran off with a man
from Virginia, she had had three sons, including
Terry.

This family background led to a boy who seemed to
have no control over his emotions or his thoughts,
much less his actions. "Anything that presented itself
to him, he would do without the slightest thought
about consequences," Principal Grist said. "He was in
fights constantly, and once a new boy came to school,

and Terry just walked up to him and slapped the fire out of him." This led to an assault charge, for which Bell received a thirty-day suspended sentence. In the breaking and entering into an elementary school in Washington, for which he got his ten-year sentence, Bell's actions were more antisocial than greedy. "It fit the pattern with Terry," Grist said. "He broke a window and kicked in a door—things that were just destructive, that he didn't have to do, and had nothing to do with the theft."

On July 23, 1974, Terry Bell was convicted of breaking and entering, which canceled his suspended ten-year sentence on a 1973 breaking-and-entering conviction, as well as the suspended sentences for previous assault and trespass charges.

"He's a cute little boy," a clerk in the Beaufort County Courthouse said as she looked up his criminal record, "but he sure is ornery."

On his first night in the Beaufort County jail, Alligood locked Bell up in the cell, but Alligood would not do so again until the night of August 26. There is great latitude within the North Carolina jail system on the treatment of "trusties." No regulations govern their freedoms within the jail, and Terry Bell began a very special relationship with Clarence Alligood: Alligood, unlike nearly everyone else in Bell's life, was nice to him. The jailer gave him the freedom of the corridors, brought him sandwiches, talked to him a great deal. "He was almost like a father to me," Bell said, but those who knew about Bell were to speculate often that the relationship might have been far deeper than paternal.

Bell's duties in the jail were routine and minimal. When Alligood came on duty at night, Terry Bell would mop and buff the floor. During the day, he would take Joan Little her food, slipping it through an opening in the bars, and leaving without a word.

William Griffin had called Bell a "very prejudiced person," and Griffin never used that description unless he had overwhelming evidence of it.

On the night of August 26, when Alligood came on duty, the topic of conversation with Bell turned to sex. Bell teased Alligood about "not being able to get it up," and the jailer told the boy that "he knew where he could get him some." This Bell told to Jerry Paul and Morris Dees, of the Joan Little defense, and put the conversation in an affidavit. The information was also on a tape of a conversation between Jerry Paul and Terry Bell, although Morris Dees had pulled a so-called Rosemary Woods trick by accidentally erasing part of the tape.

Of the principals in the case, only Golden Frinks would express the theory that others hinted at, both prosecution and defense. "Just picture a man in close contact with Joan Little for over seventy-five nights," Frinks mused, "seated in front of a television monitor, watching this brown-framed body of a very young girl of twenty years. His eyes constantly fastened on this body, his passion was raised to alarming proportions.

"Terry Bell became the cover-up of the cover-up. If they'd have let Terry Bell testify, he would have told it all. He would have told how he was a homosexual, and how Alligood was part of the setup, how they had a little old crazy thing going when they had a drink or two down there. Alligood had the potential for this. How all of them down there were using Joan, getting 'em a little pom-pom, except Alligood.

"Terry Bell did not crawl across there to see all this happen *by accident*, because Terry Bell was in on the whole thing. He saw the whole thing, and when he told it, someone said to him,

" 'You damn fool, if you tell that, you'll be involved, and you'll involve all the rest of us.'

"Alligood probably said to Terry Bell,

" 'Just watch me, I'm gonna make her give me some,' and he had Bell crawl up in the rafters. The jailer got the icepick, probably said to Bell,

" 'Watch me. I'm gonna scare that little nigger gal to death.'

"And when it turned on Alligood, Bell thought, 'Oh, my God, I didn't know this was gonna happen,' and he went down and cleaned up the cell! Threw away parts of the evidence!

"Mrs. Williams, Joan's mother, knew about Terry Bell from the beginning. She said, 'I know something I ain't gonna tell Golden Frinks *or* Jerry Paul.' The problem for us was that the Terry Bell story came too late."

Terry Bell's "confession" did not come to the attention of the defense until July 1, 1975, only two weeks before Joan Little's trial was set to begin. Jerry Paul sought out William Griffin in Wilmington, North Carolina, and they talked for three hours. Paul's reason for seeing Griffin was that he had the results of John E. Reid's polygraph examination of Joan Little, taken in Chicago on June 27 and June 30, 1975.

Joan Little had not been an easy subject for Reid. She came to Chicago with two defense attorneys, Karen Galloway and Marvin Miller, and it was clear to Reid that she deeply resented her trip. Her attitude was "poor," Reid said. She had a "bitter" expression on her face, and "she looked at me as if I were Alligood." So Reid told the attorneys that there was no point in the test unless she relaxed. So the lawyers took her out to lunch and talked to her. When they returned, Joan Little "cooperated to a certain extent," and the examination was administered: fifteen questions, four irrelevant "known-truth" questions, four control, or "cheat-and-steal" questions, and seven questions pertinent to the crime.

Relevant Issue Questions

1. Did you take that ice pick from the jailer's office? Answer: No. (Truthful)
2. On August 27, 1974, did you offer to have sex with Clarence Alligood? Answer: No. (Truthful)
3. Did you plan to escape when you talked to Mrs. Eubanks at 10:00 P.M. on August 26, 1974? Answer: No. (Truthful)
4. Did you plan to attack Alligood with the ice pick before he came into your cell on August 26, 1974? Answer: No. (Indefinite)
5. Did Alligood force you to have sex against your will? Answer: Yes. (Truthful)
6. On August 27, 1974, before Alligood came to your cell, did you plan to stab him with the ice pick? Answer: No. (Truthful)
7. Did Alligood bring that ice pick to your jail cell on August 27, 1974? Answer: Yes. (Indefinite)

Control Questions

1. Besides Kool-Aid and a small amount of gasoline, did you ever cheat anyone out of anything else? Answer: No.
2. Did you withhold any information from anyone about this case? Answer: No.
3. Besides what you told about, did you ever willingly take part in an unnatural sex act? Answer: No.
4. Besides Alligood, did you ever try to physically harm anyone else in your life? Answer: No.

Irrelevant Questions

1. Do they call you Joan? Answer: Yes.
2. Are you over 18 years old? Answer: Yes.

3. Are you in Chicago right now? Answer: Yes.
4. Did you ever go to school? Answer: Yes.

But Reid was still dissatisfied and asked that Little be brought back after the weekend, so he could doublecheck his results. When they returned on Monday, June 30, Joan Little this time was exhausted. She had been on the rally circuit all weekend, and Reid patiently advised the attorneys to get a hotel room and let her sleep for a while, because an exhausted subject was just as bad as a bitter one. She returned hours later. Reid checked his findings and then wrote to Jerry Paul:

"There are no indications in this subject's polygraph records that she brought the fatal weapon, the icepick, to her cell on August 27 before Guard Alligood arrived, and there are no indications in this subject's records that she planned to stab Guard Alligood with the icepick before he arrived in her cell. There *are* indications that Guard Alligood did force his sexual attentions upon Joan Little against her will. Furthermore, there are no indications that she had planned to escape prior to the time that Guard Alligood entered her cell."

Paul's intention on July 1, of course, was to persuade Griffin to dismiss the charges against Joan Little on the strength of the Reid polygraph. Griffin, in fact, had offered twice, once in November in Chapel Hill and again in April at the preliminary hearing, to drop the charges if Joan Little would submit to *his* polygraph examination, but in November Paul refused the offer and in April did not respond to the renewed offer, and so there never was an agreement. On July 1, the lawyers went around and around about the difference between an *offer* and an *agreement,* and whose polygraph, if any, was valid. This dispute was to surface in the first week of trial in the shape of a formal motion to dismiss for the prosecution's "failure to abide by its agreement"—a motion denied by Judge Hamilton Hobgood.

In his answer to the defense motion, stating that he knew nothing about the questions asked the defendant or the conditions of the Reid test, Griffin wrote:

"The fear of being found untruthful is one of the most important bases for the effectiveness of the polygraph, and this factor is absent in an *ex parte* polygraph examination where such fear may be diminished."

The same objections might certainly have been leveled against the polygraph of his star witness, Terry Bell.

Two hours into the July 1 negotiation, Paul said to Griffin, "Billy, I'm going to trust you. You've got Terry Bell. Now I think this guy's crazy, but I think there's something to Terry Bell having seen what happened."

Paul's hunch was based on his discussion with Bell six months earlier. In that interview, Bell had been talkative, had told of cleaning up Joan Little's cell after the killing, and in an unguarded moment, spoke of blood squirting from Alligood's head onto the wall, as he fell across the bunk. Bell had actually demonstrated to Paul how Alligood fell on the bunk and described a position in which the body ended up in a position different from the one in which it was found by the authorities. How could Bell have known this if he had not seen something?

"What if I told you that Terry Bell *had* said that he'd seen the incident?" the district attorney replied, and proceeded to tell Paul the whole story, including the fact that Bell had shown up as a liar on the state's lie-detector test.

In the days that followed, Paul sought to get Terry Bell under the scrutiny of his experts in interrogation.

He motioned the court for permission to take Bell to
Chicago for a Reid polygraph, but permission was
denied. He also went to Washington, and in Red
Davis's office, alone with Terry Bell, Paul implied that
if Bell testified, the defense lawyer would pin the rap
on the boy. *Implied* is the operative word, because
Paul knew by this time that Bell was dangerous, and
if the lawyer had said such a thing outright, he was
likely to hear his words right back if Bell took the
stand.

To Paul's threat, implied or actual, Bell replied,
"Try it and see how it looks," and then told Paul to
go to hell.

While William Griffin did what he could to prevent
Bell from coming under the control of the defense, the
confusion over the possible eyewitness led to yet another request for a delay in the trial, already continued in November, in January, and in April. The
request this time, although never formalized in a motion to the court, came from Griffin, but the mood
among the judges by now was passionately against any
continuation of the agony for the State of North Carolina, and it had nothing to do with legalities. "Get
rid of it. Justice be damned. Who cares about determining the guilt or innocence of Joan Little? Get shed
of it!" was the mood as Griffin described it.

And it was at this point that Griffin's request
elicited the comment from Susie Sharp, the Chief Justice of the North Carolina Supreme Court,

"Mr. Griffin, this albatross around the neck of
North Carolina must be removed. This case must be
tried."

The sentiments were echoed by Judge Hamilton
Hobgood, by then designated as the trial judge for the
case.

"I am not going to allow a postponement if it is
humanly possible to avoid it," he said. "The only

thing that could force a postponement would be the inability of Joan Little, myself, the chief defense attorney, or the chief district attorney to attend."

The guilt or innocence of Joan Little was paling fast in relation to the priority of getting the trial over as fast as possible. The Terry Bell piece, Paul would argue later, was an important way in which "the truth got lost amid the games-playing," but the blocking of Terry Bell as a witness against Joan Little was a move in his client's favor, and before the furor subsided, Paul would appear as the biggest games-player of them all.

In the week before the trial, Terry Bell was moved to the Polk Youth Center in Raleigh. The transfer infuriated John Wilkinson, who by this time was the prosecution's guardian for Bell, for it brought a new danger to the star witness.

"I felt that he should have been kept in Washington and allowed to talk when he was ready to talk," Wilkinson said. Immediately before the trial, accompanied by an SBI agent, Wilkinson went to Polk Youth Center to talk with Bell.

"It took us a half hour to get him," Wilkinson said, "and catcalls for Terry Bell went all over the prison. Terry Bell! Terry Bell! You could hear the shrill name bouncing off the walls. By that time the trial was conceived as a racial issue, and when we sat down with him he said it was as much as his life was worth to say anything. There wasn't but one way to interpret that: he was in danger from other inmates, and he said as much.

"There wasn't any danger for you before," the SBI man protested. "You said that earlier."

"Yes," Bell replied, "but it's changed now."

With the prosecution and the defense "ringing him out," as Red Davis put it, a strange protector for Bell emerged. All parties in the case—defense, prose-

cution, and Judge Hamilton Hobgood—began to receive letters from one Clifton E. Whitt, an eighteen-
year-old inmate, pleading for the safety of Terry Bell
in prison, claiming that his life was in jeopardy. Both
Jerry Paul and an SBI agent would interview Whitt;
and on the evidence of the interviews, the letters, and
further letters between the teen-agers in the possession
of Bell's lawyer, Ed Rodman, both sides concluded
that Whitt was Bell's lover in prison. Whitt was
physically bigger and a little older than Bell, and it
was within Bell's character that he always needed
someone to advise him. Paul surmised from his talk
with Whitt that the eighteen-year-old was working out
"scenarios" for his intimate, so that Terry Bell would
not have to take the stand.

"With criminals," Paul said, "it's like playing with
a Doberman pinscher. If you're going to do it, you'd
better wear gloves, because they can be vicious. Somebody's always trading something. Everybody's got an
interest, and trades are the common way of dealing."

But the threat to Bell could not be minimized, and
later the teen-ager would outline the dimensions of it
to the author.

"The blacks were talking to me all the time. They'd
say, 'It'd be best if you didn't testify. You do, 'n' come
back here, 'n' somebody's just liable to cut your
throat.'

"I had two fights with blacks in the prison yard.
One told me what I'd better not do, and I hit him. A
group of whites started to gather around to protect
me. I was well known, had loaned money out to people when they needed help, and they said in return, if
it came to the point where I needed help, they would
protect me.

"The blacks wanted to start a riot out there over
the case. There's a field out there at Polk Youth Center. The whites gathered in one corner, and the blacks

in the other, and when that happens out there, you know something's going to happen. It stayed that way for quite a while, until news came that she had beat it. Afterwards, blacks came up to me, said,
" 'It's a good thing you didn't testify.' "
On July 14, 1975, the opening day of the trial, in a copyrighted story for *Newsday*, the author revealed the existence of Terry Bell. In the story, Red Davis confirmed Bell's importance to the case, and said that while what the trusty saw that night was mysterious, "he told things about that night that he could not have known unless he saw something."

Throughout the six weeks of the Joan Little trial, an appearance by Terry Bell on the stand lingered as an expected dramatic moment. He was named high on the witness list released to the press, and how could the boy fail to appear? He was the only other witness to the events of that night—if not to the killing itself, at least to Joan Little's access to the icepick and, equally important, to Clarence Alligood's state of mind on the night of the crime. But as the state closed its flimsy case without calling him and Joan Little withstood her cross-examination, it became clear that the courtroom was not always the best place for all elements of a criminal event to be explored. For within the forum of the law, Terry Bell had become too dangerous for both the prosecution and the defense. Had the state called him, the defense would have impeached him as a "boy without conscience," would have suggested that for some psychotic reason Bell himself had finished Alligood off, perhaps as a shark goes berserk at the smell of blood, for Joan Little consistently maintained that Alligood's body had more puncture wounds than she remembered giving it. They would have played the tape of Paul's talk with Bell, in which the boy admitted kidding Alligood that

night about not being able "to get it up," and would
have portrayed Bell as a psychopath and a peeping
Tom and probably a homosexual, crawling in the
rafters like any voyeur that night, and maybe even
part of Alligood's scheme. So the certainties of what
the defense would do on cross-examination to impeach
the star witness outweighed the prosecution's need to
have Bell testify about her access to the weapon. So
Terry Bell had "ruined himself."

"We would have lost for sure, if we had put him
up," Griffin said.

The defense, on the other hand, was not concerned
with telling the complete story of that night. This was
not staged entirely for the entertainment of the masses
—Joan Little's acquittal had to be secured—and as
much as Jerry Paul would protest that all he was concerned with was the truth, his training dictated otherwise. Once the defense team concluded that Terry
Bell could not hurt them *legally*, they lost interest in
him. Terry Bell had to be left to literature.

In the winter of 1975 the author went to see him at
the Goldsboro Youth Center. He has the look and
bearing of a bantam Irish fighter of the 1930s (though
John Wilkinson would say that there were no Irish in
Beaufort County), short, perhaps 5′4″, clear blue eyes,
a diminutive tuberous nose that would be hard to
break in a fight, shoulder-length blond hair parted in
the middle, with well-attended curls, even though he
arrived for the talk from the milk barn in a CAT hat
and knee-length barnyard boots. His mumbly speech
is hard to understand, even for one used to Southern
mumbles, and it is contentious.

"I ain't got nothin' to say about it."

They went round and about on that note for quite
a while, until Bell finally allowed that Alligood was
"the best one they had in that jail," and then out of
nowhere,

"If I were out on the street now, she wouldn't be alive."

It was this passion—hate for Joan, love for Alligood —that campassed the mystery. He had been in that jail only a month before Alligood was killed. Were Alligood's kindnesses—a sandwich here and there, the laxity of rules, the talks—enough to fire this kind of sullen passion? There was more. His actions spoke for themselves: he had been ready to go to jail for the rest of his life if only he could convict Joan Little.

"I knew Clarence Alligood well enough," he said. "He wouldn't do such a thing as that. If anybody would have been back there screwing her, it should have been me. I had the keys. I could have gone back there anytime. She was attractive enough. Why not?

"That she was black didn't faze me. I grew up around blacks, was raised with 'em. She killed him. That was the point."

How then could Alligood have ended up in such a state?

"She played sick. That's the only way I know of that he could have gone back there."

Then he told the ostensible Terry Bell story, the one that the defense and the prosecution had come to believe, but not the author—not entirely: that Terry Bell, alone, brooding through the year of Joan Little, had written a counterscript. The part about the access to the icepick seemed solid enough: Joan Little on the phone at ten-thirty, a half-hour after Alligood came on duty . . . Peachey coming in from patrol in the county to use the toilet, and cautioning Alligood about letting prisoners use the phone—it was against the sheriff's orders . . . another deputy sheriff, Robert Jackson, coming in, saying to Joan, "How can you get so tan in here without the sun?" . . . Terry Bell sitting on a stool, drinking a Pepsi, noticing that the jailer's desk drawer was cracked open three or four inches, and, in view, two cans of shoe polish, some papers, and an icepick—noticing this before Alligood told him to hurry up and finish his drink . . . how they left her alone in the office, still on the telephone, went back to his cell and talked for five minutes (about sex?) before Alligood locked him in his cell for only the second time since Terry had been there . . . how Alligood came back a few minutes later and bummed a few cigarettes and a light for Joan . . . and the next thing he remembered was being awakened by Peachey five hours later with the news . . . how they told him to clean up the cell after the body had been taken away, and how he did so, slowly, deliberately, noting the placement of everything (the cell was "spit-polish clean" when assistant prosecutor Sam Grimes arrived there later in the morning) . . . how he played detective.

"I was looking for clues, and I found several fingerprints on the bars, and several spots of blood that they hadn't seen. And then, I got outside and went looking for her, found several footprints in a sandpile over by the Seaboard Savings and Loan. This was as daylight was breaking."

. . . How back in the ID room in the sheriff's office he had seen the pictures of Alligood's body hanging up to dry and how he studied them . . . and how two weeks later he was transferred away to a youth camp.

Then the germination of the counterscript.

"Around January [1975] I saw that the rate she and Jerry Paul were going, she was going to get out of it. Everybody was saying so. The more I thought about it, the madder I got. People would say to me that this or that happened, and I would say, naw, that's not how it was. You weren't there, and I was.

"I began to make notes, drew a map of the cell and put all the pieces of evidence in it, made a sketch of how the body was found. And then the idea of the rafters occurred to me. I'd been up there three or four times, changing the light bulbs, and had crawled over to the women's section and looked down. My finger-prints would be up there. I just thought about it and wrote my notes about it for six months, till I got where everything sounded right to me, and then I sprung it on 'em in June."

He had sprung it on Red Davis on the night of June 12, 1975, and Davis had said, "That sounds good to me, but Jerry Paul and them are hard to convince, so I got to test it on a lie detector." Davis had asked him that night if he'd ever had sex with Joan Little, and he said no.

"When Red Davis asked me to take the test, I said, 'Can't hurt anything to take it. It ain't legal to begin with.' So I answered Yeah to all the questions the next day" (including whether he'd had sex with Joan Lit-tle), "and it didn't bother me a bit."

The test took place in the Washington office of his then appointed lawyer, Ed Rodman, and was only a part of an intense two days of interrogation there. The interrogation was taped and remains as "highly privileged" material in Rodman's possession. When the wires and electrical currents of the polygraph con-cluded that Bell was being "deceptive," the subject was confronted with the results, and he broke down in tears. He had made it all up, he said, because he hated Joan Little so much.

"I was ready to go down the drain with her, just to get her convicted. Still I figured they would believe her before they believed me. I wanted to testify for the state, but if I couldn't convict her, I wanted to screw everybody up." And with a smile, "Man's got his ways," he said philosophically.

With this admission of a "fraudulent" counter-script, Rodman, chairman of the State Bar Associa-tion's Ethics Committee, advised his client to destroy all his notes regarding the evidence in Joan Little's cell, and Terry Bell did so under the gaze of his lawyer. It would be a sore point later for Rodman, for had Terry Bell ever taken the stand, Rodman would have been required under an order by Judge McKinnon to turn over all substantive evidence to the defense, and the destruction of evidence is not considered ethical. It would be the court's prerogative, not Rodman's, to judge whether evidence is fraudulent or not.

The author would have believed the counterscript explanation entirely, had it not been for a telephone conversation with attorney Rodman late in 1975. The lawyer had been protective of any substantive information on the Terry Bell mystery. He considered it all "highly privileged." The author had appealed to his high purpose on the basis of simply setting the record straight. In frustration at the end of the conversation, the author had said,

"Well, Mr. Rodman, I'm going to have to write a chapter on Terry Bell anyway."

"You write what you have to write," the lawyer replied. "It will probably make sensational journalism. But don't write something that will send a young boy to his death."

"I don't have anything in my possession that would do that," the author said in astonishment.

"Well, I do," Rodman replied, and hung up.

CHAPTER 11

RICHARD WOLF

A trial is a magnificent art form. It has the best elements of drama: passionate adversaries, the issue of blame to be resolved, surprise, acting and overacting, comic relief, competing strategies and tactics, ploys, feints, subplots, and a captive audience—the important audience of twelve with four substitutes waiting to rush into the fray. All this was drawn in the extreme in the Joan Little trial, with the rare addition that the chief defense attorney didn't really believe in the jury system at all. The only thing the trial lacked was an appropriate courtroom. The brand new Wake County Courthouse would never do. Its sterile, fake-wood paneling behind the judge, the washable synthetic-burlap wallpaper, the harsh fluorescent lighting, and air conditioning should have been scrapped for nostalgia's sake: whirling fan overhead, open windows allowing the heavy July heat to press down on a leathery audience, the judge framed between two globe lights on poles, and the adversaries, coats off, rolled-up sleeves, sweat staining the backs of their shirts, delineated by wide galluses, cooling themselves with corn-husk fans. It is no accident that a trial is the climax of so many stage productions, movies, and novels.

On the eve of the trial Jerry Paul wrote an open letter to all who had helped in the Joan Little Defense. It was an expression of thanks to some thirty-

nine people who formed the nucleus of his entourage,
but by no means encompassed it: lawyers, psychologists, security men, publicity agents, spiritual advisers,
the defendant, doctors, a literary agent, and movement activists, even those who opposed him:

> "Golden Frinks is the hardest one of all for
> me," the letter read. "I felt as though I'd lost a
> father when he opposed me. It was me he was
> against, not the fund for Joan Little. He did
> some good, and we must recognize this. Also had
> it not been for the battles he fought long ago, we
> would not be here today. Over him, I have cried
> much and been hurt much. But I could not let
> my personal feeling harm Joan and others. I hope
> someday I can show Golden that despite what has
> happened, I can and will still stand behind him."

Paul also made mention of his 13 year old son,
David, who, a month after the trial, would have a
relapse of his leukemia.

> "David Paul is a kid who faces death each day
> and wants his father home. He has been able with
> courage to put this aside because in his own way
> he believed in what we were doing."

This was apt, for the Defense in many ways bore the
character of a children's crusade. The minions included black radicals and hippies, feminists and spir-
itualists, and, as is their wont, children often fight.

> "My background," Paul wrote his troops, "is basi-
> cally that of a football player and coach, and that
> knowledge is what I have used to set up the struc-
> ture. A head coach has assistants who are respon-
> sible for carrying out duties necessary to win

games. The players carry out what they have been taught. . . . Many times I have acted on the spur of the moment, because often I did not know what to do until something ripened. At my age, I often felt inadequate to make certain decisions, but as a head coach must do, decisions must be made—right or wrong—and I accept that responsibility. If I did not have the guts to do this, then I have no business being here. Often I have been scared, and lost and had to check out my own nerve and wanted to throw in the towel. But somehow, because of others, I did not.

"I realized long ago that this was out of my hands, and God or whatever you might call Him was using all of us for a purpose. Too many things have worked out right, when I stumbled, for there not to be other forces at work."

But just as Paul could be sentimental, he could be curt: "If you have any difficulty with my instructions, say so now and pack your bags."

The gamesmanship of it all did not escape the prosecution either. After it was over, William Griffin would say sourly,

"The rules of the game have become more important than the game itself."

The first two weeks of the six-week match were consumed with jury selection. It was easy enough to elicit a contemptuous remark from William Griffin about the methods of the defense in picking the jury. He lapsed easily into characterizations of "farce," a theatrical term, or "charade," an acting term, or this "hokum of scientific jury selection," or "this garbage of using a psychic and all that junk." But it was somewhat more difficult to get a description of his own model jury. His shorthand was always "honest, decent people," but that was vague. Griffin elaborated, but only slightly: a person who worked at a job for a long time, family, children in school, no difficulty with the law, churchgoer—implicitly a male model. Once, however, he slipped into specifics.

"If only we could have gotten one strong juror on that panel—like that Sunday-school teacher who worked for IBM. Now that's the kind of person the state wants on there."

The extent of the state's preparation for jury selection had been a letter sent out to acquaintances around Wake County by Lester Chalmers, the assistant prosecutor provided Griffin by the state attorney general. Chalmers had once been district attorney in the county, and he knew bondsmen and insurance people well enough to ask them to review the jury summons list of three hundred county citizens. But, judging from Chalmers's performance, his probing did not go beyond whether those on the list were of the honest-decent-people standard. In any event, Chalmers's effort did result in a system of zeros, *x*'s, and question marks, but for all the state's griping about the defense's "pseudo-science," most of the blacks finally seated on the Joan Little jury had a zero, meaning good, beside their names on the prosecution list. There were just too many of that type of honest-decent people, that's all.

In conversation about jury selection, an overpowering lawyer's blindness emerged in Griffin. One of the prime reasons for going to trial on the charge of first-degree murder, Griffin felt, was that on a first-degree charge the state had nine peremptory challenges, the defense fourteen, whereas if the charge had been second degree murder, the state would have only four challenges and the defense six.

"With only four challenges, you've got to accept just about anybody who's put up there," Griffin said.

So, on the weakness of this legal punctilio, the public, for seven long months, was allowed to imagine Joan Little being gassed in the death chamber. Griffin never understood that the Joan Little case had long since traveled beyond legalities, that the courtroom was simply the stage for a far broader spectacle in which only lawyer-publicists belonged, and that the horror of the audience outside, stretching now beyond state and national boundaries, was sustained as much by the danger to Joan Little's life as anything. Had Griffin acceded to reducing the charge to second-degree murder or manslaughter back in November, the nation would never have heard of Joan Little and the case would have been handled "the country way" from start to finish. Remember the first line of the Julian Bond promotional letter:

"Twenty-year-old Joan Little may be put to death because she defended herself against the jail guard who tried to rape her."

Would the letter have raised $350,000 if the opening line had been:

"Twenty-year-old Joan Little may get five years for manslaughter because the state says she used excessive force in stabbing a jailer in the heart with an icepick when he tried to rape her."

And so, when Julian Bond would be asked during the trial if this whole show was not "artificially produced," the answer had to be that the state was just as much responsible for any artificiality as the defense.

As the veniremen began to take the stand, the prosecution evinced its greatest interest in the attitude toward capital punishment. Griffin later would be "disgusted" at the judge's allowing the defense to "rehabilitate" potential jurors who had expressed reservations about the death penalty. The question of whether the veniremen would execute Adolf Hitler or the killer of small children Griffin found "way out of bounds."

What then was in bounds? Lester Chalmers, who once had defended the Grand Dragon of the Klan before HUAC, became the high priest of the country way, with his high-pitched voice and convoluted sentences. He insisted on assaulting reservations over the death penalty this way:

"If the judge told you that you were to consider this case solely on the facts, and not consider punishment, could you disabuse your mind of the idea that a conviction on first degree would result in the death sentence?"

Broken down by a linguistic analyst cum playwright, the script might read:

Degenerate Witness: Don't want nothin' on my conscience about the death penalty.

THE STATE [thinking that to oppose the death penalty is an abuse of the mind]: Can you disabuse your mind of the abuse?

Rehabilitated Witness: Yes.

THE STATE: Certified death-qualified.

Defense: What if you had three killers of children, including your own children, one killer is caught, and by a guilty verdict and a sentence of death, the killing of more children could be averted, would you support the death sentence?

Recidivous Witness: Yes.

THE COURT: Is it your irrevocable belief that you could not and would not return a verdict of guilty under any circumstances, if that guilty verdict would mean that it was the duty of the state to pronounce the death penalty?

Buffaloed Witness: [Inaudible.]

As for the serious question of mental abuse and disabuse, a defense sociologist, Dr. Robin Williams, had been asked at the preliminary hearing if it were possible for a person to remove prejudices from his mind when he entered the jury room.

"When a person is clearly aware of his prejudices and strongly motivated to overcome them," Dr. Williams replied, "he can be successful in controlling them and not letting them affect his judgment. But many presuppositions and prejudices we are not aware of and therefore cannot control, no matter how sincere or highly motivated we are. . . . This would be equivalent to asking a person to wipe out of his mind unconscious feelings, and this is literally impossible. . . . I am sixty years old now, and I think I was forty-five at least before I understood how limited I was in being able to know what my own prejudices and biases were."

If the venireman survived his death-qualification test (and he or she did so entirely by the whim of the judge, for there never was a coherent answer to the judge's Witherspoon question that hadn't been contradicted earlier), the poor soul faced the defense platoon: five lawyers, three social psychologists, three statisticians, a body-language expert, and Richard Wolf, a psychic, or "a sensitive," as he preferred to be called. It must have been traumatic for the witness in the box when, after the interrogation, the platoon huddled around the defense table and whispered, before their decision was announced.

Considerable expertise went into those discussions in the huddle.

Step 1: A month before the trial, Courtney Mullin directed a telephone survey of nine hundred Wake County citizens, using the same questions as had been asked during the surveys of Eastern counties. The important conclusion from the survey was that, contrary to what one Yankee psychologist on the team expected, there was considerable open-mindedness and even liberalism in the Wake County jury pool. The results were computerized, and with a computer technique called "Automatic Interaction Detection," or AID for short, the Wake County population had been separated into population subgroupings. Within AID, the "dependent variable" combined rape attitudes with views on guilt or innocence, and helped devise a "scale of favorability" toward Joan Little.

Step 2: The defense persuaded the judge to allow a questionnaire to be mailed out with the summonses to the three hundred potential jurors for the case. The three hundred were required to answer under the command of the law. These questionnaires were analyzed, and the veniremen rated preliminarily. The conclusion of the experts from Step 2 was KEEP SLOTS OPEN. BE PATIENT. THERE ARE GOOD PEOPLE COMING UP.

Step 3: When the venireman actually took the stand, the experts judged whether the person was acting as his profile suggested. The experts, except Richard Wolf, kept a score sheet, with age, race, and sex, realities that a witness could not lie about, assigned high numerical value. Then, to determine attitudes, the lawyers asked a series of questions, looking particularly for "authoritarianism." The expert there was Richard Christie, a Columbia psychologist, whose research into the authoritarian personality dates back to the 1940s, and whose testing of a "recipe for a jury" began with the Berrigan trial.

It was the view of the psychologists that the inclination to believe authority, not only in the South, but nationally, was extremely strong. The phenomenon was referred to as "prosecution orientation," and in the Joan Little preliminary hearing Stanley Milgram's *Obedience to Authority* was cited as proof. Milgram had run an experiment in which a subject was put in a glass booth, with wires running from his fingers to a black box outside. On the box there was a lever and markings of 100 volts, 200 volts, 300 volts, and a red line, above which was written "Danger, XXX Do not go beyond here." In fact, no electrical shock whatever was delivered by the black box. A wide range of people, including professionals of different kinds, were brought in as experimenters, and told to shock the subject every time he made a mistake. In one case a businessman had the lever up to 300 volts with a bumbling subject, whereupon the subject started hammering on the glass, shouting,

"I have a heart condition. Don't go any further."

"Do I have to go on?" the businessman asked Milgram.

"The experiment must proceed," was the answer, and the examiner pushed the lever into the danger zone. This happened repeatedly.

So to test for authoritarianism and prejudice, the Joan Little veniremen were asked questions like these:

- Are respect for the law and obedience the highest virtues children should be taught?
- Does it bother you that male jailers have custody of women prisoners?
- Do you think women are occasionally taken advantage of in jails?
- Do you feel property values go down if blacks move into a neighborhood?
- Do you think blacks on welfare could get along without it if they tried?
- Are you the kind of person who makes up her mind fairly early about things?
- Do you think men make better decisions generally than women?
- If you were on a jury that acquitted Joan Little, would you be embarrassed to go back to your neighborhood or to your job?
- What do you think about interracial marriage?
- Have you ever been locked in a closet and couldn't get out?

As the answers came, the platoon rated the witness on the score sheet and passed their judgments down to the statistician, who punched away on his pocket calculator. At the end, Jerry Paul might look around to the statistician for a judgment and might receive back the whispered enjoinder, "Need religion." Meanwhile, the body-language specialist would notice a slouching or ramrod posture, the set of the jaw, the verbal tone of the response as opposed to its content, arms folded tightly across the chest (especially important with women) or open and gesticulating, the eyes in relation to the questioners: white males often looked sideways and suspiciously at the defense during the examination, whereas blacks looked everywhere in the courtroom except at the prosecution during the capital-punishment interrogation. (The author always made a point of slouching as much as he could when he talked with the body-language man in the halls during the breaks.)

This was all well and good, but Richard Wolf, the sensitive, could cut through all of that. In the face of clairsentience, clairaudience, and clairvoyance, what defenses can stand? Wolf called his process the "science of perception" and described his role as "people watcher."

"I work within a scientific process," he said. "That is not to say that my vision is always right. What I see is right, but I sometimes miss in how that fits into the legal deliberations. You see, the body is an armor. With my awareness of people, I feel them. I see pictures coming off them. In a couple of minutes, I can usually give an opinion of whether this person is useful or not."

What were some of the pictures the sensitive received during jury selection? With a deep sigh, a long pause, head in hands, Wolf tried for a rerun.

Middle-aged woman: "I saw that she was unhappy at home, dissatisfied with her sex life. She had a husband, but the husband was not coming through. Now Alligood was sixty-two—her husband is younger than that, and he isn't even getting it on. So I saw the woman thinking: if my husband isn't even getting it on at his age, how could Alligood . . . and her being a bad girl . . . there's only one way the thing could have happened. For her to recognize Alligood as an ogre is to acknowledge there's something wrong with her life and her husband, and she had a subconscious wish to reject that information."

Marcia Pearce (eventually chosen; a thirty-two-year-old woman, a fundamentalist): "The profile of her indicated that she wouldn't be the best type to have on the panel. But I could tell that she had been through a tremendous amount of pain and sorrow in her life, and thought she might have a certain hostility toward males."

(When Pearce was asked if she thought respect for the law and discipline were the highest virtues a parent could teach her children, she had broken down in sobs, declaring, no, "love and salvation" were the most important.)

White man: "He was clean, well-dressed, but I saw a picture of him with other dirty men behind him. They were saying, 'Let's get the niggers.' I heard the words."

Wolf normally sat at the end of the defense platoon on the bench within the bar, farthest from the defense lawyers' table, and nearly beside the prosecution. As the veniremen passed across his screen, Wolf would write notes to Jerry Paul (why couldn't he telepath them?).

- On a woman wearing a red coat: "She's playing the Little Red Riding Hood game. Here we go again"—an odd note for a sensitive called Wolf.
- "This man frequents prostitutes."

- "Small exec trying to climb, wants to be on, so he can tell his friends."
- "Bullshit dude."

This provided some distraction to the social scientists and statisticians, stiff anyway from the hard wood bench and long day, and as Wolf's notes would come down the line, each team member would latch onto them with glee, laugh, and poke the next colleague in the ribs. Wolf was not amused at this treatment of his clairvoyance, though he eschews hexes. Not that he took himself altogether seriously. He could laugh when a person would greet him, "Hey, Richard, what's happening in the stars today?"

Occasionally, as the sensitive admitted himself, his projector flashed up the wrong picture. Once, contrary to the psychologist's negative profile of a woman, Wolf argued strongly that he was feeling good vibrations, and that this woman would relate extremely well to Jerry Paul.

"We only had to ask her the first few questions, not even the subtle questions, for her to reveal her prejudice," the psychologist said. "Richard was quiet for a half hour after that."

July 15, 1974, brought the first explosion of the trial. Jerry Paul was examining a potential (and eventually chosen) juror, Jennie Lancaster, twenty-five, about what magazines she read when the judge sustained an objection to that line of questions. Lancaster was the twelfth person to be examined.

PAUL: There is no reason why we should be bound to the traditional way of picking the jury.
COURT: Probably isn't, but that's exactly what we're going to do as of this minute on.
PAUL: To do that denies us due process and denies us the opportunity to pick good jurors.

COURT: Do you want to put that in the record?

PAUL: We have developed a method of selecting the best jurors. For the court to ignore the advances made in social sciences and other sciences as an aid for selecting fair jurors is to return to a hundred years ago and makes absolutely no sense whatever.

COURT: . . . I want you to move to the court that you be allowed to continue as you have started. . . .

PAUL: That's what we're doing now.

COURT: Denied.

PAUL: Any questions the state asks they are allowed to ask. I think the court has shown bias in this case in favor of the state.

COURT: You can put that in the record.

PAUL: And isn't giving us a fair trial.

COURT: I'll let you put that in the record.

PAUL: Our questions are only phrased a little bit differently. The only difference is our questions are not traditional.

COURT: That's right. . . .

PAUL: The only reason I can see that your honor is now cutting us off is because we are gaining an advantage and your honor is favoring the state, and your honor is proceeding in such a manner to insure Joan Little's conviction.

COURT: All right, you got that in the record.

PAUL: At this point we ask your honor to recuse yourself because I don't think you are capable of giving Joan Little a fair trial, and I don't intend to sit here and see an innocent person go to jail for any reason, and you can threaten me with contempt, but it does not worry me.

COURT: You got that in the record.

PAUL: And to sit there and say like the Queen of Hearts—Off with their heads—because the law is the law—is to take us back a hundred years.

COURT: All right.

PAUL: . . . There has been one roadblock after another and one attempt after another to railroad Joan Little, and I'm tired of it.

The Queen of Hearts speech had a transparent air, as if Paul and the judge had rehearsed it backstage in advance. Another defense lawyer even called the speech "calculated" at the end of the day, and the calculation seemed to work, for thereafter the defense lawyers asked their nontraditional questions with impunity.

Lewis Carroll pictured the Queen of Hearts as "the embodiment of ungovernable passion—a blind and aimless Fury," and Judge Hobgood obviously did not think of himself in that light, so he sentenced Jerry Paul to two weeks in prison for contempt, to take effect at the end of the trial.

"They're dreadfully fond of beheading people here; the great wonder is that there's anyone left alive," Alice would think to herself in Wonderland, after she, at least, had escaped the fury of the Queen of Hearts.

Of the 300 citizens summoned to the voir dire, the defense judged that about ten percent were "excellent" in their terms, and as the days of jury selection wore on, the statisticians would calculate the percentage of their "excellents" yet to be examined. This gave the defense a sense of pace and controlled the temptation to accept a prospective juror who looked "pretty good." Meanwhile, the defense worked industriously to husband its peremptory challenges.

William Griffin was to say later that if a defense lawyer is patient enough, if "he wants to work on a man long enough, he can always find something that will get the person off." The defense lawyers were patient enough, and they used three questions effectively to strike "pretty good" jurors from the panel *for cause* rather than peremptorily. (Challenges for cause, of course, are unlimited.)

1. How would you vote right now on the guilt or innocence of Joan Little? Unless the juror answered with a swift and clear-toned "innocent!" the defense argued that the person did not understand the presumption of innocence in the law and should be struck. Judge Hobgood accepted many of these challenges, rather than explain the legal concept.

2. Would you trust the word of a policeman over an average citizen? This went directly to the evidence, as the state's case, such as it was, would be made by police officers; it also tested authoritarianism.

3. Would you expect Joan Little to take the stand? This addressed the state's responsibility to prove its case "beyond a reasonable doubt," and Joan Little had no responsibility to prove her innocence. Without a spontaneous understanding of that, the judge often excused rather than explain.

Suddenly, by the fourth day of jury selection, with four jurors selected out of sixteen, the defense had used only one of its fourteen peremptory challenges, and the prosecution had used four of its nine peremptory challenges—all against blacks, which, of course, the defense semaphored far and wide. At this point the prosecution gave up on the process. Griffin's complaints against "improper questions" and a growing tendency of the judge to excuse jurors on his own for (in Griffin's view) insufficient reason floated away unnoticed. Thereafter the three prosecutors took turns sitting in for the examination, their visages showing boredom, their objections halfhearted.

"We were in a corner and we couldn't get out of it," Griffin said. "It was senseless to stay in there and beat our brains out. In a real sense, Hobgood picked the Joan Little jury."

Still, the fact that the prosecution used all its peremptory challenges against blacks did not help its image and lent verisimilitude to the nostalgic charges of racism in the street rallies outside. Inside the courthouse, Jerry Paul chose Lester Chalmers, his easiest target, as the villain of the first week.

"He has shown an attitude of disrespect, contempt, and most affirmative racism toward black people during the trial," Paul told the TV cameras. He made a flamboyant request to Judge Hobgood to instruct Chalmers to be courteous to whites and blacks alike, but neither Hobgood nor Chalmers responded.

Jury selection lasted two weeks, and the usefulness of Richard Wolf was demonstrated in yet another way. During the preliminary hearing in Washington, the defense had been delighted that Wolf had drawn two Beaufort County sheriff's deputies to him as a tail, simply because he looked weird. Now, as the jury-selection process droned on and the national newspapermen had squeezed every inch of newsprint out of it, they turned to Richard Wolf as a "sidebar" to the trial, and thus gave the lawyers a needed breather. Wolf found no indignity in this.

"For me to have press coverage is not unusual," he said. "I knew it was an asset. There was a wonderful use of the media throughout the whole thing."

On July 25 the Joan Little jury was secured. It included five blacks, eight women, five people under thirty, two young women who worked at a vegetarian restaurant. Of the two young white males on the panel, one ran a stereo shop, the other was a lawyer who had been at Duke Law School with Karen Galloway, the defense lawyer. (Later, the juror, Paul Lassiter, would say privately that he was rooting for Galloway to do well in the trial, and she had.) The one juror who might have held traditional white values was a forty-eight-year-old white farmer's wife, but when she had been asked what she would do if a would-be rapist attacked her, she replied,

"I'd kill him just as dead as he stood there."

Anyway, she was excused midway in the trial, when a member of her family became ill. She was replaced by the first alternate, a twenty-two-year-old black male who had majored in black history at a predominately black community college. One of the jurors, the author learned, was a modest drug user, and it even happened that, mysteriously, the juror's supplier sat one day on the defense bench to reinforce natural inclinations.

Into the examination of alternate jurors, after the defense had exercised only its fifth of fourteen peremptory challenges, John Wilkinson rose wearily to say,

"Let the record show that the defense is using *its* preemptory challenges to excuse *whites*."

Suddenly all those virtues that the defense had touted from the beginning: having a cross-section of the community represented in the jury room, having the range of prejudices expressed in jury deliberations, removing presuppositions from the judgment of defendants, now could be turned around. One study cited by a defense witness in the preliminary hearing had been the conformity experiments of Solomon E. Asch. Asch had put long and short lines on display and instructed six of the seven subjects to give the wrong answer as to which was long and which short. The final subject was not instructed, and the uninstructed subject would generally agree with the majority, rather than the evidence of his own eyes.

Commenting on the Asch study, Dr. Robin Williams had said:

"The isolated and unsupported individual will be powerfully influenced by a majority judgment against him, and when asked after the experiment, 'Why on earth did you say that line is longer when it is clearly shorter?' the reply was, 'Well, everybody else said that and I began to mistrust my own judgment. I lost confidence in myself. I thought maybe there was something wrong with my eyesight.' "

But there would be no isolated and unsupported individual on the Joan Little jury, and William Griffin would say,

"Let me ask *you* one question: was the Joan Little jury a cross-section of the Wake County population?"

And yet, he had given up. He was in a corner and couldn't get out. But there was no reason why he could not have probed for hostility against whites by black witnesses, for sentimentality about feminist issues in female witnesses, for a *disinclination* to believe law enforcement officers when there was a conflict in testimony with an ordinary citizen—and thereby have an equally valid challenge for cause. He could have shown that liberal and feminist prejudices and presuppositions were just as strong as rascist ones.

There was no reason not to do this, except that Griffin's mind didn't work that way. The prosecution, trading in kind with the defense, could have paralyzed the system completely, but the spectacle of both sides pitting equally sophisticated social scientists and sensitives against one another would have to wait for another time and place. Griffin was the system incarnate. His reason for being there was, in his own terms, to uphold the dignity of the legal process and, short of that, to get this unpleasant business over and return to his garden patch.

Richard Wolf is unusual looking, to be sure: a long, almost horsy face, framed by hair, curled and hot-combed to his shoulders. His soft speech has a slight lisp to it, and when he is asked a thoughtful question he sighs; his head goes into his hands; his eyes close; and he pauses for some time, as marvelous guesses about what was flashing through his mind would occur to the author. When an amused twinkle crosses the corner of his eye, it is an enormous relief from his intensity.

Born in Detroit, he became interested in Eastern religions at seventeen and began to work with astrology. He had two years of psychology at Highland College, but considers himself self-taught. He was moved by the *Autobiography of a Yogi* and began to have experiences that made him aware that he had spiritual gifts, the gifts of dreams and visions, the perception of angelic forces, the judging of spirits. He cares about people, found that he could reach out to them and touch them "in [his] mind's eye."

He surveyed the panoply of wise men in world history and chose Jesus Christ as his teacher, but felt that there were many wise men in the world and there was no reason why one couldn't learn from them as well. So he synthesized Eastern concepts and techniques of meditation into his "religious system." He borrowed from the *Tao Te Ching* ("Tao is the water running down the mountain. Tao is the leaf falling in the wind.") and he wanted his life to go like the wind as well. He borrowed from Hinduism, seeing *devas*, or angels, in everything in the world, including the flame of a match. Everything in this world displaces energy. If one principle dominates this system, which covers all points on the mystical spectrum, it is Spaceship Earth: the Family of Man, one spirit, one consciousness, one mind.

"Oh, we may think in different styles and different forms, but we are all one, and each human being has a responsibility for the next human being, the common bond of man and the spirit of life."

Within each individual there are energy dynamics, he feels, and taken together, in the Family of Man, there are basic elemental forces at work. The energy in the individual can be positive—"I can look at a person and see his heart. It's shining. There's an

openness"—and the collective forces can be positive—
"I love North Carolina. There is an incredible
amount of light energy here, such beauty." But, in
turn, the energy can be terrifying—"I can see an In-
verse Pentacle on a person's forehead, the mark of
Satan"—and collectively, there are negative, base,
unhealthy forces, setting up the likelihood of destructive, violent earth changes to come.

Of all the energies that man possesses, his sexuality
is the strongest. It is creative energy itself, and spring-
ing from love and caring, it can have "life echoes" for
seventy or eighty years. But the misuse of that creative
energy, the making of sex into an object, is a death
process, unhealthy for the individual because of its
consequences for the astroculture of man. And so, as
intimately as Richard Wolf became involved in the
defense of Joan Little, he never lost his distance in
viewing the significance of the case in his mind's eye:

"They were trying Joan; they were trying Alligood;
they were trying North Carolina. People were pointing fingers, saying this is right and this is wrong, you
and you are bad. That is almost inexcusable. No man
is higher than the highest man. No man is lower than
the lowest man. The responsibility for the death of
Clarence Alligood, the death of any person in any
war, is in the whole consciousness of man, and every
single person in mankind is responsible.

"In the pornography of man's consciousness, in the
death throes, in the shit of man's consciousness, Alligood and Joan were just players."

The author had had an experience with the pornography of man's consciousness midway through the
trial. One day, the chief security officer at the courthouse handed him a letter, postmarked Philadelphia,
and addressed to him, simply "c/o Joan Little Trial,
Raleigh, N.C." Inside was an article of his, and across

the entire face of it was scrawled every putrid word imaginable in the English language, and some that the graffitist probably thought were dirty, like "panacea." A sampling was: "Filthy, sordid, bizarre murder by debauched prostitute. Nigger, whore, nympho, shit, slop, slime on the prowl. Keep the heat on the nigger-savage menace. This was planned, sordid, repugnant, pervert, degenerate bitch, cesspool slop by birth. 95% of crime, violence, debauchery, dope, VD, rape, illicit, shoplifters, muggers, copkillers, gangs, whores, etc. is *nigger*. Put one nigger in established, civilized, law and order locality and in 30 days or less you have a ghetto, slum of filthy stinking, destructive cesspool slope. . . . Destroy the nigger ravage menace . . ." and so it went.

Joan Little received about a dozen letters a day during the trial, and Richard Honeycutt, the administrator of the defense, always screened them for just this kind of trash.

One of the social scientists on the defense team, half-joking, had defined Wolf's functions as threshold: (1) he wrote the most interesting notes during jury selection; (2) he was a welcome diversion for the press; and (3) he gave the best backrub in the Western World. On the scale of significance, the third function, as house therapist and shaman, was the most important and not to be taken lightly. The defense team was a collection of diverse, opinionated individuals, all aware that this might be the high point of their lives and their careers, and Richard Wolf floated about the group as a mediator and a "people watcher." "I brought an aggravated person to an understanding of why other people were acting the way they were." But Wolf's solace was most important to Jerry Paul and Joan Little.

With Paul, tormented physically by old football

injuries, migraine headaches, and prostate problems, mentally by family problems, and professionally by the task of shepherding this case to a successful, splashy conclusion, Wolf was invaluable.

"I could see the pain in his eye alignment and in the muscular picture of his body," Wolf said. "The tensions and stresses were terrific, and I could stop him from having so much pain. If he was having a migraine, I would massage his head, and in the course of the trial I probably took him to the chiropractor eleven times. After a court day, we played games together. It was fun and interesting. If someone was bothering him, I'd say, 'Jerry, are *you* doing such and such . . . ?' and he would look at me and laugh and that helped him loosen things up. For me to just stand on the side of things was for him to know that I cared and was a support to him. Without me there, playing games, helping him to relax, making sure that his needs were taken care of, putting my love into the fountain of life, it would have been much more difficult."

With Joan Little, whose counterpose to her public stoicism was severe emotional outbursts behind the scenes, Wolf was the comfort.

"She could be very giving, and she could be very selfish and self-centered. She had qualities that some people would deem undesirable, and I helped her to understand both sides of her character. I did an astrological chart on her, which is an excellent psychological diagnostic tool, and points to potentiality, possibilities, and probabilities, and I told her she would be acquitted."

What would he have done if he had had a vision that she would be convicted and die in the gas chamber? "I wouldn't have accepted it," he said. "Negative information like that does not have to take place that way, and it would be almost criminal for me or any psychic to tell that. I would be under force of obligation not to tell it." So Wolf had no desire to act as a psychopomp as well.

Wolf and Joan had also discussed her dreams, and of the Joan Little dream that the inmate Jacquatta Davis had related—of the grotesque black figure hovering over her—Wolf said,

"That's not surprising. We're dealing here with coarse, base elements: life, death, a gross form of sexuality, fear . . . and an archetypal shadow, threatening blackness, darkness can enter as a negative elemental force.

"She had a hard time handling all the attention, and just as much as calming her during the ordeal of the trial, I helped her cope with the earthquake after acquittal, talked to her about what people would expect of her, told her, 'If you want to use people because you're Joan Little, you're in a position to do that for a little while. If you want to help people because you're Joan Little, you can do that too for a time.'

"So I helped her deal with the psychological dynamics of what she went through. If you killed someone, what would you have to deal with? She was exploring subconsciously any area where she might have contributed to the event, and this was difficult for her. Now it is true that she had, in her own mind, acted in a seductive manner toward Alligood in those eighty-one days, to secure favors, particularly the use of the telephone. She's programmed to act that way. A woman's a woman, and in today's culture a woman can't just ask for favors—she's got to be a little seductive to get them. Everyone plays that seductive game, everyone.

"Still, Joan was feeling guilt about this. *But*, there's a difference between seduction for favors and seduction for sexual reasons. Alligood simply mis-

understood. It's not his fault. His action came as a
result of cultural indoctrination. Neither he nor Joan
was responsible. Both were influenced by the attitudes
of the culture, and Alligood's misinterpretation of the
normal seductive process, his misuse of sexual energies, his death process of treating sex as an object, cost
him his life.

"I don't think Joan comprehended Alligood's misunderstanding until I explained it to her. It was important that she comprehend it; otherwise, this guilt
could have been very negative for her whole life."

As to the practical value of Richard Wolf to Joan
Little's performance on the stand, Wolf had worked
with Joan's hot temper (unlike the lawyers for Inez
Garcia) but had he, in fact, used hypnosis?

"The thought process is electrical, and it is possible
to bypass a potential electrical hazard, to bypass certain circuits with certain thoughts on different chan-
nels. This doesn't mean the hazard is eliminated; it
simply means it's inactive for a period of time. It's like
putting a plastic cover over the panic button. Still, if
just the right stimulus came, she still might push the
button. This panic, or anger, comes most of the time
from surprise or not understanding where people are
coming from. Just as I made her understand Alligood,
so I made her understand William Griffin—that he
was just doing his job. Once she understood there was
nothing personal, that Griffin himself was trapped,
then she could forgive him and the other prosecutors,
and she did forgive them. It gave her a healthy attitude toward the prosecution. So it would have been
very, very difficult for them to aggravate her on the
stand.

"We meditated and prayed together, just sitting in
a chair holding hands, sitting quietly. I directed the
meditation. This was not hypnosis; she didn't lose
touch with reality, but it was an altered state of con-

sciousness. It released tensions and cleared the mind. It centered the mind, and, once the mind was centered, we might say a prayer for Jerry and Karen. So the whole process released negative energies."

On October 19, 1975, two months after the acquittal, Richard Wolf took note of foreboding occurrences. The astrological marking was Sun Conjunct Uranus. In Scorpio, Square of Saturn and Leo, a sign of great troubles, involving earth changes. That night he had a dream. It took place in an operating room— "My head is my operating room"—and on the operating table was a sleeping bag. He saw an animal, a dog, in the sleeping bag. It got out and crawled through a window, and Richard could see that the window was broken. So he followed the dog, and they were friendly, even though the dog kept changing colors. Eventually the pooch led him to a place where he could see a sea of heads, lifted up to the sky. A light came from the sky, and the heads were slowly going up to Jesus.

When Richard woke up he remembered the dream and interpreted the dog as the animal side of man and the meaning of the dream that man should be comfortable with his animal side, but "lift up and purify." Unless man did this, the negative energy would overwhelm, and earth changes affecting hundreds of thousands of lives would result. This was disturbing enough, but that day, purely by accident, Richard found a button on the street. It read: Weathertamer.

That night, at 3:00 A.M., Wolf drove to a pornographic bookshop and dirty-movie house called Chateau II Theater on Downtown Boulevard in Raleigh. He broke a window in the back, entered the place, and went berserk, tearing porno books in half, ripping up film, smashing projection equipment. A vigilant Raleigh policeman noticed a car behind the Chateau

II, investigated, and arrested Richard Wolf at gun-
point. The sensitive was relieved. He said later that
his biggest worry was that no policeman would come,
and he would have to use the Chateau II phone to call
them. He was booked and later indicted for felonious
breaking and entering and malicious destruction of
private property.

The man who became his lawyer was James Rowan,
the smoothy in Jerry Paul's law firm, and in plea discussions with a Wake County prosecutor, who bragged
about his solid case against Wolf, Rowan threatened
to spend two weeks picking a jury, arriving at twelve
conservative hard-shells. "Your people can't stop this
pornographic stuff," Rowan said. "Richard was just
doing his little part." The prosecutor, who had been
instrumental in drafting the Wake County pornographic statutes, relented, agreeing to drop the felony
charge if Wolf would plead guilty to trepass and
make restitution of $750 for the magazines and films
that were "no longer salable."

Richard's day in court was February 3, 1976. He
took with him the *Scientific American Book of
Mathematical Puzzles and Diversions*. The night before, he'd stayed up to 4:00 A.M., trying to make a
Japanese Flapping Bird out of paper, the instructions
for which were in the chapter on Origami. Richard
Wolf's plea was before Judge Henry McKinnon.

It was a civilized procedure throughout. Wolf even
chatted jovially with his prosecutor beforehand, asking him if he hadn't just been on a skiing vacation,
and the prosecutor said in surprise, "Why, yes, how
did you know?" to which Wolf just smiled. On the
stand, he spoke of the breakdown of "loving values"
in our society "in this Bicentennial Year." The negative forces were taking over, and it was "my responsibility and the responsibility of other psychics to notify
the people, and to notify the state officially, that earth

changes are coming within the next two years. These changes do not have to come, if people learn to love and to reach out to other people." Wolf noted that certain pornography was produced by the Satan Publishing Company and that he was simply striking at satanic forces. His action was directed at the area "I think will be responsible for man's downfall." He said he did not like to have to notify the state in this way and confided to Judge McKinnon that "sometimes being a sensitive is not easy." But it had been his duty to speak out, and his act was related to the survival of thousands. Only once did he mention Joan Little. North Carolina had been "subjected" to the case, and while numerous people pointed fingers at Joan Little and Clarence Alligood, the incident was simply a "breakout" of an unhealthy consciousness existing all over the world. Likewise, the X-rated movie houses and pornographic bookstores were not supported by one man's consciousness, but many.

In the course of Wolf's notification, Judge McKinnon listened judicially, although he allowed himself an injudicious twinkle in his eye. Around the court, from the collection of bailiffs and lawyers with their accident cases, there were titters of muffled laughter, but it was strained amusement. There are two subjects at which people laugh very nervously: sexuality and prescience, and Wolf's case involved both. Would the sensitive feel compelled to continue to notify the state? No, he replied, once it was officially on the record he did not feel the "necessity." Was he prepared for the consequences of his act?

"I must render to Caesar what is Caesar's, and to God what is God's. But for me, God comes first, and the court's province ends with 'In God We Trust.' I have done what I had to do, and I must accept what the court has to offer. That is its right."

It was, therefore, a pure act of civil disobedience. In sentencing the sensitive to a two-year probation, Judge McKinnon made reference to exercising Caesar's right. There was opportunity for Wolf to air his views without resorting to violence and the destruction of property, and McKinnon cautioned him "to avoid bad company and bad habits" during his probation, but the judge did not define them.

When it was over, Wolf sighed, "What a relief to know that that is now on the record!"

As the bald *nebbish* of a probation officer was processing his forms, Wolf asked if he had ever studied for the ministry.

"As a matter of fact, I did get my degree in divinity. Why do you ask?"

"I was just curious," Wolf sparkled.

CHAPTER 12

DEPUTY SHERIFF WILLIS PEACHEY

ONE could usually tell when Judge Hamilton Hobgood was about to crack a joke. He telegraphed his kindly little smile beforehand, and it was impossible not to like him. His relaxed, benign temperament was perfect for this trial, and not Jerry Paul, not the "judge watcher" sent down from New York, not even the author could make him mad when, after the trial was over, he asked the judge if he wasn't afraid of getting a reputation like Judge Julius Hoffman, of the Chicago Eight fame.

One morning at the start of the day, the judge had an announcement.

"Well, I just received a message from the Moon; took a dollar and thirty-nine cents to send it to me," he said.

"What did the Man in the Moon say, if it please Your Honor?" said John Wilkinson, the straight man.

"Says, 'Going to blow up Raleigh.' "

"Maybe he'll miss his aim and hit New York instead," Wilkinson replied, turning as always to see if his wit was fully appreciated by the clutch of reporters.

The blasé attitude toward the handful of threats during the trial was remarkable. They were simply ignored. The chief security officer felt blandly that with the security on the floors above and below the third floor, a bomb blast would not affect the proceedings, but in one bomb scare the tenth floor evacuated, imagining, no doubt, the "towering inferno," reduced to Raleigh scale. The two telephone threats to assassinate Joan Little, the sheriff's office handled routinely, simply working with the private security guards that the defense had hired for Joan Little. If all else failed, Joan Little might hope to stop a bullet, Theodore Roosevelt style, by the copy of *To Kill a Mockingbird* that she clutched to her heart now as she passed the photographers on the way into the courthouse, the picture of innocence.

In the absence of Terry Bell, the state's case rested on showing that (1) Joan Little had access alone to the icepick at 10:30 P.M., (2) she was in her cell five hours later when Alligood was stabbed, and (3) she stabbed him either by design, or with malice aforethought, or by using force beyond what was required to repel his attack. But in order to be persuasive on the third point, the state had to provide evidence for the first two, for one can not logically conjecture guilt beyond a reasonable doubt: it must be proven. But without Terry Bell, direct proof of her access to the weapon was lost, and, therefore, the case had to concentrate on the evidence as it was found at 4:00 A.M. August 27.

A parade of law-enforcement officers took the stand: Sergeant Jerry Helms, of the Washington Police Department, who discovered the body when he brought the screaming, drunken woman in to lock her up; Detective Danny Respass, of the same department, designated as an "expert" photographer and fingerprint man, who took the photos of the body; the SBI officers called to the scene later in the morning. But also there were the doctors who examined Alligood's corpse.

It was quite easy in the Joan Little case, amid all the talk about *her* rights as a woman or prisoner or black or human being, to forget that another human being had been stabbed to death, and there was nothing elevating about that whatever. She might, of course, have been convicted for manslaughter, the standard for which was simply the use of excessive force in repelling an attack, sexual or otherwise. (However, Judge Hobgood would later charge the jury on manslaughter that if she killed in the heat of passion, after adequate provocation, if she had a reasonable apprehension that she would be sexually assaulted and believed it necessary to kill in order to save herself from death or sexual assault, the killing was excusable.) Had she been charged straight off with manslaughter, and a non-death-qualified jury asked to concentrate only on the severity and placement of the wounds, she would have had a far rougher time . . . and the proceeding would have been in Beaufort County.

To accentuate the possibility that *Alligood*'s civil rights may have been violated, the prosecution brought Dr. Charles L. Gilbert to the stand on July 30. Gilbert had examined the body in the "autopsy suite" of Pitt Memorial Hospital in nearby Greenville. Under examination by Lester Chalmers, whose talent for convoluted language was excessive—"Dr. Gilbert, do you have an opinion satisfactory to yourself . . ."—the pathologist sketched the placement of the wounds on a blackboard, four bunched around the heart, two around the right temple, two in the right shoulder, and two on the right thigh. The doctor's opinion was that Alligood died from a stab wound through the chest wall into the left ventricle of the heart, seven to ten centimeters deep, at an angle straight in. The other wounds were more shallow and angled up or down, as if rendered in a struggle, and the two wounds above the right ear did not penetrate the skull and therefore could not have been the killing wounds. Alligood, Dr. Gilbert guessed, might have lived two to ten minutes.

Then the glaring fluorescent lights of the court were turned off, and on a screen set up near the defense table, Dr. Gilbert lectured about four color slides of the body, as it was photographed in the autopsy suite. The doctor's demeanor was academic, his voice a high-pitched monotone, a natty professional plying his expertise. The moment was grotesque. The body appeared massive, almost whalelike, heightened by the fact that on the first slide, taken from the side, only the torso appeared, with the head and feet cropped, and this made the chest and belly seem even more huge. Beyond that, a gray bag had been placed over the genitals, and there was a greenish tint to the color slides, somehow an appropriate color for an autopsy suite. Joan Little sat behind the screen, her eyes fixed downward, as the doctor droned on clinically, using a flashlight beam to fix the wounds on the torso.

With the lights back on, Jerry Paul tried to diffuse the power of this testimony by raising several ancillary points. If the wounds had rendered Alligood unconscious, could he not have been suffocated to death before the wall of the heart collapsed? Technically, yes, Dr. Gilbert conceded; it would not take much to suffocate an unconscious victim, but there was no evidence of this, like ligature marks on the neck. What about this half-cocked theory, brushed at halfheartedly by the prosecution, that a violent death might cause a man to ejaculate, having nothing to do with sexual stimulation? Dr. Gilbert had never seen it in over two thousand autopsies he had performed. While he found spermatozoa in the urethra, had he found any on the thigh?

"No."

"Then it had been wiped off?"

"Yes."

Paul noted that Alligood's liver weighed 2090 grams, rather than the normal 1600 grams, conjuring up the butcher's counter for laymen. That was often associated with a nutritional deficiency, the doctor answered. "Could it also be caused by excessive drinking?" Yes. Paul also extracted the information that the examination showed an enlarged prostate, which could cause an infection in the urinary tract, and make urination difficult and painful.

But the weight of the testimony did much to make this a more solemn proceeding, and Golden Frinks should have been proud.

"I don't like killing no way," he had said.

Ideally, with a brutal killing such as this, Sheriff Davis of Beaufort Five-O should be able to call in "Forensic" immediately and those white-coated wizards of the laboratory, dangling stereo binoculars, brown bottles of phenolphthalein, and "identi-kits," should soon solve the mysteries of motive, intent, and blame from dust, mud, or hair filaments. As Deputy Sheriff Willis Peachey would put it later:

"People get an idea from *Hawaii Five-O* that you take a print or a hair, put it in some fantastic machine, and it comes back how tall he is, what his address is, how long his penis is . . . that's stupid. It just doesn't happen that way in law enforcement."

The Che Fong of Forensic for Eastern North Carolina is James Bailey, an overworked little man who is the SBI's only crime laboratory specialist for all twenty-three counties of the East. Bailey was not called to the crime scene at the jail until 11:00 A.M., six hours after the killing, and when he arrived the place had been polished to a spit-shine luster by Terry Bell. Still, SBI involvement in a case comes by invitation only, and the SBI director, Charles Dunn, was very sensitive to local dominion.

In trying over five hundred jury cases in his seven years as prosecutor, William Griffin realized the impact of television on the modern juror. The modern juror expects the police and the state experts to perform like their television models, he related, and to present the kind of evidence that is presented in courtroom scenes for their entertainment.

"So police officers now must do things at the crime scene that are often valueless from the legal standpoint but which the common juror will demand before he votes for a conviction. Since local governments will not provide the adequate funds for facilities and training, prosecutors are having to get into the business of training the police," Griffin said.

To Griffin, the difficulty of obtaining legally valid fingerprints, acceptable in court as proof positive, is the least understood problem in criminal investigation. Of several hundred larceny and breaking-and-entering cases in the previous year, Griffin could remember only three where a valid fingerprint was lifted.

"Had one several months ago, and the SBI man came in shocked and excited: '*Voilà*,' he said. 'Here it is, a gen-u-ine identifiable fingerprint.' "

Thus, along the road to the impression that the state had botched the investigation, the state experts were helpful. The local detective could produce no identifiable fingerprint from the bars or the bed or the sink or the clothes or the icepick. The SBI chemist's test of Joan Little's scarf, found underneath the body, was "inconclusive." The SBI handwriting expert could not say for sure that the inscription in the Bible found in the cell was written by Joan Little. All this expert testimony bore on the essential element of the case: Joan Little had to be physically put in her cell at the time of the crime. After the state rested, it was clear to all that from the technical legal standpoint, Joan Little's presence there was never established. Beyond this, the state had considerable difficulty in getting what it did have into evidence. The most vivid illustration of this was the problem of the crossword-puzzle books, novels, and magazines that were found in the cell. The magazines were pulps: *Original Secrets, Confession Secrets,* and *My Romances,* and the novels were *Ben Hur,* by Lew Wallace, and a Perry Mason mystery, *The Case of the Silent Partner* (was it about Terry Bell?). As all these books and magazines had notations in them, Marvin Miller of the defense argued that they were really "diaries" and "private papers," entitled to "an aura of protection" as a "privileged area." The case law was extensive and the argument interesting, for who says that an indigent prisoner must prepare her private papers as Charles de Gaulle might prepare his, to give them their aura of protection? Miller argued that Joan Little's diaries could not be seized without a warrant, and as no warrant was secured, the diaries were inadmissible. But John Wilkinson scoffed at the ridiculous notion that the state needed a warrant to search its own cell after a brutal murder had taken place, and he persuaded Judge Hobgood that the books were abandoned and therefore seizable. But it was a close question and it looked for a while as if only the dead man's wardrobe would be available to the jury.

With all these disabilities, the case of North Carolina fell to Deputy Sheriff Willis Peachey of Beaufort County, who became the chief investigative officer on the early morning of the crime. He has the look of combat about him: short, athletic, cauliflower ears, closely cropped hair, a glower in his brown eyes that comes from seeing people at their worst so often, and a curt delivery which relates only the necessary and nothing more. After a stint in the Marine Corps, where he saw six months' combat in Vietnam, and a year of long-distance trucking, Peachey joined the police department of nearby Belhaven, North Carolina. His salary was $103 a week, which came out to $1.35 an hour, and for a year he worked 8:00 P.M. to 8:00 A.M. and went to school at Martin Technical Institute from 8:30 A.M. to noon. After two years at Martin Tech, he received an applied-science degree, and along the way had taken courses in criminal investigation, criminal evidence, and testimony in court. Schooling was fine, but Red Davis's attitude toward it was:

"Haven't seen any results out of schooling. Don't care how many qualifications or degrees a man's got. He's got to put them into practice."

In his two years on the Belhaven force, Willis Peachey had been on one homicide case, where a black shot another black, and Peachey caught the murderer down the street with the murder weapon. He also remembered vividly the first case he ever testified about in court, when at one point he called the victim coherent, and at another point, incoherent, and the defense lawyer had pointed out the discrepancy. The judge had cleared the courtroom.

"He turned to me, said, 'Officer, you will not answer any questions unless you fully understand what the question is.' He trimmed me down good, and I remembered it. Now I don't answer questions no more unless I know what I'm talking about."

Peachey's career on the Belhaven force ended on a noble note. A year before the Alligood killing, he and all five policemen on the Belhaven force went to the town council complaining that their chief was corrupt —he had assaulted a female and broken into a store, to name a few of the chief's indiscretions—and the officers, led by Peachey, demanded that the council fire the chief or they would quit. But the town council did not want to be browbeaten into a decision, so the five quit, and Peachey joined the Beaufort County sheriff's department, with a raise to $7,200 a year.

In August 1974, Peachey lived six miles east of Washington at Douglas Crossroads, and on the night of August 26–27 he had been on routine patrol. Close to 10:30 P.M. he was swinging through town, on his way to the eastern part of the county, and stopped at the jail to go to the bathroom. He entered the jailer's office; Terry Bell was sitting on a chair drinking a soda, and Joan Little was on the phone, with her back to him. Alligood just standing around. Peachey greeted the three, and it was deemed important by the deputy later that Joan Little did not respond. She was talking in a very low tone of voice, "sort of a mumble, very low," Peachey testified forebodingly.

"I would like to ask you one thing, Mr. Peachey," Jerry Paul baited him, "and see if you'll tell me the truth . . ."

"Objection," Griffin interposed.

"Do not say that about *any* witness," the judge cautioned. "It's improper."

"Excuse me, judge. I apologize. Why did you make a point of saying Joan Little didn't greet you?"

"Because in my opinion, the other times I had talked to her she was more jovial and outspoken. She always spoke to me, and the reason I made a point of it is because I felt like at this particular time, she was completely different than any other time I talked to her."

"Yet her back was to you, and you can't say she heard you speak, so your point is actually worthless," Paul snapped.

Before leaving the jail, Peachey scolded Alligood, reminding him of the sheriff's rule about prisoners using the phone at night, but he did not persist. "I

didn't want to make an issue of it." Eventually he
went home and went to bed. At 4:00 A.M. the phone
woke him, and he was at the jail by 4:20 A.M. Jerry
Paul suggested that the scene that morning was one of
mass confusion.

"I would not say mass confusion," Peachey replied.
"There was some confusion, but not *mass* confusion."
Peachey would relate an example of the excitement
later: at 5:30 A.M. a call came in that Joan Little was
seen on Seventh Street, and nearly all the officers at
the jail rushed to their cars and over to the Cobbs'
house Back of Town.

"If you walk in one morning and find a close associate dead on the floor, killed in a brutal manner without his clothes on, there's bound to be a certain
amount of confusion. We had never dealt with anything like that before."

Whatever the state of things, no clear plan of action
was agreed upon. Sheriff Davis quickly found himself
too busy with other things—the Alligood family, the
press, issuing bulletins, making calls to San Antonio,
Texas, for another set of keys from the jail contractor
—to take charge of the investigation. So the deputy
took charge somewhat, without being officially designated as the investigator, and without official authori-
zation, he fell short of acting like the man in charge.

"I didn't have no business being in charge of
nothin'," he would contend.

"Just a rookie down there with three years' experience, the last deputy to be hired. Had I been told I
was in charge, I could have applied my training, but
this was not done. I was really a victim of circumstances." Peachey was always careful not to cast asper-
sions on Red Davis, for after his testimony in the Joan
Little case, some had tried to have him fired for
"undermining the sheriff's department." "Luckily for
me," Peachey said, "the sheriff happened to be in

court on the day I testified. He had a lot of things on his mind that morning."

From the stand, Peachey defined three priorities when he arrived. First was to determine if Alligood was alive, and it became moot when a doctor told him at 4:30 A.M. that the jailer was dead. His second concern was the other prisoners, and while it took two hours and an acetylene torch man to accomplish their security, the pressing nature of this concern soon diminished. His third concern was the whereabouts of Joan Little.

"It was a very simple situation. The jailer was in the cell with his pants off, dead, and the girl in the cell was gone. The only real question was whether there was a third party, and I figured that if she had an accomplice, it would be her boy friend, Julius Rogers. So in that first hour, among other things, I was getting his license number and vehicle, and talking to the Chapel Hill police about whether he was at home up there."

Peachey arrived at these conclusions out of his own instincts, rather than through any briefings or orders or natural chain of command, and Paul kept badgering him about whether these decisions did not mean he was the officer of record.

"How did you determine that Object Number Three, to find Joan Little, was something you should do . . . or did you just make that up?"

"Your question is vague to the point that I don't understand what answer you want me to give."

"Let me ask it this way, and see if you can understand. I'm asking if this decision was based on some information as a trained police officer . . . or was it just a wild hunch on your part?"

"I made the decision that this was important to do."

"How did you get to make that decision, if you weren't in charge?"

"I made the decision for myself, not for the other people."

"Is there no organization in the Beaufort County Sheriff's Department, no organized method for viewing a crime scene and determining what steps to take? Is that what you're telling me?"

"On this particular morning, there was no organization, no sir."

Not until the SBI arrived at 10:30 A.M. was he officially designated as chief investigator, Peachey testified, but Sheriff Davis contends the time was closer to 8:00 A.M. The difference did not matter, for that still left four crucial hours in which the actions taken were haphazard, and that later gave the Joan Little jury its easiest out: to find that the investigation was botched, the essential elements of the crime were not established, and thereby the state's circumstantial case could not be taken seriously.

Clearly, Peachey did not focus on the marshaling and protection and recording of the evidence as his foremost responsibility. Sgt. Helms and the rescue squad personnel were already there. Sheriff Davis and the doctor soon arrived. Three other deputies came in shortly thereafter, and then Detective Danny Respass, of the Washington Police, a man with eight years' experience, arrived with his camera. The others stood back while Respass took six pictures of the body and the cell area, but no one was telling him what to photograph.

"Why didn't you have Detective Respass make a full photograph of the way Mr. Alligood was gripping the icepick?" Paul asked.

"If I had been entirely in charge and had gotten the photographs taken that I myself would like to have had, he would probably still be developing them. I asked him to take photographs. He took them and he left."

"So you don't feel he took sufficient photographs?"

"There could have been a hundred more taken, and it wouldn't have hurt a thing."

"Was anybody else telling him what to photograph beside you?"

"Not to my knowledge."

"So that was your responsibility?"

"I don't see how you could figure that, no sir."

"Did you have any responsibility?"

"I had a responsibility as a deputy sheriff to assist in any manner that it was told to me and any manner that I thought was best."

In fact, Respass took an entire roll of film that did not develop, because someone else had loaded the camera improperly, so the net result was only six photographs. But the parsimoniousness of Respass's photographing would not be unusual in Eastern North Carolina. In one of William Griffin's larceny cases, a police officer was asked why the prosecution had not presented any pictures of the crime scene.

"We're so tight in our budget," the policeman had replied, "that we have to save our film for homicides."

When Respass finished photographing, he reached down, removed the icepick from the dead man's right hand, and handed it to Peachey.

"Now, after you put the icepick in your pocket, did you put it in your pocket in such a way to make sure that no fingerprints were smudged or rubbed off that might have been on the icepick?"

"Detective Respass and myself discussed the surface of the icepick, and it was his opinion that there would probably be no prints, or it would be impossible to take prints from this. That is why the careless manner in which I handled the icepick."

Respass then handed the deputy Alligood's glasses,

which were on the floor beneath the victim's head, then the clothes on the floor—the underpants, the green trousers, a purple negligée—and Peachey stuffed them in a white pillowcase.

Then a strange thing occurred. Peachey put the pillowcase down in the cell, and headed for his wall locker with the glasses and the icepick. Along the way he encountered Gordon Edwards, a TV cameraman, who had heard of the killing from a dispatcher in the Pitt County sheriff's department. That Edwards could simply waltz into the jail at 5:15 A.M. and begin filming is indicative of the lack of control, though Red Davis would argue that he was glad in retrospect that the cameraman had gotten in: it proved the sheriff's department was not trying to hide anything. Edwards was clearly one of the boys, and shortly after the Joan Little trial he became a deputy sheriff in adjoining Pitt County. But even stranger was the fact that the pants, underwear, and negligée that Peachey had stuffed in the pillowcase before going to his wall locker had magically leapt back out onto the floor, for they appeared on the floor in Edwards's TV film— later shown nationwide on CBS News. Peachey said on the stand he wished he knew how that happened. So there was a break in the chain of custody for these items, and, beyond that, a discrepancy between the Respass photos and the TV film planted a fertile doubt that perhaps some arranging of the evidence took place.

But the humbling of Willis Peachey was based more on what he did not do than what he did do, and in this Jerry Paul played shamelessly to the television-bred expectations of the jurors. Peachey could have sealed off the women's section, but he did not. He could have issued instructions for no one to touch anything without his say-so, but he did not. He could have required more photographs, etc., etc. But the real deficiency was the absence of specific items in the cell which were not taken into custody or measured or diagrammed, and Paul followed a set pattern, ending usually with: "So there is another piece of evidence missing." The bloodstained sheet was not retained, nor the mattress, nor Alligood's glasses, nor clumps of bloodstained toilet tissue found in the sink bowl, nor the blankets found on the floor and tied to the bars. Joan Little's scarf was presented to the court in a different state than it was found in the cell. There were no measurements of the blood spots on the floor or the bloodstain on the wall.

"If we had done everything that we possibly could have done that morning, gone over the cell with a fine-toothed comb, sent every single item to the SBI for examination," Peachey said, "I think I still would have been on the stand eight hours. There's always something to get at. They tell you in school, 'Always prepare yourself for an out-of-town attorney who's smart.' Regardless of how right you do something, lawyers are gonna make it wrong. That's what they're paid to do."

In it all, Paul baited Peachey mercilessly:

"By some disorganized decision-making process, you were the man in charge of the investigation, weren't you?"

"Well, you and the other deputies didn't fight about who was going to keep the icepick, did you?"

"Why is it you can remember every detail the state wants you to, and can't remember things I want you to?"

"Some of this evidence you were very careful to pre-serve and note its location and the condition it was in. Other evidence you did nothing to protect. Is that correct?"

"So you went in and got her personal effects and did nothing to preserve the evidence, is that correct?"

And his last question to Peachey was "Are you aware, Mr. Peachey, that that is the hundredth time you've said 'I don't recall'?"

In his humiliation of Peachey, Jerry Paul occasionally lapsed into the ridiculous. The deputy conceded at one point that with a pack of Salem cigarettes found on the sink in the cell, he counted the individual cigarettes "as part of a lead I was running down" and put the pack with personal articles of Joan Little. He did not know where they were a year later. Jerry Paul rolled his eyes over the ceiling at yet another "piece of evidence from the crime scene" no longer in Peachey's possession. At another point, Paul was shocked that Peachey, immediately upon finding Alligood's body, had not "taken steps to see if Joan Little was injured." But the Episode of the Hairy Serendipity was the highest slapstick of all.

Alligood's shoes and socks were entered into evidence, and put on the dais in front of the witness. Paul wanted to know if the deputy had marked in his notes which sock came off which foot. He had not, because he had not taken the socks off. History would have to go without the information. Had he examined them visually? He had. Had he examined the socks with a microscope or a magnifying glass? No. And then, as if he were Sherlock Holmes pulling the wax vesta from the mud, before the very eyes of Inspector Gregory, Paul pointed at the sock, his face beaming broadly:

"There is a hair right there on the bottom of the sock. You see it?"

Deadpan Peachey braced himself for the inevitable. William Griffin had given Peachey only one warning: "Don't give any smart answers." So for the next five minutes Peachey's competence hung on the hair.

"Now watch me closely, please; if I picked this hair

up like this. You see it?" With his thumb and index finger curved delicately together, as if he were a plump English lady at Ascot lifting her teacup, Paul removed the hair from the sock.

"Now why didn't you see that hair on the bottom of the sock when you examined it?"

"The only explanation I could give is that the hair was not there," Peachey replied.

"You've never seen it?"

"I've never seen the hair."

"Yet you admit it's there."

"I see it there; no doubt about that."

"All right. Look at it closely, Mr. Peachey."

"He looked at it closely one time," the judge interjected.

"Does that appear to be white in color or black?"

On and on the questions went. Did it appear to be Alligood's hair? Was it a white or black person's hair? As a "trained investigator," could he have sent the hair to the SBI lab for examination, to determine if it belonged to a white or black person . . . *if* he had seen it?

"If your honor please, since you won't let us have that hair examined, I move that that hair be identified separately and sealed and placed in the record and preserved," Paul said.

"For the future?" the judge asked.

"For the record," the lawyer replied.

"Put the hair right up here and I'll get it. Put it right here now," demanded the judge.

"ORDER IN THE COURT," the bailiff demanded, as muffled giggles filled the room.

"Take that, get it sealed and mark on it, 'Hair taken from the sock, one of the socks identified as Clarence Alligood's socks by Mr. Jerry Paul at two-fifty-two p.m. August 1, 1975, and sealed in an envelope by direction of the court.' "

Later, Peachey wondered what happened to the hair.

"Why Jerry Paul wanted to plant a hair on those damn socks . . . He planted that hair on the socks. I've got a source—I'm not going to tell you who it is—but he saw Paul put that hair on those socks. It wasn't nothin' but somethin' to try to rattle me."

The social scientists on the defense team had made a great deal of the "authoritarian personality" during jury selection, but in bolstering the impression of Peachey as an oafish, incompetent bumbler, the defense displayed an authoritarianism of its own. It brought to the stand one of the most notorious professional witnesses in America, Hubert MacDonnell, who came from out of town—Corning, New York, to be exact—and had the biggest briefcase of all, and so met at least two conditions of John Wilkinson's tripartite definition for a court expert.

MacDonnell's reputation in the field of criminalistics rests on his scientific knowledge of crime-scene investigation, and while his technical grounding is solid, he is not as well respected for acknowledging human failings on the part of police officers, or for countenancing other interpretations of a crime scene than his own. He wore a green suit on the day of his appearance, and a green tie, unknotted. This caused immediate suspicion in some observers who by this time were in tune with the proceedings, and were making snap judgments about people willy-nilly, by the way they looked or talked. What sort of person, the whispers went, wears a tie, but doesn't knot it?

MacDonnell, who insisted on the pronunciation Mac-DON-ell, had no hesitation about listing all his professional qualifications. He was professor of criminalistics at Elmira College and Corning Community College, Director of a Laboratory of Forensic Science, and past chairman of the Department of Chemistry at Milton College in Wisconsin. He was chairman of the criminalistics section of the American Academy of Forensic Science, and over the years, had been retained in over twenty-six states as an evidence analyst by both prosecution and defense. He would move from the Joan Little trial to the Robert Kennedy assassination investigation in California, as one of the six experts pondering whether there was a second gun after Sirhan Sirhan's. He taught courses in death investigations and bloodstain interpretation and had invented two different fingerprint processes, which, he said, "have been adopted worldwide." In 1969 he landed a grant from the Department of Justice to study the "flight characteristics" of human blood. In all, these were more impressive credentials than Peachey's two years at Martin Tech, and MacDonnell probably made more money as well, judging that the professor's appearance in the Little trial alone earned him about one-sixth of Peachey's annual salary.

William Griffin found MacDonnell's appearance "pure Hollywood, real TV stuff," but he realized that the mere presence of an expert, who could so unabashedly rattle off so many multisyllabic professional associations, could have an impact on a jury. Now this was the kind of testimony that jurors of the television age expected! In the past, Griffin had seen the appearance of psychiatrists produce the same effect, "even though from the legal standpoint their testimony might be valueless."

The "professor," as the defense lawyer always called him, began his testimony by comparing the bloodstains on Alligood's undershirt and sport shirt. The thrust of this went to the issue, hardly central to the case, of whether the outer shirt was buttoned or unbuttoned, and MacDonnell concluded from the absence of blood in a buttonhole that the shirt was unbuttoned. His analysis of a large, yellowish stain with a dark brownish border on the left shoulder area of the sport shirt was somewhat more interesting.

"It is consistent with hemolyzed blood or blood which has been diluted with water, blood that is very thin, in contact with water, which ruptures the cells very quickly. There is a rather technical explanation for that, but I don't think it's important." (He was happy to give the technical explanation later in his testimony.) "The blood cells rupture, and when the diluted blood is on a garment, by capillary action the water evaporates at the front or extremities of the stain so that blood is concentrated on the edges and you get a darkening there. Normal blood that is not diluted would do just the opposite; it would coagulate or clot. The serum then being thinner, without red cells, would give a yellowish external area of the circumference. So this appears to be a very small amount of blood in a rather large amount of water."

Although the judge would not permit a conclusion from this, it added some picture of Alligood's death throes. The wounds to his head would be bleeding the most, for as MacDonnell would say later, icepick wounds to the chest are self-sealing. So there was a splashing of water over his head, where the wounds were bloody but superficial, the dying man trying to clean himself up and make himself presentable to the first officer to find him. But Peachey would wonder if a man in that state wouldn't first want to put his pants back on, and if Alligood splashed water all over himself, why wasn't there water on the floor?

From this, MacDonnell moved to blood spots. For evidence of blood on the cell floor, the court had to rely on the Respass photos, because Peachey had not taken notes on the shape or size of the blood spots around the cell (although TV film of the blood was available). In this, the state nearly lost these photos as well as admissible evidence, because the State Bureau of Investigation had given the defense a set of photographs with developer splashed on them, creating small dark spots. To the untrained eye, these spots could be misinterpreted as blood spots, and the defense raised the specter of "retouching" the negative. Defense lawyer James Rowan motioned to strike the photographs altogether, but without them, the state would have virtually nothing left in evidence, so Judge Hobgood, probably feeling sorry for the state by now, denied the motion. The professor said the spots were probably due to a "bad day in the darkroom."

From the shape of the blood droplets on the floor, MacDonnell discoursed on the difference between dripping and splattered blood.

"The basic difference is in the size of the spots of blood. Normal droppings of blood result in a very uniform drop size whether it is bleeding from a hand or object. Blood drops produce very uniform size spots. In order to have blood produce smaller than normal droplets, there has to be some energy added to overcome surface tension, the force that holds liquids together. A shaking or a flicking of the arms or head or whatever slapping motion with some degree of force is necessary to break up the blood into smaller than normal drops. Medium-velocity energy is consistent with beatings, whereas high-velocity energy is consistent with gunshot or explosive forces."

So splattered blood drops are elliptical, whereas dropped blood drops are circular, and both were present in the cell. This proved that there had been a struggle. But upon questioning about a blood drop in the hallway outside the cell, the audience, thoroughly entranced by this time, got a glimpse of how Professor MacDonnell spends his time in his Laboratory of Forensic Science. William Griffin wanted to know if the drop in the hallway could not have run off the tip of the icepick.

"There wouldn't be enough blood on that icepick in my opinion to leave a drop this size if the blood originated on the icepick within the cell. The surface area of the icepick is so small and blood runs off so rapidly that I doubt a drop of that size could appear outside the cell. We have conducted many experiments dipping knives and icepicks and other things into blood and then walking to see how far the trail of blood goes."

This was all interesting, amusing, and diverting (James Rowan had been told to absorb that afternoon with MacDonnell, for the next witness was not quite ready yet). In the style of its presentation, rather than its content, the testimony was devastating to Peachey. It created the psychology that anything less than the MacDonnell standard of an investigation was inadequate to conviction, and Griffin missed an opportunity to grill the professor on how often, in real life, the professor encountered *his* Holmes-like standards of professionalism at a crime scene.

"In any serious crime, particularly homicide, the investigating officer should cord off the area," MacDonnell catechized. "The entire scene should be photographed. This, of course, follows the determination that the victim is beyond medical help. That determination should be made with as little alteration or movement of the body or materials as possible. Each and every item should be photographed. I personally prefer overall wide-angle photographs, and if practical a motion picture coverage of the scene, walking in with a motion picture of the quiet scene. From motion pictures, many times you will pick up things that are not included in one of the panoramic photographs.

"Each item should be bagged and tagged. It should

be noted where it was found, by whom, and witnessed by another officer or investigator. These items should be sent to the crime lab for examination and evaluation. No material present should be overlooked. Depending upon the nature of the crime, some common sense has to be used as to what has potential value, but it is much better to throw out evidence later because it has no value than to have discarded something and find out later that you want it. Each criminal scene is different, and I don't think there are any general rules beyond that: just to collect everything after it has been photographed."

MacDonnell reached the depth of his condescension when he was asked about the photographs provided by Respass.

"Photographically, I would not pass one of my students who took those pictures."

"What grade would you give the Beaufort County Sheriff's Department on their investigation of the crime scene?" Rowan asked, but the professor was not allowed to answer. Willis Peachey said that since the Alligood killing there were plenty of plastic evidence bags available in the sheriff's office.

It would be hard to decide whether Hubert Mac-Donnell or William Kunstler provided the best sideshow of the trial. After Alabama attorney Morris Dees was kicked off the defense for subornation of perjury, Paul invited Kunstler down. Paul's reasoning was that if Kunstler was barred, it would be a valid ground for reversal on appeal, should Joan Little be convicted, for any defendant is entitled to the best defense possible. If he was admitted, then Paul would have an "eloquent foreign attorney" to remind the jury that the eyes of the world were on them.

So William Kunstler came to Raleigh on August 5, 1975. Before the court session, outside the Wake

County Courthouse, he gave Golden Frinks a bear
hug in front of the television cameras, lifted him off
the ground, both laughing raucously, and gave
Golden his best television exposure of the trial. Inside,
when Judge Hobgood refused to admit him to the
defense team as a "foreign attorney," Kunstler leapt
to his feet.

"Thank you, judge. I am glad to see the quality of
justice has not improved in North Carolina," he
shouted.

"Any more remarks like that and you'll be on the
fifth floor," said the judge.

"Take me up there, judge. I think what you're
doing here is outrageous," and Kunstler's wish was
granted. He had to rot in jail for two hours for his
outburst. As the deputy sheriff reached for his arm,
Kunstler, like a good civil disobedient, said with dignity, "You don't have to remove me. I'm happy to
go."

Later, after release, he informed his press conference that, while he pulled his time, he had spent
twenty minutes reading a lousy novel and fifteen
minutes reading the trial of Christ, in which he per-
ceived similarities to this trial. On the late evening
news the same day, Kunstler was pictured sitting next
to another client, Jack Scott, the sports activist, who
was announcing at a Pennsylvannia news conference
that he would not cooperate with the FBI in its Patricia Hearst investigation.

As Willis Peachey had been "flustrated," as he
would say, from getting his theory of the crime expressed compellingly in the courtroom, the author
returned to the Holiday Inn in Little Washington,
and they talked, as the sound of clapping floated in
from a luncheon for Miss America that was taking
place in the adjoining room. That night there would

be a beauty contest, and some thought that this year, Beaufort County would produce, at the very least, a Miss North Carolina, although Joan Little is likely to remain the most memorable Miss Beaufort County for some time to come.

Peachey's demeanor on the stand had been deadpan and dispassionate, and it seemed to reflect his true attitude towards the case. He was never mad at her, he said, and had treated her just like any criminal, black or white. "I have never condoned the fact that he was in that cell with his pants off. Had she been captured that morning, she probably would have pled guilty to manslaughter, and it would have been all over with."

About the reports that Joan Little was in danger of her life, Peachey shows only a flicker of emotion: "She was never in danger. We're not in Alabama. Despite how we were written up in national magazines, a pistol was never taken from its holster in those searches. A shotgun was never taken from a car, and there were no dogs. And if someone had done that in Los Angeles, brother, the police would have had all their mess out."

Peachey remembers the search of Paps Barnes's house vividly, because the lot fell to him to search upstairs.

"It's a wino's house, and every time we went in, there was this retarded woman upstairs, frigging one of those winos, and we assumed that the calls to the sheriff's office, saying Joan Little was in that house, came from someone who was upset with that woman."

And then the man in Beaufort County, who had interviewed close to fifty witnesses in the case, and who knew more about the case than anyone in the county, concentrated on his theory:

"She found out that her boy friend was shacking up with another woman. She also found out that day that she wasn't going to make bond, and she wanted to get out. There had either been advances before or that evening, and she had an indication that she could get him in that cell. So she got the icepick at ten-thirty and planted it in the bedroom. He came in, done his thing, and when he ejaculated, she popped it to him, sitting right there on that damn bunk. He didn't move around. MacDonnell might be a good criminologist, I'm not denying that, but all the flopping and carrying on, beating and banging around in there, that she described on that stand, and yet on the floor of the small cell, was a blanket folded perfectly.

"If I live to be sixty-two, I'm going to try doing what she said Alligood did: icepick in one hand, with the intent to commit rape, take my pants off, all the time watching somebody dangerous while I'm doing it. You ought to try it. No, it was premeditated murder, in my opinion.

"I think he was probably leaning back against the wall, might have even had his eyes closed, and I think she went for his head first. He didn't ever fight or nothing. He was so surprised. If there had been a big fight, there would have been blood all over the place, and there were only a half a dozen blood spots on the floor.

"He didn't do a thing but lay down and die. He reached down and grabbed his pants, because his last dying thought was that he didn't want to get caught with his pants off. And she went to the basin, washed the blood off her hands with that toilet paper, and left."

CHAPTER 13

JOAN LITTLE

PERHAPS an indistinctness of character is needed for a person to become the receptacle for such important issues, whose case would so touch the guilt of the South, whose fate concerned so many, whose name lubricated the flow of so many dollars and pounds and guilders. The confusion even over what to call her—Joan as her birth certificate read or Jo Ann as people addressed her—seemed to symbolize the degree to which her identity was elusive. Interviews with her failed to get at that essential core of character, and the result was always unsatisfying. Her learned coolness and natural toughness lend a bored dutifulness to her responses. Later, after the verdict, when she overslept and missed her interview on the *Today* show, the author understood: she didn't have to do this anymore. In the end, he concluded that with Joan Little, it mattered not so much what she was, as how she was seen.

Jerry Paul had seen her as a mimic and impersonator, and his psychiatrist had said that she had no personality at all. Celine Chenier found Saint Maria Goretti, fighting off a rapist, but, unlike Saint Maria, surviving that attack only to endure an attack in the courts; William Griffin's informant—for Griffin would hardly venture such a characterization himself—found her to be "nothin' but a whore." Golden Frinks saw a

black Esther, inspiring her people to defend themselves in oppression and in prison; John Wilkinson, as
the scorned woman whose wrath exceeded Hell's fury.
And perhaps she saw herself as Jael.

For the marker in her Bible had been a clipping
from the August 6 *Washington Daily News* relating
the story from Judges 4:18 of the woman inviting the
fugitive Sisera into her tent:

> And Jael went out to meet Sisera, and said
> unto him, Turn in, my Lord, turn in to me; fear
> not. And when he had turned in unto her into
> the tent, she covered him with a mantle.
>
> And he said unto her, Give me, I pray thee, a
> little water to drink; for I am thirsty. And she
> opened a bottle of milk, and gave him drink, and
> covered him.
>
> Again he said unto her, Stand in the door of
> the tent, and it shall be, when any man doth
> come and inquire of thee, and say, Is there any
> man here, that thou shalt say, No.
>
> Then Jael, Heber's wife, took a nail of the tent,
> and took an hammer in her hand, and went softly
> unto him, and smote the nail into his temples, and
> fastened it into the ground; for he was fast asleep
> and weary. So he died.

Were it not for the fact that throughout the Joan
Little saga the Bible was made so much of, this story
might be of only passing interest. But the saga was
Southern, and to a Southerner no sinister or foreboding references in the Bible could be read to indicate
wickedness rather than salvation. Sentimentality over
religious passion can set people free, as Jerry Paul had
proven many times in his practice. So when Joan Little took the stand on August 11, 1975, Paul would
have her read the inscription in the Bible found in

her cell. The scrawl and the touching manner in which it was read were intended to melt the coldest heart on the jury—if there was any cold heart:

"This Bible was given to me on the fourth of July 1974, by Mr. Charlie Oden, to help me to endure the stress and hardships I was going through. It has helped me to make a lot of decisions and has comforted me when I had no one to turn to, so I called on God. Since the sixth month, 6, 1974, I have really learned the true meaning of faith and prayer. Faith more than anything, St. Luke, 5th Verse, 50th Chapter to 54th Chapter; also St. Mark, 14th Chapter from the 27th to the 32nd Verse; also John 14; also Jeremiah, the 3rd to the 14th Verse. These are just a few of the readings that have caught my attention during this time. I only pray that more young people can convert themselves before it is too late and turn more toward Jesus Christ for support and strength in these troubled times of today. I am no Christian or anything, but I am praying every day and night that I may get closer to God. To those of you that are without mothers and fathers, just think how blessed you are to have someone to love you and to be there when you really need them. Others, God is your parents for ever and ever and he'll always be there so you are never alone. Pray with all your heart and soul and he will answer your prayers. He can help you when no one else can or will. God will never turn you down. He is a forgiver of all sins. Each and every day, praise God and the many blessings he gives you and always believe in God and through God all things are possible if you only believe. Thank God our Father.

"Joan Little, 5th month, 8th, 1974"

Just as the prosecutors paid no attention to the Jael clipping, neither did they pay any attention to the citations in Joan's Bible. Had they done so, their summations might have been more powerful. To begin with, they would have found that there is no St. Luke 5:50–54; the chapter ends with the thirty-fifth verse. Could she have meant St. Mark 14:50–54, the only chapter of the four she mentioned with that many verses?

And they all forsook him [Jesus], and fled.
And there followed him a certain young man, having a linen cloth cast about his naked body; and the young men laid hold on him:
And he left the linen cloth, and fled from them naked.
And they led Jesus away to the high priest: and with him were assembled all the chief priests and the elders and the scribes.
And Peter followed him afar off, even into the palace of the high priest: and he sat with the servants and warmed himself at the fire.

Therein lie the themes of betrayal in adversity, nakedness, warmth, and flight. And in Jeremiah 3:14:

Turn, O backsliding children, saith the Lord: for I am married unto you; and I will take you one of a city, and two of a family, and I will bring you to Zion.

The Lord speaks to the backsliding, offers the chosen deliverance. In John 14:

And whatsoever ye shall ask in my name, that I will do, that the Father may be glorified in the Son. If ye shall ask any thing in my name, I will do it.

The theme of possession and mission. And, most important, St. Mark 14:27:

And Jesus saith unto them. All ye shall be offended because of me this night; for it is written, I will smite the shepherd, and the sheep shall be scattered.

The theme of vengeance and chaos.

If the prosecution had argued that she was motivated by a distorted faith, in which a wrathful Jehovah possessed the sinful and the downtrodden and sent them on missions of vengeance, it would have been stronger than what they did argue with the pitiful Peachey as their instrument. A distorted faith would certainly have fit her family background. For her mother, Jessie Williams, was a religious fanatic. She would often consult a "root worker" or conjurer, who could purportedly cast spells through the use of roots with mystical powers: tree bark tea to bring back a wandering lover, quinine and mistletoe to accelerate birth, yellow root for a good appetite, snake root for anemia and diabetes. This voodoo of rural Southern blacks is deeply believed, according to Golden Frinks. Not Pentacostal, not Methodist or Baptist, the practice is inspired by the sections of the Bible dealing with leprosy and magic, and it is not unusual that a root man would be paid "to throw" for a person—or put a hex on an enemy. Frinks had said to Ms. Williams before the trial,

"Now Joan's going to trial. We've got people praying for her all over the country, and we've done all we can do now. If you know any place you can go, where you can find a root man who can do anything else, you go do so."

Joan Little was an "outside child," and as the oldest of her mother's children she was forced into the role of baby sitter for her mother's five children by Joan's father and four by her present husband. As her mother was off with her religion, and her father by this time off in Brooklyn, New York, where he is a security guard, she turned inward . . . and to others, "an older crowd," the family social worker called them, "the scrapings." She began to run away from home often, and often the social worker, Jean Nelson, would go looking for her with her mother. Nelson found Joan an "escape artist" and "a regular Houdini," for she had a talent for hiding herself. Once Ms. Nelson and Ms. Williams went looking for the girl in the house on Pierce Street, Back of Town, and nearly giving up after a thorough search of the house, Ms. Williams eyed a deep pile of dirty clothes in the corner, stripped the layers away, and found Joan curled up in a ball at the bottom. In another search for her, again nearly giving up, Ms. Williams looked for a third time in a closet, and pulled Joan from the top of it, where she had "receded into the wainscoting." So Jean Nelson had been amused when she heard that Joan Little had eluded the authorities in Paps Barnes's house by hiding under a feather mattress.

At fifteen, her legal problems began. She lost interest in school, and Jessie Williams, fed up, had no qualms about asking a judge to declare her a truant and commit her to the Dobbs Farm Training School in Kinston, North Carolina. But Jean Nelson, who was handling the commitment, learned that a root worker in his sixties had offered Joan and another girl $20 if they would be "intimate" with him. The idea was that with the money Joan could hop a bus north. So Nelson had a warrant sworn out against the root man for contributing to the delinquency of a minor and had Joan locked up for a few days, until she could be taken to Kinston. The Dobbs School required a Wasserman test before they would take her, and when Ms. Nelson took her to the hospital for it, Joan Little first faked a suicide by popping a white powder into her mouth and letting white saliva dribble from her mouth, and then, when that didn't work, she grabbed a pair of surgical scissors and threatened the social worker with them.

"I treated her like a child, just told her to put them down, and eventually she did," Nelson said. On the trip to Dobbs, Ms. Nelson, who always thought Joan Little had unusual intelligence, told her she should straighten out, because "some day you could do a lot of good."

Joan had had her first sexual encounter at age fourteen, and at fifteen she contracted syphilis—a fact that Alligood would surely have known from jailhouse talk or from her records. (Jerry Paul would gloat later that the prosecution could have gotten Joan Little's health records into testimony as illustration of Alligood's state of mind on the night of the incident. Instead, the judge had ruled both the health records and the Dobbs School records irrelevant when William Griffin tried to introduce them simply as another piece of evidence in the state's case.) The former sheriff of Beaufort County, Red Davis's predecessor Jack D. Harris, had wondered, as if in exoneration of Alligood,

"Why would he want a woman like that, all eat up with syphilis like she was?"

Joan Little walked out of Dobbs after several weeks there. With a friend, several miles down the road, they saw a man filling up his gas tank, told him that their boy friends had left them on the side of the road, and asked him to take them home to Washington, which he did. Realizing that the legal arrangement would not work, Jessie Williams sought an official release from the Juvenile Petition, and packed Joan off to Philadelphia to stay with relatives.

"She always wanted to be a city girl," Jessie Williams had said, and it is likely that in the big city Joan Little lost any foot-shuffling ways that the strict segregation of Washington, North Carolina, encouraged. She enrolled in Simon Gratz High School and was placed in the twelfth grade. But within three weeks of graduation she developed a thyroid problem, and a doctor told her that if she did not have it operated on it would choke her to death. So, without graduating, she returned to North Carolina and had the operation at the Duke University Medical Center.

As a teen-ager, Joan Little had worked tobacco in the summers and waitressed at several local cafés, but after her operation she went to work in the Washington Garment Factory for four months, until September 1973, when, now aged eighteen, she went to work with Julius Rogers. Rogers was twenty years older than she and, among other things, had been a sheetrock finisher for fifteen years. Rogers taught her the trade. On the stand, the defendant described her trade this way:

"A sheetrock finisher goes into apartments, and after the hangers go in and hang the sheetrock, the finishers go in and tape it out, put mudding on it, bed it in, skim it out, and then sand it down so that the painters can come in and have it ready for vinyl as this courtroom has, or whatever."

This work and love took her first to Greenville, and later to Chapel Hill, where she lived for five months. But toward the end of 1973 the criminal difficulties came in a sheaf. In Jacksonville, North Carolina, she was charged with the possession of stolen goods, and a sawed-off shotgun belonging to an associate was found under the seat of her car, but the case was not prosecuted. On January 3, 1974, she was arrested in Washington for shoplifting, but with John Wilkinson as her attorney the charge was dismissed. Six days later she was arrested again for shoplifting in nearby Greenville, and this time was convicted, receiving a six-month suspended sentence. Six days after that she was arrested and charged with three separate felony charges of breaking, entering, and larceny. She was indicted by the grand jury on March 15, and the trial was set for June 4.

On June 3, 1974, Joan Little and Julius Rogers, along with two juveniles, Brenda Ann McCray and Mary Snipes, drove from Chapel Hill to Washington. They took a room at the Cumberland Motel, and later Brenda McCray and Mary Snipes told the SBI that Joan Little talked to them of how nice her bondsman, Jennings Bryant Freeman, was and, because he was so nice, she was going to have sex with him. The following morning Joan Little called Freeman, had him pick her up at the shopping center, and drive her to the jail. Although Mary Snipes was listed as a possible witness at Joan Little's murder trial (but not Brenda McCray), neither girl was called to the stand. Still, William Griffin got into this matter in his cross-examination of the defense's star witness:

> GRIFFIN: Now at the time that Mr. Freeman turned you in, did you tell him that you would have sex with him if he signed your bond for no fee?
> PAUL: Object to that.
> COURT: Overruled.
> LITTLE: No.
> GRIFFIN: You did not tell him that?
> LITTLE: No.
> PAUL: If your honor pleases, may we be heard on that?
> COURT: Well, she's answered that.
> PAUL: Yes, but this type of character assassination has nothing to do with this trial and what they are trying to do with this girl.

The objection fit into Paul's general strategy: identify for the press and the jury any suggestion of old-time racism or modern character assassination. He had postulated many times to the press that the prosecution was racist and its only hope to convict Joan Little was to assassinate her character.

Interestingly, Brenda McCray and Mary Snipes ended up in jail as well on this jaunt to Washington. They claimed to the SBI that the daytime matron of the Beaufort County jail had tricked them into a cell and then charged them with being runaways. But the significant event of their stay in jail was that, according to their testimony to the SBI, a white, male, blond trusty had exposed himself to the two girls and claimed that if they would "give him some" he would let them out of jail.

Joan Little was convicted on June 4 and, unable to make a bond of $15,000, she was locked up in the Beaufort County jail. She specifically requested that she remain in the Beaufort County jail rather than be moved, as was customary, to the Correctional Center for Women in Raleigh. The reason for the request, she told the clerk of court, was that, close to home, she could work on raising her bond. But she might also have thought her time would be easier in a small-town jail, where the officials were amateurs, rather than in the main women's facility, where the officials knew most of the tricks.

In her eighty-one days in jail, the rules were bent as a matter of course in a way, one could argue, that humanized the situation both of the jailer and the inmate. Alligood allowed her to make phone calls after he came on duty at 10:00 p.m., even though Sheriff Davis had specifically forbidden it. He brought her sandwiches and Cokes and cigarettes late at night, as she would read her romance magazines or her novels, *Ben Hur* or a Perry Mason mystery, or do crossword puzzles, or listen to the all-night radio show from Greenville. But if these could be said to be human touches, there was another interpretation. Describing Alligood locked in Joan Little's cell, his life ebbing away from a fatal icepick wound to his heart, defense lawyer Milton Williamson argued in his summation:

"All those sandwiches, all those Cokes and cigarettes . . . wasted. All his schemes and designs . . . wasted."

In those eighty-one days, Joan Little grew increasingly lonely and frustrated at Julius Rogers's withdrawal and, in turn, she appeared to be undergoing a religious awakening. In a long rambling letter to her friend in Chapel Hill, Mrs. Anna Eubanks, dated August 10, she wrote:

I received your letter and was glad to hear from you. It shows that everyone hasn't forgotten me. I knew Rogers was going to do a lot of drinking and I knew something was wrong because I dreamed he was sick. I told my mother something wasn't right. Rogers knows what he is doing. He is a mature man so you should not have to almost beg him to call or write, Mrs. Eubanks. I have written him four letters, and he has answered one. So I gave up on him a good while ago, but I'm not saying that I have forgotten him. I loved him before coming here, and I love him now, but he is letting me down and himself. I knew he doesn't have the money to get me out, but at least he can work so that I would have something to come back to. Rogers has that don't-care mind now. When he gets like that he drinks and won't work like he supposed to and won't eat anything. I know him better than anyone. He is a man you thought him to be. It's just that he is worried about me. He won't be satisfied for a while but there is a reason for him acting the way he is. He's not sleeping at all either, but tell him not to

worry, I will be home real soon. I'll call you next
week, and I will have good news for him, I am
sure. Court is going on this week, high court. I
will explain better after I call. One reason I think
he is not in touch is because I found out he hasn't
made one car payment since he has left. Mr. Freeman asked for his address. I didn't give it to him
because I don't have nothing to do with that car.
So tell Rogers, he knows, but tell him I'm in jail.
That's enough. I am almost crazy in here. I felt
better after I got out, so I don't really know what
to say, but I pleaded with him, because I was with
him, to cut down on his drinking, but if he cares
anything about hisself or me he would. Rogers
has a short temper when he gets that mind he has
now. He wants one thing now and that isn't
working out for him the way he thought but the
way he is going, we will lose everything we have
and never have anything unless he is sick or has
already gone on his way. Now I am coming for
my clothes, so just bear with me, until I get there.
Call my mother, please. I asked him to go to do it
some four weeks ago. He hasn't yet. I know he has
$1.50 for a phone call. It's very important and
with what she tells him, she will make him happy
to hear it. I am trying not to worry but I know
Rogers. I don't care what he is doing, but at least
he can care for himself. Your letter touched me
and just the thought of knowing somebody cares,
even if they can't help, means a lot. I never
thought you would write me. Thank you. You
don't know how much it means. I have everything
I need for right now. My mother brings some of
her clothes plus I had packed a small suitcase.
The jailers are very nice to me so I am feeling a
lot better now. I was only worrying why no answer from anyone, and my belongings. What did

he do with that. I guess half of my stuff is missing, but that's okay. I can buy more. Rogers has let me down, but he is not my husband, and I can't put my problems all on him, so I guess if I go to court I have to go alone, but I'm not afraid any more. Did he pay the fine in Jacksonville for me, or do you know? When I wrote him the last time, I told him he could call me any time after 10 p.m. The jailer would let me talk to him. They all are really nice. At least I have gained a little weight since I have been in here, and my skin has cleared. My health is fine, and I feel good every day. Last week and this week I had almost too much company. They are having court for two weeks. That Judge isn't playing either, but I am praying. We had an attempted jail break here. Two guys tried to get away but they didn't. The Lord has a way of showing you all the evil in the world and what he wants you to do with your life, but I am not complaining. There are some people who are in worse shape than I, so I consider myself as being blessed. God never lets anything happen without a warning. He knows just what he has to do to make everything right. As long as I have faith in him, I know I don't have anything to worry about, because God is a way-maker, I know. He's answered my prayers for many times, and when I don't have anything to do, I pray to God, talk just like he is sitting right here beside me. I'm not alone. God is always with me, so by me being in here alone, it gives me a chance to get closer to the Lord, so when I feel lonesome and think I can't make it, I put it in the Lord's hands. He knows just how much you can bear and he don't put no more on you than you can stand. Just pray for me and Rogers and please, help him too, help him. He needs somebody now, and it seems he has turned all his trust to you. Tell him, please, stop drinking and work. Please do not give me anything else to worry about. I have enough as it is, and he already knows that I love him, and I think about him everyday. Tell him just to keep the life and think of me as being right there. I have him there in my heart, and even though he hasn't called or anything I haven't lost my faith in him. It is the little things that mean so much. Until I hear from you again, I close, leaving my love and blessings.

Jo.

It could have been argued, far more forcefully than the prosecutor chose to do, that the seeds of crime were contained in that letter.

In the first five weeks of the trial, the defendant moved in and out of sight at a distance, separated by the bar in the courtroom and by her security guards at other times. She was always nicely dressed, usually in shimmery synthetics, sometimes in a schoolgirlish, sailor-boy costume. But she projected an interesting sensuality: the feline smoothness of her walk, the full lips, the shiny skin tones, her street wisdom and her stoicism. Her unusually large, limpid, dreamlike eyes were hypnotic, like balls moving on parallel pendulums. By white classical standards, she was most unattractive, but black had become beautiful since classical times, and her desirableness was evident to all. She showed emotion only at times when she smiled at Jerry Paul or when she was "with her own element," as one of the TV sketch artists put it. With them, she relaxed, and a softness came over her face, but generally her expression was blank, and the same sketch artist, who had covered the Watergate trials, saw far less emotion in this defendant than Haldeman or Erlichman had shown at their trials.

All the preening and coaching, the practicing on Jerry Paul's couch, and the press interviews were directed toward the *sine qua non* of the trial: her story of the attack from the stand. It began at 2:00 A.M., August 11, 1975.

LITTLE: I was laying on my bunk in Cell Number One. I was reading and listening to the radio.

PAUL: What were you listening to on the radio?

LITTLE: There is a program that comes on from Greenville that stays on till six o'clock in the morning, country western music, and that's what I was listening to.

PAUL: Now when he came back with the sandwiches and cigarettes, Miss Little, did he come here to the bars or did he enter into the cell?

LITTLE: Came into the cell.

PAUL: And what did he say at that time, if anything?

LITTLE: He said that he had brought the sandwiches and that he was going to talk to the dispatcher and that he would be back, and I took the sandwiches and he kept standing there, and he said that—by that time I had changed into my gown, and he was telling me that I looked real nice in my gown and that he was gonna, you know, wanted to have sex with me again.

(Again? Paul had steadfastly maintained throughout the year that this had been the only advance Alligood ever made, and he was not about to follow up now on the slip. The prosecution characteristically did not follow up later in cross-examination.)

Under cross-examination, Griffin did elicit that Alligood left her cell "in a hurry" at this 2:00 A.M.

visit. The doorbell to the jail had rung, and it was against the rules for him to be back there at all.

GRIFFIN: There was nothing unusual about him coming in there at that time of night, was there?

LITTLE: If you call it unusual, it was unusual because he wasn't supposed to be there.

PAUL: After he said he was going to the dispatcher's office and brought you the sandwiches which you put in Cell Number Two, when was the next time you saw Mr. Alligood?

LITTLE: When he came back the third time, when the incident occurred . . .

COURT: How's that?

LITTLE: When he came back the third time, that was when the incident occurred.

PAUL: Where did he come from? Did he open this door here? [Pointing to the jail diagram.]

LITTLE: Yes.

PAUL: Did he come inside?

LITTLE: Yes, sir.

PAUL: Where was he the first time you saw him?

LITTLE: Just standing there just outside the bars of Cell Number One.

PAUL: Outside the cell door?

LITTLE: Yes.

PAUL: Would you describe for me the expression on his face?

LITTLE: He had a sort of, I'll say, a silly-looking grin on his face.

COURT: Had what kind of grin?

LITTLE: Sort of silly grin.

COURT: Silly grin.

PAUL: All right, did you notice anything else about him?

LITTLE: No, not at that time.

PAUL: All right, where were you when he came and stood in the doorway?

LITTLE: When he first came into the automatic door and stood at that door, which was the first time that I had seen him, I was up. I had gotten up off the bunk at that time and stood up.

PAUL: All right, where were you standing?

LITTLE: Just approximately middleway the bunk.

PAUL: What did Mr. Alligood say to you at that time, Miss Little?

LITTLE: He said that he had been nice to me and that it was time that I be nice to him, and that he wanted . . .

PAUL: Speak up.

LITTLE: He said that he had been nice to me and it was time that I be nice to him.

PAUL: Anything else?

LITTLE: That he . . . that he wanted to . . . wanted me to give him some pussy . . .

PAUL: Anything else?

LITTLE: Not at that time.

PAUL: Now, how were you dressed at that time?

LITTLE: I had on a gown and a pair of panties.

PAUL: Anything else?

LITTLE: . . . and a . . .

COURT: Had on a gown and what?

LITTLE: I had on a gown, a pair of panties, and . . .

COURT: Panties.

LITTLE: And a scarf that had a lot of colors in it.

PAUL: Where was the scarf?

LITTLE: It was tied around my head.

WILKINSON: May it please the Court, should the attorney come back to the table.

COURT: He may be going to point out something.

PAUL: I am going to point out some stuff, your honor. I realize Mr. Wilkinson is trying to disrupt . . .

WILKINSON: Objection.

COURT: Members of the jury, do not consider that conversation.

PAUL: Now, Miss Little, what did you say to him?

LITTLE: What did I say to him?

PAUL: Yes.

LITTLE: I told him, no, that I didn't feel I should be nice to him in that way, and I asked him to leave.

PAUL: Did you continue to stand there or did you move?

LITTLE: He came, he started . . . he was standing there and he started to take off his shoes outside the corridor.

PAUL: He took off his shoes out here?

LITTLE: Yes.

PAUL: Did he take them both off?

LITTLE: Yes.

PAUL: Then what did he do?

LITTLE: He started in towards the cell and I backed off to the back wall.

PAUL: You backed up. Where did you back up to?

LITTLE: To the right side of the bath.

PAUL: And what did he say?

LITTLE: He said that I may as well do it because if I told it to Ellis [Ellis Tetterton, another jailer] or Red [Red Davis, the sheriff], none of them were gonna believe me anyway.

PAUL: Did he say anything else to you?

LITTTLE: He didn't say anything at that time. He just came towards me.

PAUL: What did you do?

LITTLE: I stood there scared, and hoping that he would turn around and leave, and he started feeling all over my breasts.

PAUL: Describe for me how he started feeling all over you.

LITTLE: He just started touching me, fumbling over my breasts.

PAUL: What were you doing at this time?

LITTLE: Standing still, scared stiff. I didn't know what to do.

PAUL: What physical actions were you doing if any?

LITTLE: I had started to cry.

PAUL: What did Alligood say while he was standing there feeling your breasts and you were crying, and he is fondling you, what did he say to you?

LITTLE: He didn't say anything. He just continued and he started . . . He reached down and pulled up my gown and put his hands between my legs.

PAUL: Did he say anything that time?

COURT: Wait just one minute. Put his hands where?

LITTLE: In between my legs.

COURT: All right, now, let me say this to you. It is apparent to me looking up that some of the jurors are straining to hear. So please speak up just a little louder. All right, go ahead.

PAUL: Now, Miss Little, while he was doing that, and he was feeling between your legs, what did he say to you at that time?

LITTLE: He told me that he knew that I had did it before and then he backed up away from me.

PAUL: What did he say?

LITTLE: He said he wasn't gonna leave, and he came more forcefully in what he tried to say.

PAUL: Did you still have your gown on?

LITTLE: No.

PAUL: How did your gown get off of you?

LITTLE: He slipped it over my head.

PAUL: Were you crying while he was doing that?

LITTLE: Yes.

PAUL: All right, now, have you left out anything that he said to you?

LITTLE: No.

But from defense notes on conversations with Joan Little, she had left out a few exchanges, that had a slightly meaner cast.

"What's wrong, do you think you're too good for me?" Alligood had said. "I know you do it with others. Regardless of what you say or what you tell, they will not believe you, so you had better do what I say," he said.

"Hell, no, I ain't gonna do no shit like that," she replied, and reached down to pick up her gown. When she stood back up and looked at him . . .

PAUL: As he came back towards you what did he do, Miss Little?

LITTLE: He just started taking his pants off, and when he took his pants off, then he came towards me and he said . . . he reached for me. I told him no, I wasn't gonna do anything like that, and then that's when he tried to force me towards him and when he was trying to force me towards him, I tried to get away and reach for my gown and that's when he snatched it out of my hand and told me that I wasn't gonna put my gown back on. And at that point, I noticed that he had an icepick in his hand.

PAUL: What hand did he have the icepick in?

LITTLE: In his left hand.

PAUL: What did he do then?

LITTLE: He grabbed me around the neck with his right hand.

PAUL: And did what?

LITTLE: Pulled me towards him.

PAUL: Towards him? Where was he?

LITTLE: Standing middleway of the bunk at that time.

PAUL: What was he doing while he pulled you towards him?

LITTLE: He had me by my neck, right by the back of my neck, holding me, pulling me towards him, and he had the icepick at my head.

PAUL: Did he sit down?

LITTLE: Yes, sir.

PAUL: He had his hand, as I understand it, his right hand on the back of your neck?

LITTLE: Yes.

PAUL: Left hand, icepick?

LITTLE: Yes.

PAUL: Can you tell me whether or not at this time he pulled off your scarf and set it down beside him, is that what happened?

LITTLE: No.

WILKINSON: Objection.

COURT: Sustained. You're testifying now. You are putting words in her mouth.

PAUL: Now, Miss Little, will you explain to me when Mr. Alligood took your panties off?

LITTLE: He didn't.

PAUL: As he pulled you towards him and sat down on the bunk, explain from that point on what happened.

LITTLE: He pulled me down to the floor . . .

COURT: Stop. He pulled you on the floor, not the cot, but to the floor.

LITTLE: To the floor, yes.

PAUL: And he was sitting on the cot at this time?

LITTLE: He was sitting on the cot . . . He said he wanted me to suck him, and I told him, no, that I'm not gonna do it. He threatened me with the icepick, and I then did what he told me to do.

PAUL: Did he have an erection when you began to suck him?

LITTLE: No.

PAUL: Did he later have an erection while you were sucking him?

LITTLE: Yes.

PAUL: Where was the icepick while you were sucking him?

LITTLE: In his left hand.

PAUL: Describe the manner in which the icepick was in his left hand.

LITTLE: He had a grip on it just like this. [She indicates with her fist next to her temple.] It was down by his side, right in my face.

PAUL: Now, Miss Little, how long did you have oral sex with him?

LITTLE: Maybe three, four, five minutes.

PAUL: What were you watching while you were having oral sex?

LITTLE: I was looking at that icepick, because I didn't know what he was gonna do. I didn't know whether he was going to kill me or not.

PAUL: What happened after you had oral sex with him for a while?

LITTLE: He loosened the grip on the icepick.

PAUL: Speak up, please.

LITTLE: He loosened his grip on the icepick and I grabbed for it and it fell to the floor.

PAUL: Speak up.

LITTLE: He loosened the grip on the icepick and I reached for it and it fell to the floor.

PAUL: Then what happened?

LITTLE: He went for the icepick.

COURT: He did what?

LITTLE: He grabbed for it.

PAUL: And what happened?

LITTLE: I grabbed for the icepick. [And she broke down in sobs.]

COURT: [To the jurors] All right, go back to the jury room for fifteen minutes. [And the jury retired for a brief recess.]

The author had asked Jerry Paul whether in the year of bolstering for this performance on the stand there was not a danger that Joan Little would not get too familiar with her story. Would she not get bored with it and lose the spontaneous emotional reaction to it that was so central to her deliverance? Paul shook his head.

"She never told what happened in that cell. I was the only one she told it to, and she told it to me only one time before she took the stand. I had never asked her, didn't want to, and my orders to her were not to tell it to anybody. And she didn't want to tell it. I had her see a psychiatrist, and she said she didn't want to tell it to no damn psychiatrist. That part of my program was a failure, so I had to be my own psychiatrist. She got into such a thing about the story that she quit going over to the office. So many people over there were hounding her about it. She'd come over to my house. But that wasn't so bad, because we had a great time. I taught her how to question witnesses. I'd bring in prospective witnesses. I'd start 'em, and Joan would finish 'em.

"So, yes, I did not want her to rehearse the story of the attack. It was a negative program, really. I simply stayed away from it, requiring her to keep these emotions bottled up for a year. There was no way to re-create the scene of that night if she was a drone or a plastic figure on the stand. Not letting those emotions come out until she took the stand was a way of capturing realism."

Just to make sure that the jury knew how upset Joan Little was during the recess, a woman on the defense team was instructed to go to the women's toilet next to the jury room, make loud sobbing noises, and flush the toilet quite a few times.

PAUL: All right, Miss Little, where did the icepick land when it fell?
LITTLE: On the left-hand side of the sink between the bunk and the sink.

PAUL: Tell the jurors what happened then.

LITTLE: I reached for the icepick and he reached for the icepick. I got the icepick first.

PAUL: Speak up, please.

LITTLE: I got the icepick first, and when I grabbed the icepick and I hit at him, he fell backwards, and I came up with my feet, and he was sitting on the bunk facing me, and I was standing there facing him.

COURT: Did you actually hit him with the icepick when you hit that first time?

LITTLE: I don't know. [Invariably, on the stand she said she hit out "at" him, as if she was using the icepick like a tennis racket, but in the defense notes she had said, "I kept hitting out, *aiming for his chest*," which was obvious enough from the four stab wounds around his heart . . . unless, of course, one were to give credence to the shark theory concerning Terry Bell.]

He was sitting on the bunk, and I was facing him, and he came up at me. I struck at him. At this time he came at me. Then in the course of that, he finally got up, and he grabbed me around my wrists and when he grabbed me around my wrists I had the pick in my hand with the point out towards me and the handle in my hand facing him, and I pushed him, and he came back up at me with more force and I put my feet on the bunk and he came behind me. When he came behind me he had both my hands, and I came up over my right shoulder and hit him.

PAUL: Now did you switch hands with the icepick?

LITTLE: Yes.

PAUL: When did you do that?

LITTLE: When he grabbed my hand . . .

COURT: Which hand did he grab, which wrist did he grab?

LITTLE: Both of them.

COURT: Grabbed both of them?

LITTLE: Yes. And he was in front of me and when I got a chance to push him away with my right hand and got my hand out extended far enough to put the handle in my left hand, that's when I changed hands.

PAUL: What happened then?

LITTLE: He was behind me. I put my feet on the edge of the bunk so I could place the weight of my body up against him, and I hit over my right shoulder and he turned me loose.

PAUL: Do you know whether or not you hit him when you hit over your right shoulder?

LITTLE: Not at that time. He fell forward.

PAUL: Where and how did he fall?

LITTLE: He fell middleway of the bunk forward with his knees on the floor and just on the bunk but he was raised up with his head turned . . .

PAUL: Which way was his head facing?

LITTLE: Facing the wall near the sink.

PAUL: Where were his knees?

LITTLE: As far as I can remember on the floor. He fell forward with his knees on the floor, his hands on the bunk with his head turned to the right facing the wall the sink was on.

PAUL: During that struggle, what happened to your scarf?

LITTLE: It must have come off, I don't know.

PAUL: Now, after he fell and turned loose of you, what did you do?

LITTLE: I saw blood on his right side of his face and I turned and ran to Cell Number Two.

PAUL: When you got to Cell Number Two, what did you do?

LITTLE: I reached for the first thing I saw, which was

my blue jeans, blue pull-over blouse, and my pocketbook.

PAUL: Did you see him again after you grabbed these articles?

LITTLE: As I was coming out, I didn't see him. When I got out into the corridor, this hallway outside the control door, I turned and looked around and he was standing there. He was standing at the doorway near that bath thing.

PAUL: What do you remember about him as you looked back and saw him?

LITTLE: I just remember seeing his face and seeing that grin that he had on his face when I saw him the first time.

PAUL: What did you do then?

LITTLE: I slammed the automatic door.

PAUL: After you slammed the door, what did you do?

LITTLE: I came out to this door here [the door to the women's cellblock] and it was open.

PAUL: What did you find in that door, Miss Little, if anything?

LITTLE: There was a ring of keys that had a bunch of keys on it.

PAUL: What did you do, and speak up?

LITTLE: There was a ring of keys and sticking inside the door, and I took the keys out of that door; came down the corridor and slipped on my pants and my blouse.

COURT: Where were you when you put on your pants and blouse?

LITTLE: Just outside the main door. I slipped on my pants and blouse, still holding the keys and my pocketbook, came down the hallway and went to this door [the door to the sheriff's office and freedom] and tried to put the key inside the door but neither of them would fit.

PAUL: Speak up.

LITTLE: Neither one of the keys would fit on that ring. So I came back to the jailer's desk, and there was a file box, a green card thing where you put files in. There was one single key laying in the file box. I took the key from the file box, went back to the door, stuck the key inside, and came out the entrance [to the basement]. [On cross-examination, Little explained that she had seen the key to the outside door used many times when she was on the telephone in the jailer's office.] I was coming up the steps to the parking lot when there were head-lights coming around from the side entrance. I went across the parking lot to Union Alley, just threw away the keys, and kept running.

The preparation of Joan Little for her cross-exami-nation was somewhat more gutty than any other stage of her preening. She naturally saw William Griffin as her tormentor. He had indicted her, had kept her in jail those six months before her release on bond, and now was trying to send her to the gas chamber. The defense sought to insulate the defendant against this tormentor, protect her from skillful prosecutorial de-vices that might anger her and set off a series of events by which she would hang herself, as so often happens on witness stands, as had happened to Inez Garcia.

Therefore, Jerry Paul was anxious to change her perception of William Griffin, to make her think of him not as her tormentor, but as a fool whom she was outsmarting, and a trapped fool at that, who had to do this job to feed his family and for whom a good person should feel a little sorry. The task was to show her how to deal with people who talked down to her.

"In the direct examination, I wanted a raw, natural emotionalism," Paul explained. "I wanted her emo-tional at certain points, because they were emotional by nature, but not too smooth. In cross-examination, on the other hand, I wanted her calm and creative. She should answer succinctly, without hesitation, and without leaving anything out, so that later Griffin might accuse her of lying."

In this preparation, Paul set a tone of partnership. He began to appreciate Joan Little's intelligence and believed that she had rejected the pattern of subservience that she had been taught growing up. "So why feed into that by acting like an authority?" he asked rhetorically. To act the part of Griffin in training, Paul characteristically had no time for amateurs. He brought in a role-playing expert from Washington, D.C., Dr. Don Clarkson, and the expert grilled her in the crudest possible language.

"Joan Little, aren't you a whore?"

"Didn't you enjoy it there, Miss Little, with his penis in your mouth like that?"

They went over the dangerous points in her narrative again and again, so that when Griffin asked the same question in polite terms, he would seem minorleague by comparison.

Her interrogation by Griffin lasted six hours, and the prosecutor approached his job, yeomanlike, by carrying her over her work record, her association with Julius Rogers, her prior convictions, through her eighty-one days with Alligood's kindnesses and his bending of the rules, over her notations in the crossword-puzzle books. So far, her consistency held.

But as he approached the night of the incident, Griffin's exasperation at her calmness and her adroitness became manifest.

"He left you alone in the office," Griffin asserted as he reached the 10:30 P.M. conclave in the jailer's office, the essential element of the state's case that gave her access to the icepick.

"I wasn't alone," she replied.

"Yes, you were!" he shouted at her. Paul objected

and was sustained. Getting closer to the climax of the trial, the consummation of the entire Joan Little crusade, Griffin's voice became increasingly shrill. Paul objected to his "hollering" at the witness, and the judge calmly noted that shouting was a two-edged sword, which the jury would no doubt take into consideration.

GRIFFIN: But there he was, fully dressed at that time, did you see an icepick in his hand at that time?

LITTLE: No.

GRIFFIN: What did he say to you?

LITTLE: He came in and he stood at the door and he said it's time that you be nice to me because I been nice to you.

GRIFFIN: What did you say?

LITTLE: I told him, no, that I wasn't gonna be nice to him.

GRIFFIN: Is that the words, is that the exact words that he used?

LITTLE: Yes.

GRIFFIN: Is that the exact words that you used?

LITTLE: Yes. [In defense notes, she told him "Get the hell out."]

GRIFFIN: What was the next thing he did?

LITTLE: Took his shoes off.

GRIFFIN: Did you say anything to him when he took his shoes off?

LITTLE: No.

GRIFFIN: Not a word?

LITTLE: No.

GRIFFIN: Didn't you say what are you taking your shoes off for, what are you gonna do, get out of here; you didn't say anything like that?

LITTLE: No, sir.

GRIFFIN: At that point what did he do?

LITTLE: He came towards me and I was standing

there near the sink, and he started feeling on my breasts.

GRIFFIN: Both hands, speak up, both hands?

LITTLE: Yes.

GRIFFIN: Where was the icepick at that time?

LITTLE: I hadn't seen it, Mr. Griffin.

GRIFFIN: You did not see any weapon at that time?

LITTLE: No sir.

GRIFFIN: Did you slap him?

LITTLE: No sir.

GRIFFIN: Did you knock his hands away from your breasts?

LITTLE: I just stood there.

GRIFFIN: What, did he still have his clothes on at that point?

LITTLE: All except for his shoes.

GRIFFIN: What did you say to him?

LITTLE: I asked him would he please leave.

GRIFFIN: And what did he say?

LITTLE: He said he wasn't gonna leave.

GRIFFIN: Did you do anything at that time?

LITTLE: Started crying.

GRIFFIN: How long did he stay there with his hands on your breasts?

LITTLE: Maybe two or three minutes; I am only guessing.

GRIFFIN: Would you show us how he had his hands on your breasts?

LITTLE: He just started feeling over me.

GRIFFIN: You didn't slap his hands away from you; you didn't push him away from you?

LITTLE: No sir.

GRIFFIN: After feeling of your breasts there for two or three minutes, what did he do?

LITTLE: He reached down for my gown.

GRIFFIN: Did you strike him, hit him, push him?

LITTLE: No.

GRIFFIN: Did you say anything to him?

LITTLE: No, I just stood there.

GRIFFIN: You just stood there; how long did this continue with him holding the gown up and he had his hand, his left hand between your legs?

LITTLE: Maybe a minute.

GRIFFIN: You never screamed, hollered, shouted, pushed him away, struck him, or anything during this period of time?

LITTLE: I was scared, and I didn't know whether to scream or what, because he could have killed me right then and there.

GRIFFIN: He didn't have a weapon, did he?

LITTLE: He was bigger than me.

GRIFFIN: He had not threatened you, had he, had he said anything except make a proposition to you?

LITTLE: He said some things later.

GRIFFIN: He had not threatened you; he had not said he was gonna hurt you; all he said to you in effect was that he wanted to have sex with you, is that right?

LITTLE: Yes sir.

GRIFFIN: And you didn't holler, you didn't scream, you didn't fight him off, is that right?

LITTLE: No I did not, but if you had been a woman you wouldn't have known what to do either, you probably wouldn't have screamed either, because you wouldn't have known what he would have done to you.

(In the preening of Joan Little for this performance, the mock interrogators for the defense had asked her why she did not scream, and her first answer was: "What for?" And so Jerry Paul had her retire to the bedroom, write out the questions she thought Griffin would ask and later had her write out the answers she would give. Then, first, he would be the prosecutor, and she would read her answers; then, their roles reversed, "to see," he said, how the answers sounded to her. To the question of why she didn't scream, Paul had said to her, ("Who are you, Joan? What do you come from? Why do you think you didn't make a fuss?" and in this way extracted from Joan Little a realization of her paralysis at this moment. Once the desired response was arrived at, he made her practice its delivery over and over. The technique, Paul said, was intended to point out the stupidity of the question, and make Griffin look foolish, which it did.)

GRIFFIN: What did he do then?

LITTLE: He started taking off his trousers.

GRIFFIN: Now I want you to stand up and show us how he took off his trousers. Did he reach down around his ankles like that to get them off?

LITTLE: No, he just unbuckled his trousers and took them off.

GRIFFIN: How about his shorts, his underwear, how did he take them off?

LITTLE: Mr. Griffin, I don't remember that.

GRIFFIN: Well, you found out later he certainly didn't have them on, didn't you?

LITTLE: I found out later?

GRIFFIN: Well, you said you had oral sex with him. You knew at that time whether or not he had them on, didn't you?

LITTLE: Yes.

GRIFFIN: Could you tell after he got his pants off whether or not he was erect?

LITTLE: No.

She testified that Alligood had taken her gown off over her head, and thrown it on the cell floor. She had reached for it on the floor; and "When I reached down for it and came back up holding the gown, he snatched it up, and that's when I saw the icepick in his left hand."

GRIFFIN: Did he say anything?

LITTLE: Say exactly what he said?

GRIFFIN: Say exactly what he said.

LITTLE: He grabbed for my neck and he reached for me and told me to come over, that he wanted to have sex with me.

GRIFFIN: Is that what you said yesterday? Did he say sex or did he use some other term?

LITTLE: Mr. Griffin, the reason why I am using the word sex is because I don't want to use any other word, because it's still embarrassing to me.

GRIFFIN: I want to ask you what the word was you used yesterday, and you said it yesterday, and you can say it again for us today; what was it that he said?

PAUL: I object. She has said it once.

COURT: Overruled, she can say it on cross-examination.

LITTLE: He said he wanted me to give him some pussy.

Then she testified that the jailer forced her to her knees brandishing the icepick at her head, and sitting half-naked on the bunk.

GRIFFIN: Why didn't you twist away from him? He only had one hand on you.

LITTLE: And the icepick in the other.

GRIFFIN: Is that the icepick?

LITTLE: Looks like it.

GRIFFIN: I want you to take it in your hand and show us how he put it at your head.

LITTLE: Like this.

(And she put the icepick to her temple. Griffin thought he had her. "I thought she would croak," he said, but he did not realize that Joan Little had been toughened for this moment more than any other. Defense lawyer Milton Williamson, that wily trial attorney from Eastern North Carolina, had handed her the icepick in the mock interrogation, and she took it loosely, tentatively. Williamson scolded her, "Now, Joan, when Griffin hands you that icepick, grab it firmly with your left hand. Otherwise, the jury's going to think that you're unsure," and they went over the sequence time and again.)

GRIFFIN: What did he say?

LITTLE: To go ahead and do it.

GRIFFIN: Go ahead and do it; now he had said to you that he wanted you to have traditional sex with him, and yet he pulled you down to have unnatural or nontraditional sex with you, is that right?

PAUL: I object. She never said that.

COURT: Well, sustained.

GRIFFIN: I am trying to keep from using the word.

PAUL: Then why does he want her to use the word?

COURT: I sustained the objection.

GRIFFIN: He said he wanted you to give him some pussy, isn't that what he said?

LITTLE: Yes sir.

(Griffin's discomfort with the language of the event began to take on comic overtones.)

GRIFFIN: He pulled you down and told you to do it; did you know what he meant?

LITTLE: No.

GRIFFIN: What word did he use?

LITTLE: He told me to suck him.

GRIFFIN: And did you suck him?

LITTLE: I did exactly what he told me to do.

GRIFFIN: How long did it take for him to become erect, if he did?

LITTLE: Two or three minutes.

GRIFFIN: He was sitting upright on the bunk?

LITTLE: I wasn't really looking at him. I was looking at the icepick that was pointed directly at my face.

GRIFFIN: How could it be in your face with you doing what you have described you were doing?

LITTLE: The pick was laying right there, and all I had to do, I didn't have to turn my head. All I had to do was turn my eyes and there it was right there.

GRIFFIN: Did he have a tight grip on it?

LITTLE: At first he did.

GRIFFIN: And you reached for it, and it fell on the floor?

LITTLE: He had loosened his grip when it fell, when I reached for it and it fell.

GRIFFIN: How could you tell he had loosened his grip?

LITTLE: I kept watching the icepick . . .

GRIFFIN: Did you at any time bite him, strike him in the genitals, or in some other way disable him?

LITTLE: No.

GRIFFIN: Why didn't you do that?

LITTLE: My only reason was to get that icepick away from him so that he wouldn't have it pointed at me as he did before.

GRIFFIN: Well, he could have broken you in two without any weapon at all couldn't he?

LITTLE: A man his size . . . I would say yes.

GRIFFIN: And you had an opportunity during this period of time to disable him by hitting him in the genitals, biting him?

LITTLE: I didn't have that much power over him, Mr. Griffin.

GRIFFIN: When did you strike him with the icepick?

LITTLE: I'm not sure I hit him.

GRIFFIN: Didn't you feel the icepick go into his body?

LITTLE: No, I was so scared, I had the pick gripped so tightly, I probably couldn't tell whether I had even hit him.

(The language of the autopsy report read: "Seven puncture wounds were present over the anterior chest. Two were present over the upper sternum [breastbone] and five were present over the left upper chest about the nipple and about the sternal margins. The wounds resemble puncture wounds and measured up to 4 mm. in diameter. . . . One wound entered the left ventricle [of the heart] and resulted in severe cardial tamponade. The cause of death was severe cardiac tamponade secondary to a penetrating injury to the left ventricle.")

GRIFFIN: Did you hit him or not?

LITTLE: I'm not sure.

GRIFFIN: How many times did he come up at you with his arms outstretched?

LITTLE: Three, four times.

GRIFFIN: Three times, four times, each time he came up, did you stick him?

LITTLE: I'm not sure that I hit him.

GRIFFIN: At what part of the body did you direct the icepick?

LITTLE: I didn't direct the icepick to any particular part of the body.

GRIFFIN [after the witness described again how Alligood got behind in the struggle, how she switched the icepick to her left hand, and struck at him across her shoulder]: You came over your shoulder; where did you strike him?

LITTLE: It was on the right side of his head.

GRIFFIN: Did he say anything?

LITTLE: No.

GRIFFIN: Didn't say 'ouch, I'm hurt, I'm bleeding, I'm stabbed, you're trying to kill me'; didn't say anything like that?

LITTLE: No.

GRIFFIN: Not a word?

LITTLE: No.

GRIFFIN: How did he fall to the bunk with you between him and the bunk?

LITTLE: I came from in front of him.

GRIFFIN: And he fell like a tree. You got out from under him and he toppled like a tree, right onto the bunk?

LITTLE: A tree falls with no life at all, Mr. Griffin, and he didn't fall in that way.

GRIFFIN: And he fell and you knew he was injured?

LITTLE: Yes.

GRIFFIN: Now you say you went and got your clothes out of Cell Number Two?

LITTLE: That is correct.

GRIFFIN: And when you started out, he was standing in the corridor . . . and you walked right by him?

LITTLE: I didn't even see him, not until I got outside the corridor—and turned around and looked in and he was standing there.

GRIFFIN: Did he say anything?

LITTLE: No.

GRIFFIN: Did he make any effort to stop you?

LITTLE: No, he was just standing there, with a funny facial grin on his face.

GRIFFIN: Standing there smiling at you, silly grin, I believe you called it.

LITTLE: Mr. Griffin, as I tell it to you now, I see him the same way in my mind.

GRIFFIN: I'm asking you if he had a silly grin, is that what you said?

LITTLE: Just exactly what I said.

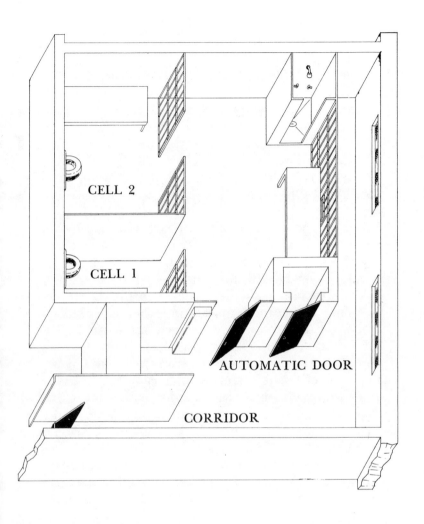

CELL 2

CELL 1

AUTOMATIC DOOR

CORRIDOR

Women's Section
Beaufort County Jail

GRIFFIN: Blood streaming from his head standing there grinning?

LITTLE: I don't remember seeing any blood at that time.

GRIFFIN: I want you to think about how many times you struck him with that icepick.

LITTLE: How many times I know for sure that I hit him? Only once.

GRIFFIN: Which one was that?

LITTLE: In the head.

And so, the excruciating part of her testimony was completed—excruciating for Joan Little, to be sure, regardless of how much was the truth, how much was packaged for her by her attorneys, how much was false; excruciating for the audience in the courtroom, including the author, for at times he, supposedly a dispassionate witness of the proceedings, wanted to cry out for it to stop; excruciating for William Griffin, who never relished his task, motivated only by the misty lawyer's belief that this was a case that had to be tried, who had, for a year, faced a battery of skilled lawyers, a platoon of sophisticated and often highly paid experts with very little help at all, and a string of innuendos about him personally. He would go home to the East and console himself with the comments of friends who cared little whether he won or lost, but only that he had gone up to Raleigh and "acted like a gentleman."

Still, her testimony trailed on for another hour with a few interesting interchanges. Griffin tried his hand at poetry, describing her running down Union Alley, swinging the ring of jail keys, "jingling like a horse and sleigh with bells on it, going to grandma's house at Christmas," but the judge sustained Paul's objection. Joan Little pled the Fifth Amendment to four questions on the breaking-and-entering case, and

when Griffin asked her if one Linda Jones hadn't been
her lover in Central Prison in Raleigh, before she got
out on $115,000 bond, she made him look silly once
again by describing the virtual isolation in which she
had been kept at that facility. She told of the two
offers to spirit her out of the country: the one at Celine Chenier's house by a woman, who, after Joan
Little refused her invitation, had replied, "Well, personally, I think you are a damn fool," and the other, a
few hours before turning herself in to the SBI, by a
man called "Bucky" who had a private plane and
good connections abroad. And finally, almost as a last
hurrah, Paul asked her,

"Did you intend at any time to try to evade the
authorities?"

"I knew that if the Beaufort County police or the
Washington policemen had seen me on the streets,
they would have shot me down," she replied. "I
wouldn't 'a' had a chance to be in this courtroom now
to tell what happened, just by reading what was in the
newspapers. They had written it up saying that I had
intentionally left a man to die and had killed him,
and I wanted the people to know that I wasn't that
type of person, to leave a person there and not try to
help him."

It had been a brilliant performance.

CHAPTER 14

LOUIS RANDOLPH

THE balance of Joan Little's defense was displayed magnificently for the jury in summations. James Rowan was elegant and dignified in explaining the concepts of law involved: presumption of innocence, burden of the state to prove its case beyond a reasonable doubt, the burden of the state to preserve its evidence, always the burden of the state. The crime scene was a "shambles," he said, and as a result the state's case was a spiderweb. Marvin Miller was adroit with the case law, as he had been throughout in arguing legalities. Milton Williamson, called by *Time* magazine the best trial attorney in Eastern North Carolina, was precise, humorous, his granite features turning wonderfully expressive as he identified the missing links in the state's chain of evidence. He invoked Genesis as the best story of circumstantial evidence ever, Joseph mourning the death of his son after having been shown his son's coat, drenched in goat's blood.

"They brought you a bloody coat here," he said, "but circumstantial evidence, to be believed, must exclude every reasonable hypothesis of innocence."

Karen Galloway was the most effective of them all, emotional, reducing jurors to tears, as she transported them into that cell that night, making them feel Alligood's power and his perversion, and making them touch Joan Little's defenselessness, her paralysis, her violation: "What was she going to do? Give him a karate chop?" Jerry Paul was apologetic for his yokelism and his passion, perceiving the hand of God in accidents favorable to his symbol and in his own faltering that somehow always seemed to come out right. He summoned Martin Luther King and Rosa Parks (who began the Montgomery bus boycott in 1955), as if all the jurors, instead of only six, were black.

"If Rosa Parks had obeyed the law of the land, if she had sat at the back of the bus, *you* wouldn't be serving on this jury today, and black children would not be going to good schools, and black people would be going to separate bathrooms or no bathrooms at all. So sometimes you have to stand up for morality and sometimes God chooses people to make points just like he chose Rosa Parks, just like he chose Joan Little."

The shambles of the prosecution was just as clear. Lester Chalmers, as the state attorney general's representative on the prosecution, addressed the jury as if he were exhorting the elders of Beaufort County in an empty courtroom, defined murder under North Carolina law as "Thou shalt not kill," mixed in "Conscience do make cowards of us all," quoted Proverbs, "The wicked flee when no man pursues, while the righteous stand bold as a lion"—forgetting that the judge had ruled out premeditation: "Her intent was to take his life at all costs"—and then, conjuring up revenge and Inez Garcia,

"Where is there evidence of self-defense? This murder was not in defense of an assault. The assault had already been committed. This murder was committed in *retaliation!*"

By contrast, William Griffin was calm and terse. He eschewed Bible-quoting: "Everyone else has quoted the Bible, and I think I'll let you go on that." If his case was a spiderweb, which was not necessarily a criticism with a circumstantial case, theirs was a good piece of Swiss cheese, with lots of holes. The icepick floated into that cell as if on a magic carpet, accompanied by a puff of smoke. Alligood looked like he'd been shot with a shotgun, not stabbed, the holes directed at his heart. Griffin asked the jury to look behind the smokescreen and the obfuscation—"a fifty-dollar word"—and to ignore the defense's red herrings. He asked them to treat the evidence like the game of Concentration, turning over the cards one by one, until the outlines of the crime emerged. "You don't have to see all the cards to get the picture." The question, he said, was:

"Are you going to construct a wall so thick and so high that no amount of evidence would ever take it down, would ever put a hole in it? Are you going to do that, or are you going to construct a reasonable wall? I submit that you've got enough bricks removed from that wall to see through it, to see what the truth really is."

And John Wilkinson sought to dissociate himself from the whole nasty business.

"I'm not carrying any cause," he said. "I shall not weep if you turn her loose—it's not my responsibility. I won't shed a tear. . . . I will not expect my black friends in Beaufort County to be mad with me. I will not expect Jerry to be mad with me. I will expect Brother Williamson the next time we're in court together over in Washington and Greenville to speak to me with his usual courtesy. I wish to say to Brother Hobgood . . . Oh, I beg your pardon . . . to Your Honor, I respect him as a man and a judge.

"No, this is not any cause to me. It's a case. I will not consider the blacks have won a victory if you find her not guilty. If you can honestly do it, go ahead. It's on your conscience, not mine. I will not expect the whites to have won anything if you find her guilty. I don't think it makes a hoot one way or the other as far as race is concerned. One of the most solid rebukes to those who seek to use this case to attack our whole system so dear to us all, white and black, is to make anything else except a search for truth depend on it."

Wilkinson fumed, smiled cherubically, railed in his grainy voice about the injustice to Beaufort County, as he limped around the bar on his game leg, whispered about the shabbiness of it all, complimented Paul as being sharp as a butcher's cleaver, and turned around and slew him with it. The speech had everything: aphorism, Shakespeare, farce, brilliance. It could be recaptured only by a Sir Laurence Olivier. He denied he is the last of a dying breed, but where else can you see this? He never looked at the jury. They were irrelevant now. He looked at the audience, the press particularly, for this was his fulfillment. But the reenactment of the crime—that was the high point, when he made Billy Griffin play Alligood and look the fool.

Tape had been stuck to the floor to outline the dimensions of Joan Little's cell for Karen Galloway's performance, and Wilkinson went to it.

"Look at this thing. Look at it on the floor, ladies and gentlemen of the jury. Look what they're trying to get you to buy: that Joan Little in this small cell, squatting down . . ." and Wilkinson painfully, slowly went to one knee, apologizing parenthetically, "I got one game leg, served four years in the army in spite of it, but I'm going to get down on the other."

Steadying himself precariously, his rear side to the audience, he went on. "Down here like that with a powerful man weighing two hundred pounds, she was able to take an icepick away from him, and it fell. Where? Under the sink, and this guy right on top of her, a two-hundred pounder."

He paused, eyed Griffin. "You don't weigh two

hundred, Billy, but come over here a moment."
Griffin acceded with an embarrassed smile, and stood
over Wilkinson, bending over slightly and stiffly—he
was no actor—and Wilkinson continued.

"And when he reached for her, she fell over . . ."
and Wilkinson himself fell over into a seated position.
"She beat him to it, and this guy on top of her, strong,
going for the icepick." Griffin did not move. "And yet
she was able to get up from there to stab him. Pick,
pick, pick, pick." He jabbed at Griffin, who tried to
laugh like a good sport and returned to his seat.

But then Wilkinson tried to get up off the floor,
and he could not! His game leg would not cooperate,
and he thrashed about on the courtroom floor for an
eternal moment, as the audience started to giggle unabashedly. Finally, he made it to his feet, his face beet-
red, angry.

"Well, ladies and gentlemen of the jury, buy it if
you want to, but if you'll believe that, you'll believe
anything. You'll have trouble getting that capsule
down reason's throat. The only possible difficulty I
can see in giving a horse a capsule is when you're
blowing on one end of the straw and him on the
other."

The jury retired at 11:15 A.M., August 15. In the
jury room, they went around the table, each juror
giving a little talk on the evidence and the issues. The
investigation of the crime scene had been botched,
they agreed. Was it a cover-up or just ineptness? Ineptness primarily, they thought, although some doubt
was raised by various photos in evidence, in which the
body appeared in different positions, as if it had been
moved. Could a prostitute be raped? All felt she
could. Did Joan Little go beyond self-defense by in-
flicting eleven stab wounds? The issue was raised, but
it never became a serious problem. A woman's right to

defend herself—they felt women always had that right, and here was a woman simply exercising it. And on the cross-examination of Joan Little, rather than being horrified at its graphicness, as many in the audience, including the author, had been, they found it limited, ineffective, not nearly so extensive as they had expected.

In judging the performance of the lawyers, their modernity showed. They were most impressed with the lawyers who stuck to the facts and least impressed with those who argued abstract racism, Biblical mumbo-jumbo, countrified down-homisms. They found Wilkinson the least effective. "The prosecution could have done without him," the young lawyer-juror Paul Lassiter said, and they resented Lester Chalmers talking down to them like a country preacher.

And they were clock-conscious. They knew someone would be timing them, and they didn't want to come back too soon. Seventy-eight minutes was dignified enough. When the stereo-shop-manager-cum-jury-foreman announced the verdict, Jerry Paul leaned over quietly and gave Joan Little a peck on the cheek. She smiled, but she would not grin broadly until she emerged from the doors of the courthouse to the shouts of the throng.

Judge Hobgood moved on swiftly to sentencing Jerry Paul to two weeks in jail for the Queen of Hearts speech. Afterwards, Hobgood must have been pleased when a juror came up to him and thanked him, not only for being so fair but for sending Jerry Paul to jail. It was all expected, and after Paul extracted a promise from the judge that he have his medicine in jail, for he was visibly a physical wreck by now, he rose to say quietly, nostalgically,

"I've spent a long time in this state fighting for social change, and sometimes I do become emotional and outspoken and heated. That heat is not hatred, and it is not spoken in anger to belittle anyone or to hurt anyone. Sometimes it is necessary that we speak out, knowing that others will become angry at us, so that a thought process will result in growth.

"If it's necessary for a person who lives under Dr. King's philosophy to call upon himself punishment or harshness for speaking out, then he knows what he's doing, and he accepts it gladly, but at no time does he hate or despise or dislike the other person. And he hopes that out of that grows the dialogue which results in better understanding."

It was Jerry Paul's most dignified moment, and he went quietly and slowly off to the Wake County Jail.

Nationwide, the euphoria of many and diverse interests who felt a stake in the outcome was tangible. The feminist paper *Off Our Backs* in Washington, D.C., wrote: "We celebrate in her victory, but know that Joan is free, not because of the judicial system in this country, but in spite of it." But *Big Mama Rag* out of Denver complained in a piece called "Little Freed, Feminism Raped" that sexism had only been "intertwined" with racism in the Little case, rather than dominating the racial issue. "The painfully obvious fact that she is a woman and was raped because she is a woman was not seen as part of Little's situation," the article read. But then if she hadn't been black, she never would have been indicted, and if she hadn't been in prison, the accident would never have happened either, and if she hadn't faced death, *Big Mama* would never have heard of her, so it was a weak argument.

But as this was a case that had operated on the plane of illusion and image, the euphoria of the verdict was soon to dissipate as both Joan Little and Jerry Paul brought their adulatory supporters back to reality. Joan Little moved from the control of Jerry

Paul to the control of Carolina Black Panther head Larry Little (no relation), and she went off on a national speaking tour. In Chicago, where the Panther organizers warned the press beforehand about asking "dehumanizing questions," she proclaimed that there were a million innocent black persons in American prisons, and "I was only one out of a million that was able to escape." Federal and state statistics showed that less than a quarter of a million prisoners of all descriptions are kept in penal institutions. It wasn't the court system that set her free, she said, it was the jury, "people off the streets" who did it. The same week, when a federal grand jury of "people off the streets" declared that state officials and national guardsmen bore no responsibility for the events at Kent State, someone in the audience leapt up and shouted at the jury, "It's not you. It's the system!" The two thoughts seemed to cover all bases. In Cincinnati, she declared solidarity with Patricia Hearst, said she hoped the heiress got off, so that it would prove that justice existed only for rich people in America. Meanwhile, Cicely Tyson, who was considering playing Little in a film, sent her two plane tickets to Hollywood, so that the actress might get a feel for her character, and Tyson got the feel fast: Joan Little and Larry Little cashed in the tickets and went somewhere else. (Cicely Tyson denies this Jerry Paul anecdote.) *Ex Umbris et Imaginibus in Veritatem!* From shadows and symbols into Truth!

An appearance for her was scheduled for the *Today* show, and she went to New York with Morris Dees. At the appointed hour, Dees showed up at the NBC studios alone—and both he and Barbara Walters looked silly on the air, speculating on where their star might be. Later, Joan Little said she had overslept in Brooklyn, didn't feel like getting up anyway, but the rumor in Washington, North Carolina, was that she was in Washington that morning buying an automobile from a local dealer. The *Today* show caper amused the author, for he knew so many people, mostly other authors, who would give their proverbial eyeteeth to appear on the *Today* show.

Jerry Paul could not leave his victory on the level of illusion, and in many ways the author respected him for it. Life simply does not conform to the dictates of bad fiction. There are rarely quintessential victims, pure heroes, clearcut victories, for individuals and institutions are more complicated than that. The messiness is that in a case of such cosmic issues—life and death, the sanctity of the human body, the nature of punishment, the isolation of criminals, the disadvantage of color and sex—real people, not waxen figures, are present, and real people can seldom scramble up to the plane of the cosmic and stay there very long.

So Paul gave an interview to Wayne King of *The New York Times*, whose December 1, 1974 piece had done so much to legitimize the Joan Little promotion in the beginning. Paul was outrageous, and by being so deserved credit for continuing to generate the energy and the dialogue that the case had evoked from the start. Comparing himself to Elmer Gantry, who was only *part* charlatan, he talked of his boredom with the law, referred to the trial as a charade (William Griffin's term for it), boasted about holding the system up to ridicule.

"This system doesn't want justice. It wants convictions," he said. "That's why, given enough money, I can buy justice. I can win any case in this country, given enough money. I can create illusion. You must destroy the charade, and the illusion of justice."

He did more. He implied that the verdict was almost irrelevant, and suggested—as the *Times* article was written—that she might even have been guilty after all. He showed the reporter the Jael clipping which had been in Joan Little's Bible all along.

"If they hadn't made so many assumptions about the jury disbelieving Joan Little on the stand, the prosecutors would have seen that clipping and used it."

The *Times* reporter had left the Jael information at that, and his article caused a storm. Paul's supporters were horrified, and his enemies, most of the State of North Carolina, were overjoyed. He was swamped with abusive mail. The Women's Strike for Peace demanded an explanation. Editorial comment was overwhelmingly negative, but the press in its self-importance was most outraged at the notion that it had been manipulated and orchestrated by Paul. In Philadelphia, Claude Lewis, a columnist for the *Evening Bulletin* who had attended the trial, wrote: "Jerry Paul wants to be F. Lee Bailey. The surprise is that a single important victory turned a young idealistic lawyer into a publicity-seeking sycophant. . . . So practicing law can wait. All those other 'Joan Littles' languishing in jail can wait, while Jerry Paul makes his wallet fat and his name a household word."

But the *Times* piece had had a dash of journalistic devilishness to it. For one thing, it allowed Larry Little, the Panther person, to make moral pronouncements about Jerry Paul as a "con artist" who operated the defense with "cases of champagne," bought with "people's money." That a bit actor, side stage, would be sour is understandable enough, but the *Times* piece arrogated to him some moral standing. Little, described by the paper of record as "a surprisingly gentle man considering his revolutionary outlook," deserved no such standing, for the week after the *Times* piece appeared he sprained Joan Little's ankle in a fight, and she ran back to Jerry Paul for protection.

Beyond that, Jerry Paul's point was deeper than the *Times* piece suggested. The Jael clipping, Paul explained, was a "coincidence," and there were more coincidences that the prosecutors missed. They had not troubled to put Joan Little's notations about Clarence Alligood in her books on a calendar. Had they done so, they would have seen that she made no notes on nights when he was off duty. From that, they might have argued that Joan Little was tracking Alligood, and softening him up for the kill. The author could add other coincidences: her citation of Mark 14:27, never mentioned in the trial, "I will smite the shepherd and the sheep will be scattered"; or Richard Wolf's perception that she had been seductive toward Alligoood to receive favors, a theme never explored in cross-examination; or Golden Frinks's revelation about the picture of the naked black body with the face smudged out, distributed by her boy friend Julius Rogers, which came out of the author's investigation; and—Terry Bell.

There were other worrisome incidents that never came out: how Paul dissuaded a car dealer from swearing out a warrant for Joan when the money for the car Paul gave her never reached the dealer; how Paul avoided another warrant for her arrest in Newport News, Virginia, when there had been a fight in a motel room; how Paul persuaded her boy friend to go quietly to the hospital and not bring charges against Joan during her trial after she had stabbed him in their motel room during a sexual encounter; and how she had brandished a knife at her security guard once, complaining he was guarding her too closely.

"I had good reason to be worried about her temper," Paul said later.

Still, to the defense lawyer, these were all coincidences, but the question was: how many coincidences make a pattern?

"In the law, it often happens that a lawyer can put

innocent facts together and build a persuasive case," Paul said. "You see, a racist, sexist, and law-and-order mentality can hurt even those who seek to use it. I never worried about the evidence; rather, it was only the prejudices of people that concerned me. This goes back to the argument of Socrates at his trial: there is no evidence against me, he said, but against what people are saying about me in the street, I have no defense.

"So with the prosecution's mentality, lawyers malfunction. They can't think straight. By the state being that way, they failed to give an airing in the Joan Little trial to these coincidences."

In short, a circumstantial case is a competition of illusions, and the state simply failed to create as powerful *an illusion of her guilt* as it might have; it was Paul's illusion of her innocence that had carried the day.

But Jerry Paul's trashing of the case in the end had a deep motivation. There was a good deal of sanctimonious talk, reminiscent of Watergate, about how the verdict showed that "the justice system worked." Her judgment supposedly showed the fairness of the New South, and this claptrap touched a core of rage in Jerry Paul.

"I wasn't going to have that. No way I was going to put up with that. Before I let the system claim she got a fair trial, I'd destroy the whole mess. We got justice, but we took it, it wasn't given to us. The price was too high: in dollars and in human suffering, for Joan, and quite frankly, for me as well. Towards the end I was in so much pain every night that I had to fight to put one foot in front of the other. Towards the end, I was like the fullback in the fourth quarter, just bowing his neck and going for that goal line, and prepared to take whatever punishment it took to get there. But that doesn't make sense."

What had it all been worth?

Had it been a "pseudo-event," that synthetic novelty defined by David Boorstein as a happening packaged for the media to sound like news, where no true significance exists, and consumed by the public in its appetite for the sensational? How most North Carolinians wanted to believe so and were delighted with Jerry Paul's shattering illusion after it was over. Once the author had asked a lawyer friend to introduce him to a judge who had played a role in the case, and the lawyer's refusal was conveyed by his wife:

"He feels that the Joan Little extravaganza treatment inserted significance where it did not exist, that the case was ordinary and unproven, that the law understandably could not thereby convict, that she is no heroine nor this a *cause célèbre*. He would do nothing to encourage or contribute to the writing of such a book on principle. . . . It would be part of a treatment he already considers inappropriate."

The author could not agree, though he respected this "dissonant" position. The case had focused attention on Eastern North Carolina, a homogeneous area controlled by whites in a traditional fashion, full of shantytowns, where abuses of blacks in the courts were real and provable. It was an area of the South largely bypassed in the civil-rights activism of the sixties for the "sexier" targets of Alabama and Mississippi, and bypassed in part because of the liberal image of North Carolina, projected by the intellectual oasis of Chapel Hill.

The case had fired important debate on the issue of a woman defending herself against sexual assault, even to the point of killing her attacker. Even if, as the lawyers manfully argued, the law always has accepted that right as an extension of a citizen's right to defend herself—or himself—against *any* threat of bodily harm, the Joan Little case had lodged the right firmly both in the law and in the public mind.

The case opened the North Carolina jail system to scrutiny, revealing that there are more prisoners per capita there than anywhere in the nation; that in Jones County in the East, one person in ten is in jail; that the overcrowding in the nineteenth-century Bastille in Raleigh, otherwise known as Central Prison, is a disgrace; it brought to view a Prison Commissioner, David Jones, who advocated public executions and was a candidate for Governor. In one judicial district, consisting of two rival eastern counties, a prosecutor has put twelve people on death row in less than two years—a figure that exceeds the entire death-row population of twenty-four of the thirty-four states that had the death penalty at the time.

Paul had played to a synthetic nostalgia that the nation had for the Old South: the South of one-dimensional good and evil, racist towns, redneck sheriffs and jailers, railroading prosecutors telling nigger and Jew jokes, black shantytowns, quintessential, slavelike victims, and civil-rights crusaders. Paul genuinely sees the South in those archaic terms; his perception of his region fits the nostalgic view of the rest of the nation. Perhaps a subtler man could never have achieved Paul's triumph. But it is certain he knew that casting the case in those old-fashioned terms would make a lot of local people mad, and this would make his opponents careless and redound to the benefit of his client.

The media event that he was to stage could work only because the media were one-dimensional, that the images projected by the case came to the public in ninety-second doses across the television screen, and the public in the seventies demanded nothing more subtle. The author later learned personally how difficult, perhaps impossible, it was in television production to digest a complicated court day into a ninety-second television package. There was simply no time for complicated images, much less reality.

Thus, the nature of modern communication was Paul's first and most important collaborator, and the national public a voracious consumer. And Paul's preening of Joan Little had been matched by the public's willing beatification of her.

And he had been lucky. That the case was circumstantial with Joan Little the only living witness to the incident was his biggest piece of luck. Without the woman's element of rape in the case, there would have been no celebrity of Joan Little, for there were plenty of traditional civil-rights cases around in the South and in the nation—and, after all, wasn't it International Women's Year? Without the capital-punishment element, kept alive by the prosecutor's insistence on the first-degree-murder charge, despite Alligood's obvious misconduct, there would have been no national commotion, for Paul would never have been able to raise $350,000 to defend a client charged with second-degree murder or manslaughter. So circumstances, a woman, and the gas chamber—not Jerry Paul—made the Joan Little case. It was the same Jerry Paul who said those outrageous things after the verdict, as before; it was just that the feminists and the lawyers were the goats, instead of the rednecks. Still, he had won after fighting tenaciously and ruthlessly for Joan Little's freedom, and it was a modern verdict suited to a modern age.

In the spring of 1976, the author made his last pilgrimage across the sandy tobacco land to the Original Washington, that pleasant, progressive little town in Eastern North Carolina where Cecil B. De Mille grew up. There had been changes in the year since he had first visited there, not Wolf's "earth changes," perhaps, but Washington was not really the same. There was a new Police Center now, an attractive combed-cement structure located on the border between downtown and Back of Town. A new housing project had been completed, and several dirt streets Back of Town were being paved and guttered. One of these was Fourth Street, running in front of the Randolph Funeral Home, the Forty-second Street of the black community, according to John Wilkinson, the street where Julius Rogers had his bistro and Golden Frinks his Resurrection City III.

In November 1975 there had been an election. Max Roebuck retired as mayor and did not run again. He looked dad-burn happy when he was pictured turning over the gavel to the new mayor. Eleven candidates ran for the five seats on the city council, and two of them had figured in the Joan Little case. One was Louis Randolph. The talk before election day was that Randolph would not do very well because of his efforts to raise money for Joan Little's defense. Some people were even saying that Randolph would be hurt by the family problems of Clarence Lightner, Raleigh's black mayor. When the mayor had his wife tried for receiving stolen goods, his daughter charged with using fraudulent credit cards, his son charged with possession of drugs and later with contempt for giving a judge the finger—all during Lightner's term as mayor—it was bound to hurt black politicians statewide. But when the results were tallied, Randolph had again, for the second election in a row, polled more votes than anyone else.

"My people came through for me," Randolph said as he slouched his massive frame back in his well-worn executive's chair. "They had me leading the ticket, and I felt good about that. Most people thought I'd done a good job during the Joan Little crisis because we had no disturbances as such. I've been accused of a lot of things, mostly of fostering the interests of only black people in city hall, which is not true, but no one accused me of not promoting peace and tranquillity in the community."

The other candidate of interest for city council was the bondsman, Jennings Bryant Freeman, who seemed to some to have aged a great deal during the year of Joan Little, as he waited for the shoe to drop, but it never had. Freeman had been in the electrical business once, and his main campaign promise was to do something about the high electric bills.

"He knew he was going to get a seat on that council," Randolph said. "Oh, he was going to do big things for Washington, and I told him, 'Welcome to the club, brother, cause I'm gonna be on there too.' But his talk about the high light bills didn't do him a bit of good." Freeman came in next to last in the field, polling 258 votes compared to Randolph's 937.

In December, the five elected councilmen met and in a three-to-two vote elected Richard Tripp, a retired employee of the Voice of America, as mayor. He had been out of the United States for fifteen years with the Voice and had returned to Washington only a year before his election to the council. The loser was not Randolph, but a white businessman, who had received fifteen percent less of the vote than Randolph. But Louis Randolph was elected mayor pro tem, and his reaction carried its usual resignation and infinite patience.

"Mayor Tripp is retired, and everybody figured that a retired man would have more time to devote to the position. I was almost mayor, and a lot of people were upset that I wasn't elected. They questioned the qualifications of the new mayor, but I don't know that I'm that qualified, even though I have had a lot of experience in government and in dealing with people. Fortunately or unfortunately, we have a system where the five top vote-getters elect the mayor from among themselves, and after the people go to the polls in Novem-

ber they have no more say-so. But being in a little
more responsible position now as mayor pro tem, I can
make a little more of a contribution to the community."

Randolph's office seemed a bit tidier in the Bicentennial Year, and when the author greeted him this
time Randolph slipped off his diamond ring and
dropped it in his coat pocket. "I don't know about
you," he said with his Casbah smile. It had been a
successful year for him, not only in politics but in his
profession. At the national convention of the National
Funeral Directors and Morticians Association in San
Francisco, he had been elected man of the year. At the
banquet which honored him, Randolph had made an
appeal for contributions to the Joan Little Defense,
and got a good response.

All told, in the year of the Joan Little "crisis," Randolph and friends raised close to $5,000 for the de-
fense, but there had been a problem along the way.
The contributions of Washington citizens solicited by
Golden Frinks were not reaching the legal office.
Frinks was called in, and he explained to Randolph
that there were two funds: one for the defense and the
other the SCLC operational fund.

"Very pointedly, I told Golden we were not going
to watch him collect money for the Joan Little Defense and do something else with the money. Oh, it
was just a drop in the bucket, compared to what it
took to defend this child, but it was people's hard-
earned money, and they didn't want to see it go down
the drain for no partyin' and motel rooms and such
foolishness.

"So I put the word out, and Golden was just phased
out. He couldn't collect any more money, and without
revenue, you can't do nothin'. The day of the militant
is over. The day of people brickbattin' your windows
and shooting into your house is over. Don't destroy

my property, because you got me to reckon with, and I just don't want to have to sit up in my window all night with a shotgun.

"Golden told me later that I put him out of business, but if I don't believe in his tactics, I don't believe in 'em. I didn't help do nothin', just did what I thought would be best for Joan Little. Not that the man hasn't done a lot of good, but it's a new era now, totally new. When Golden started out he took a lot of people for a ride. But people found out. They don't stay ignorant forever, you know.

"Kids are thinking about getting a job, being responsible, getting an education now. We just had someone in Washington signed a four-year football scholarship at the University of North Carolina! That used to be unheard of. They've found this marchin' just doesn't pay off. This twelve-inch Afro and one-inch mind stuff—let's reverse this thing."

The Joan Little case had turned out the way Louis Randolph expected in the beginning. He had raised money, and he had spent hours with Courtney Mullins identifying blacks on the jury lists, and while he was happy to do this he wondered what all the money and effort was for. "Washington is not the one-horse-town–mudhole that a lot of people wrote about," and he felt she would have been acquitted at home. But he was realistic enough to know that if the trial had been in Washington, it would have taken its place beside Dayton, Tennessee. "We probably would have had more outsiders here than there were in Raleigh. It would have been a more dramatic show here, and we just weren't ready to handle it."

But Randolph was saying more. He was saying that once the trial was moved away, the local citizens felt no stake in the outcome any longer. With the pressure off, Washingtonians lost interest.

"People were saying, 'I'll be glad when they get through with this Joan Little case. That's all you can see on TV.' Truthfully, the city of Washington has felt no ill effects. Progress is taking place when the town can afford it. People are going about their business, doing what they've normally done through the years. So the case didn't mean much to Washington. Meant more on the national and international level than it did to us."

Unwittingly, he was supporting Golden Frinks's point: that when the case was moved away, it lost its potential for social change in Eastern North Carolina. From this perspective, Randolph could judge the players with detachment. He meant no reflection on "our local law-enforcement officers" when he said Red Davis blew the investigation. He intended "all due respect to her lawyers" and thought Jerry Paul a knowledgeable lawyer, but he didn't like "clowning" and thought Paul could have done better by being a little more conservative. By lambasting "the system" after the acquittal, Jerry Paul had been "immature," for his posturing had killed the receptiveness of judges to grant Joan Little a new trial in the original breaking-and-entering case, or at the very least, killed the chance for a reduced sentence. "Jerry's not mature, not mature as I would want a lawyer to handle a case for me, and let's face it, the system is here to stay." What was its value then? "It opened the eyes of the country to how people are being taken advantage of, not here necessarily, but all over the country . . . Look at the Alabama prison system."

Twice, Louis Randolph had seen Joan Little since the verdict, and he was astonished at the change in her. Here was truly an earth change: it was like the transformation between elementary school and college. She was a totally different person now, so much smoother and more articulate in the way she handled herself, and he credited Karen Galloway with the accomplishment.

"Karen worked with that child. She cleared Joan of

her childhood instincts, and developed what had been left out in her upbringing here. Joan had begun to understand what womanhood is all about, what being black is all about, what life is all about.

"No, I don't think she'll revert back to what she was. She's seen there are better things in life than running down Fourth Street boozin' it up. Things have been instilled in her now that she'll never forget."

The author rose to leave, thinking of the long drive ahead of him, back to the Piedmont. He asked Randolph to give a call the next time he was in Chapel Hill for a Board of Governors meeting at the University. As he started out of the office, the mortician called after him,

"Think they're going to make a movie of the Joan Little story? She's gonna make her some real money, huh?"